THE YESHIVA AND THE RISE OF MODERN HEBREW LITERATURE

JEWS IN EASTERN EUROPE

Jeffrey Veidlinger
Mikhail Krutikov
Geneviève Zubrzycki

Editors

THE YESHIVA AND THE RISE OF MODERN HEBREW LITERATURE

Marina Zilbergerts

INDIANA UNIVERSITY PRESS

This book is a publication of

Indiana University Press
Office of Scholarly Publishing
Herman B Wells Library 350
1320 East 10th Street
Bloomington, Indiana 47405 USA

iupress.org

Manufactured in the United States of America

First printing 2022

Library of Congress Cataloging-in-Publication Data

Names: Zilbergerts, Marina, author.
Title: The Yeshiva and the rise of modern Hebrew literature / Marina
Zilbergerts.
Description: Bloomington : Indiana University Press, 2022. | Series: Jews
in Eastern Europe | Includes bibliographical references and index.
Identifiers: LCCN 2021032845 (print) | LCCN 2021032846 (ebook) | ISBN
9780253059444 (hardback) | ISBN 9780253059437 (paperback) | ISBN
9780253059413 (ebook)
Subjects: LCSH: Hebrew literature, Modern—History and criticism. |
Jews—Europe, Eastern—Intellectual life—19th century. | Yeshivas. |
Europe, Eastern—Intellectual life—19th century.
Classification: LCC PJ5019 .Z55 2022 (print) | LCC PJ5019 (ebook) | DDC
892.4/7—dc23
LC record available at https://lccn.loc.gov/2021032845
LC ebook record available at https://lccn.loc.gov/2021032846

To Amos,

אִם אֵין קֶמַח, אֵין תּוֹרָה. אִם אֵין תּוֹרָה, אֵין קֶמַח.
If there is no flour, there is no Torah.
If there is no Torah, there is no flour.
—*Pirkei Avot 3:17*

CONTENTS

NOTE ON TRANSLITERATION

FOR TERMS AND PHRASES IN THE TEXT OF this book, I have used a simplified version of the Library of Congress systems for romanizing Russian, Hebrew, and Yiddish. Most diacritical marks are omitted, and alif and ayin are usually not indicated. For transliterating names, whenever a particular spelling has become somewhat conventional in common English-language usage (outside of academia), I have preferred that romanization over the more technically correct choices. Thus, Chaim Nachman Bialik rather than Hayim Nahman Biyalik. However, in the notes and bibliography, the book titles and names of authors are usually transliterated according to the previously mentioned romanization standard, in order to help scholars who, while able to type Hebrew letters, are not familiar with the Hebrew and Yiddish spellings of these names and titles.

ACKNOWLEDGMENTS

THIS PROJECT FIRST BEGAN TO GROW INTO A written work when I was a graduate student in the Department of Comparative Literature at Stanford University. I was blessed to receive the unwavering support there of Gabriella Safran, who was and continues to be the best adviser I could ask for. Gabriella has guided and inspired me at every turn, and I am thankful to have her as a friend. At Stanford, I also received significant support from Vered Shemtov, Steven Zipperstein, Monika Greenleaf, Charlotte Fonrobert, Hans Ulrich (Sepp) Gumbrecht, Steven Weitzman, and Mira Wasserman, who read drafts or discussed ideas with me.

I would not have been able to pursue this research without the training that I received as an MA student at the Graduate Theological Union and the University of California, Berkeley. Naomi Seidman, Chana Kronfeld, and Holger Zellentin all nourished me with their teaching and scholarship. I am most grateful to Robert Alter, whose scholarship and teaching have been continual sources of inspiration and who supported me through his advice and reading drafts. Also in Berkeley, I benefited immensely from the Posen Society of Fellows as part of the 2015–2017 cohort. I am grateful to David and Rachel Biale and the Posen fellows for the fruitful workshops and intellectual exchanges.

As an assistant professor at the University of Wisconsin–Madison, I have benefited greatly from the support of colleagues, who helped as I revised my work for publication in this form. I am especially thankful to Tony Michels, who so ably led the Center for Jewish Studies and supported me as a colleague and a friend. I will always appreciate his steadfastness and integrity. Chad Goldberg and Jordan Rosenblum, senior colleagues at the center, supported me in research and were valuable mentors. I am also grateful to Karen Evans-Romaine and Irina Shevelenko of the Department for German, Nordic, and Slavic. Further, my colleague Sunny Yudkoff provided valuable feedback and advice, as did Kirill Ospovat and the graduate students involved in the Slavic Colloquium. Judith Kornblatt read drafts and pointed me in good directions with attentive and detailed comments.

In the larger fields of interest connected to this work, Eliyahu Stern, Zvi Septimus, Harriet Murav, and Shaul Stampfer all contributed their time and expertise. As series editors at Indiana University Press, Mikhail Krutikov and Jeffrey Veidlinger were extremely helpful. Gary Dunham and Ashante Thomas have expertly shepherded the work toward publication. Important copyediting assistance along the way came from Jonah Rank and Megan Schindele.

While I cannot ever sufficiently repay them for their care and labors, I thank my parents, Natalia Nuzhnaya and Sergey Zilbergerts, for everything they have given me and continue to provide. They cultivated and preserved my facility and interest in the languages and cultures that are at the heart of this book. More importantly, their exhortations, support, and personal examples of resilience gave me the values and strength essential to seeing this long work to its completion. Their often humbling practical wisdom remains a guiding light. Similarly, my grandparents Leonid and Irina Nuzhny pushed me forward at every step, and my sister, Michelle Zilbergerts, read many drafts of the introduction and gave feedback about their readability.

Last but not least, I thank Amos Bitzan, with whom, over many late evenings, I studied this book's most central questions about the value of literature, the balance between art and utility, and of the relationship of Torah learning to modern Jewish thought and scholarship. I dedicate this book to him.

THE YESHIVA AND THE RISE
OF MODERN HEBREW LITERATURE

INTRODUCTION

ONE COULD IMAGINE FEW VOCATIONS STRANGER AND LONELIER than that of the Hebrew writer in nineteenth-century Russia. Although referring to Hebrew as having been a "dead" language in the nineteenth century is a mischaracterization, the idea of reading novels and stories in Hebrew at that time would have seemed quite unusual.[1] Hebrew had not functioned as a vernacular for many centuries. For the Yiddish-speaking Jewish population of the Russian Empire, Hebrew was the language of traditional Jewish texts and scriptures. It was the language of prayer, law, and ritual, which every Jewish man, and a few women, theoretically knew how to read.[2] Hebrew expressions and phrases permeated the rich fabric of the Yiddish vernacular spoken by all.[3] Despite the prevalence of Hebrew in the religious spheres of Jewish life, however, it would have been hard to imagine it as a language for people's everyday lived experience, let alone as a suitable vehicle for imaginative literature.[4]

Moshe Leib Lilienblum (1843–1910), one of the first modern writers of Hebrew, likened the experience of being a Hebrew writer to that of an ancient sage who was resurrected into a future in which his knowledge, skills, and entire purpose had become null. "I am one of the eternal dead of the Babylonian Talmud, whom Hebrew literature has revived," he wrote of himself.[5] Like the mythical wandering Jew, the Hebrew writer, according to Lilienblum, belonged neither to the past nor to the present, and his attachment to Hebrew literature doomed him to remain forever suspended, "fluttering between life and death for the rest of his days."[6]

If being a Hebrew writer was such an anachronism, an occupation for which there was neither need nor demand, why then, one might ask, would anyone dream of engaging in this strange and impractical activity? Modern Hebrew literature's early champions, whose choice to pursue it ran against all odds and sense, could very well be described as the "eternal dead of the Babylonian Talmud" of whom Lilienblum wrote.[7] The first writers of Hebrew in Russia were a small group of Talmud-educated Jewish men who wrote in Hebrew for each other's pleasure and entertainment. They were Hebrew literature's primary producers and, at the same time, its sole consumers. They were paradoxical individuals who were misfits in traditional

Jewish society and also the most extreme embodiments of rabbinic culture and its values. Their choice to write modern Hebrew literature was viewed as an act of apostasy, for which they were banished and punished with social and economic repercussions by the representatives of traditionalist Jewish culture in Russia. Once they freed themselves of the restraints of traditional society, however, their lives as secular Jewish writers and intellectuals were no less precarious. Stripped of the protections and special status with which traditional Jewish culture endowed men of religious letters and Talmudic scholarship, these aspiring Hebrew writers in Russia found themselves—like ancient scribes transported into the future—in a hostile or indifferent economic and literary marketplace in which their rabbinic textual skill set was utterly useless.

If Hebrew literature was a rather impractical pursuit within the sphere of Jewish life and culture, what was its status in the Russian Empire as whole? The state of Russian intellectual and cultural discourse during the second half of the nineteenth century was certainly no more conducive to Hebrew literature than was the internal opposition presented to it from within Jewish culture. In the 1850s, the main questions occupying Russia's literati were about Russia's future as a nation and an empire, aesthetic debates about Russian literature between Slavophiles and Westernizers, and general excitement about reforms and the impending emancipation of the serfs. Beginning in the 1860s, however, ideas emerging from a marginal group of radical literary and social critics known as the Russian nihilists presented new attitudes toward literature that succeeded in capturing the attention of both readers and the Russian literary establishment. The nihilists, the so-called heretics of nineteenth-century Russia, undermined the sacred value previously attributed to texts and the literary pursuit. They argued that texts were valuable only insofar as they served practical needs of society, however those needs might be conceived. Touching directly on the issues of the day, such as the dismantling the Russian social and economic order and replacing religious dogma with scientific and rationalist thinking, among other issues, the nihilists' ideas were hotly debated in most works of Russian literature and criticism in the 1860s. Despite the strong opposition to the nihilists' views from the Russian literary establishment, their argument for basing the worth of literature on how useful it was to society became an idea to be contended with.

Inspired by these new modes of thinking, Jewish writers, too, began to question their long-held assumptions about the inherent value of literature, challenging the sphere of Jewish literary production in Russia. When Jewish writers began to apply the criterion of utility to the dream of the Hebrew literary endeavor, they could find little to say in its defense. With no substantial audience or sphere of influence, Hebrew literature could hardly qualify as an instrument of social reform for the Jews living in the Russian Empire. If social influence was to be the new measure of value, why not write in Yiddish, or Russian, for that matter? It was this troubling realization that led one of modern Hebrew's first poets, Yehuda Leib Gordon (1830–1892), to declare himself the last of "Zion's poets" addressing its "last readers."[8]

Surprisingly, Gordon's sober prognosis for Hebrew literature did not materialize. Contrary to all expectation, it was nineteenth-century Russia in which Hebrew literature sprang to life, entering the most productive period in the life of Hebrew letters, known as the *tehiyah* (revival).[9] The emergence of a modern Hebrew literature on Russian soil, which happened even before the revival of Hebrew as a spoken tongue, was an extraordinary historical and cultural phenomenon that scholars still do not fully understand.[10] Why did modern Hebrew literature emerge at all, and why particularly in late-nineteenth century Russia? By what process did Hebrew resist the practical and ideological challenges to its existence? And how did Jewish writers make the case for a literature that was, by all accounts, "useless" to Jews living in the Russian Empire? These are the central questions this book seeks to examine anew.

Since the early twentieth century, scholars have attempted to explain the story of the emergence of modern Hebrew literature in Russia. A long-established narrative, championed by scholars from Joseph Klausner to Dan Miron, has described the story of modern Hebrew literature as a cultural product that is inseparable from the history of Zionism.[11] On the other hand, more recent accounts by such scholars as Hannan Hever, Shachar Pinsker, David Biale, and Kenneth Moss integrated the creation and development of Hebrew in Russia into the story of the "constitution of secular Jewish culture."[12] While each of these established streams of scholarship illuminates our understanding of important facets in the story of Hebrew literature, this book challenges both of these narratives. What I offer here is a new model for understanding the rise of modern Hebrew letters as grounded in the literary practices and metaphysics of the world of Talmud study in eastern Europe, from which the most influential first writers of Hebrew emerged.

More specifically, this book presents a new account of the rise of modern Hebrew literature in nineteenth-century Russia at whose heart is an exploration of the value and purpose of the literary word. It is an exploration that begins with the earliest layers of rabbinic literature and continues to modern philosophical and literary attitudes that found expression in the nineteenth and twentieth centuries. I argue that the pioneers of Hebrew letters in Russia emerged from the challenges of pragmatism and utility by adopting a noninstrumental model for the valuation of literature. This model was inspired neither by Zionism nor secularism but by the practices of Talmud study and the Jewish approach to texts, which Jewish writers applied to the creation of modern Hebrew letters. At first, like a stubborn old habit left over from their Talmudic past, these practices were inadvertent and ran counter to Hebrew writers' explicit ideological convictions. But by the end of the century, the noninstrumental approach to the study and production of Hebrew literature was embraced as a literary and aesthetic approach that continued to enrich the lovers of the word amid changing times, continents, and ideologies.

Understanding Hebrew Literature in Russia

To understand the development of modern Hebrew letters in Russia, we need to examine the transformation of notions of literary value that took place on Jewish culture's three founding fronts. The first is the rise of the Jewish cultural reform movement, the Haskalah, and its attitudes toward Hebrew. The second is the change brought about by the formation of the yeshiva movement and the way it revitalized the rabbinic culture of religious learning. The third factor is the influence of Russian intellectual trends, particularly nihilism and its emphasis on utility, on Jewish literary and intellectual discourse. The ways in which questions of literary value and utility developed on each of these three fronts and at their intersections influenced the course and character of Hebrew literature in Russia.

The Haskalah movement, also known as the Jewish Enlightenment, has received the most credit for giving rise to Hebrew literature in Russia. It began with the transmission and adaption of modern intellectual trends from the European Enlightenment and, to a large extent, Romanticism to Jews living in the Russian Empire.[13] Inspired by the writings of Moses Mendelssohn (1729–1786), the Haskalah's original epicenter during the last two decades of the eighteenth century had been Berlin. Toward the mid-nineteenth century, however, that shifted to Galicia and the Russian Empire, where Jewish intellectuals raised in traditional milieus, who were products of the rabbinic education system, had seized onto "enlightened" ideas to formulate their own projects of enlightenment and reform.[14] This group of writers became known as *maskilim* (commonly translated as "the enlightened ones"), and the corpus of writing they produced from 1841 to roughly 1870 is referred to as the literature of the Haskalah.[15]

The maskilim saw literature as a means toward their primary goal, which was to enact religious, educational, and cultural reforms that would pave the way to Jewish emancipation and integration into Russian society. Despite striving for Jewish integration, however, the maskilim entertained nationalist aspirations for the Jews in the Russian Empire. One central objective was to define the unique "essence" of Jewish culture, religion, and nationhood in Russia. The crucial ingredients for defining a national essence were, of course, land, a national language, and literature—and all these were perceived by the maskilim to be missing from Russian Jewish life. Although Yiddish, the one language universally spoken among Jews in Europe, could have been a fine candidate for the role of the national Jewish tongue, for the maskilim, that choice was out of the question. Enlightenment notions of aesthetics and language purity prevalent in German maskilic thinking, in particular in the writings of Mendelssohn, had cast Yiddish as "jargon"—an ugly and impure mix of Germanic, Hebraic, Romance, and Slavic elements that rendered it as a reflection not of the Jewish national essence but of the negative facets of diasporic Jewish existence.[16]

In their search for the Jewish essence, the maskilim turned to the Jewish biblical past and its language, Hebrew, as reservoirs for the essential Jewish *Geist*. In Mendelssohn's view, only Hebrew, the language in which the Bible was originally written, could reveal the universalist elements within Jewish culture, making it more compatible with the Enlightenment's conception of a religion grounded in reason, devoid of superstition and irrational beliefs.[17] At the same time, Romantic thinking among the maskilim pushed them to view Hebrew literature and poetry as aesthetic forces that would Europeanize the Jewish heart, allegedly corrupted by centuries of rabbinic legalism and the backwardness of Jewish life, and foster in the Jewish conscience the kind of cultivation (*Bildung*) that would attune it to beauty, nature, and the sublime. As the historian Olga Litvak has observed, the maskilic project of Hebrew revival "anticipated the evolution and meaning of Bildung," which became synonymous with the use of literature for most of the nineteenth century in the West.[18] In other words, the revival of Hebrew literature by the members of the eastern European Haskalah was predicated on the maskilim's belief in the redemptive powers of literature (in the supposedly pure language of Hebrew), which were to be directed toward the struggle for cultural reform and integration.

With relatively little success at enacting the cultural reforms the maskilim had hoped for, however, the revival of Hebrew literature through the rehabilitation of the Hebrew Bible became the Haskalah's main lasting accomplishment. Among the first works of Hebrew literature to emerge out of the efforts of the Haskalah was *The Love of Zion* (*Hibat tziyon*, 1853), by Avraham Mapu (1808–1867). Widely considered the first Hebrew novel, *The Love of Zion* attempted to recreate the language and setting of a glorious biblical past. Populated by strong and attractive Jews who fought battles and fell in love on the pastoral fields of Judea and Samaria, this starkly didactic novel provided a fictional counterpoint to the glum reality of Jewish life in the Diaspora. Among Hebrew literature's first creators were the polemical satirist Joseph Perl (1773–1839), the Hebrew poets Avraham Dov Lebensohn (1794–1878) and his son Micha Yosef Lebensohn (1828–1852), and the aforementioned Gordon—all of whom felt the production of Hebrew literature in Russia to be tied to Jewish cultural refinement, necessary for the dream of integrating Jews into bourgeois Russian society. Ironically, however, their literary visions were as far removed from any reality in which they hoped to enact their reforms as was the eastern European shtetl from the fields of biblical Judea.

The Haskalah's challenge to traditional Jewish society coincided with the flourishing of a revitalized rabbinic scholarly elite culture, which centered on the institution of the yeshiva (rabbinic academy, Hebrew plural *yeshivot*) and the figure of the *lamdan* (a scholar, or "learner," of religious texts, Hebrew plural *lomdim*). In yeshivas located in small towns of the Russian Empire, devout students of the Talmud toiled day and night at the study of sacred texts, practicing the rabbinic principle of Torah *lishmah* (Torah for its own sake)—the belief that the study of Torah, a term inclusive of all sacred Jewish texts, is to be carried out without any instrumental motives, only as an end in itself. The ideal of Torah lishmah, which I describe as the autotelic approach to textuality at the heart of Talmudic culture, was, as this book shows, no less formative of modern Hebrew literature than the efforts of the maskilim.

The cultural understanding of Torah lishmah is a complex subject to which several chapters in this book are dedicated. It was as much grounded in centuries of Jewish thought and rabbinic theology as it was a modern development that, like the Haskalah, flourished in the wake of the European Enlightenment. Central among the Enlightenment ideas that were incorporated into the theology of the yeshiva movement was a philosophically idealist worldview that saw the Torah and other sacred Jewish texts as the code and key to the universe's ultimate reality. Developed by the yeshiva movement's first visionaries, the Gaon of Vilna (Eliyahu ben Shlomo Zalman, 1720–1792) and his student Chaim of Volozhin (1749–1821), the notion of Torah lishmah, rendered as the cosmic centrality of texts, constituted the yeshiva movement's primary tenet of faith.[19] The institution of the yeshiva, by design, elevated the study of texts above all traditional modes of spirituality. In the minds of its critics, among the Hasidim and maskilic figures alike, the yeshiva movement had replaced the worship of God with the worship of texts.

Although the Haskalah and the yeshiva movement were ideological and political rivals, they shared one incidental point of convergence, which was the idealist faith in the value of literature. A general disregard for practicality, particularly when it came to the production of Hebrew letters, pervaded both disparate camps. Despite Hebrew's ineffectiveness in serving and disseminating the maskilic agenda, the maskilim nevertheless believed in the redemptive powers of the Hebrew language to correct the damage done to the Jewish heart and spirit by centuries of rabbinic legalism and superstition. The adherents of the yeshiva movement, also known as the *mitnagdim* (opponents, because of their opposition to Hasidism), meanwhile, privileged the life of the mind in the universe of Jewish texts so highly that they perhaps deliberately failed to consider its economic repercussions both within the yeshiva world and in Jewish culture at large. Micha Yosef Berdichevsky (1865–1921), a former student of the Volozhin Yeshiva and a trailblazer of modezrn Hebrew prose, reflected on how deeply the text centeredness of Talmudic culture had shaped its writers' experience: "The world into which we were born, in which we breathed life and in which we learned to think and live, to see and hear, to feel and sense, is solely the world of the books and its folios. Our lives are those of the script and the text, our questions are those of the text. . . . Other than the words of the texts we have neither matter nor spirit."[20]

Like Berdichevsky, most of those who became writers of Hebrew literature had been Jewish men of letters, reared in the study of the Talmud in the yeshiva. Trained in the study of traditional Jewish texts from an early age, they had internalized the love and value of the textual endeavor and took pleasure in the playful variety of Jewish hermeneutical practices, textual games, and scriptural allusion, which they acquired in their learning of the Midrash, the Talmud, and traditional commentaries.

Taking their first steps outside of the traditional Jewish world, young yeshiva-trained writers unproblematically translated their passion for the autotelic study of religious texts into the production of secular poetry and prose. The first natural step on their new journey was becoming maskilic Hebrew writers. Shulamit Magnus explains that "as men, the maskilim were heirs to a tradition of elite male writing. They themselves came from the circles of this elite, having all had traditional yeshiva education; some, like Lilienblum, having been groomed for the rabbinate."[21]

Since the path to Hebrew writing began in the elite circles of Talmudic learning, the fact that Hebrew literature was almost entirely a male enterprise was "a given."[22] There existed no formal educational framework that would endow women with the skills to be Hebrew writers.[23] Instead, within the culture of the rabbinic elite, women bore the burden of men's intellectual endeavors, often acting as the providers of financial support. By the 1860s, rabbinic intellectuals aspiring to be Hebrew writers increasingly saw the rabbinic economic order as structurally and ethically problematic. What brought their hopes of forging a modern Hebrew literature to a sudden halt, however, was not so much the recognition of internal ruptures but rather their encounters with a new worldview that shook the basic assumptions that Hebrew writers had previously held. For the first time, ideas coming from Russian intellectual circles began to challenge Jewish writers' faith in literature's irreducible worth and forced them to reckon with questions of economic productivity and utility.

The instrumentalist approach to literature of Russian nihilist critics, whose popularity lasted from the 1860s roughly to the late 1880s, inspired an entire generation of Russian and Jewish intellectuals to question their ideas about literature. Interestingly, nihilism's founders, Nikolai Chernyshevsky (1828–1889) and Nikolai Dobrolyubov (1836–1861), were themselves men of religious learning, educated in the Russian Orthodox clergy. They had severed ties with their religious upbringing, however, and had developed a materialist and utilitarian critique of literature in opposition to the theology and practices of Russian Orthodoxy and its veneration of the written word. Their arguments in favor of instrumentalizing literature's production and consumption for society's practical benefit resonated deeply with young

Jewish writers who were becoming increasingly aware of the structural economic shortcomings of Jewish educational and cultural institutions.

This book focuses on the early works and personal histories of five founding Hebrew writers and their confrontation with the utilitarian critique of literature. They are the brothers Avraham Uri Kovner (1842–1905) and Yitzhak Aizik Kovner (1840–1891), Moshe Leib Lilienblum (1843–1910), Micha Yosef Berdichevsky (1865–1921), and Chaim Nachman Bialik (1873–1934), among others. These writers, who published their first Hebrew works between 1862 and 1900, were all reared in the scholarly milieu of Talmudic culture and the yeshiva. They are united by the formative experiences of their youth, which involved a period of an all-consuming devotion to religious texts.

Faced with the tension between the unconditional veneration of texts inherited from the rabbinic tradition on the one hand and their newfound conviction that literature must serve a practical benefit on the other, the creators of Hebrew literature struggled to find a purpose for their acts of writing. While Yiddish writers found refuge from the accusation of uselessness by turning to social satire, Hebrew writers, lacking the possibility of mass appeal, struggled to find a worthy target for their literary efforts. Continually made self-conscious by the anxiety of uselessness, Jewish writers emerging from this milieu were faced with the choice either to conscript their work to a recognized social cause (and between Zionism, socialism, Marxism, and populism, there was no shortage of ideological causes in late-imperial Russia to which Jewish writers were willing to offer their allegiance) or to find a way to reclaim their artistic freedom from the pragmatic constraints of utility.

The transformations of Jewish writers' attitudes toward Hebrew literature, which the following chapters document, are best illustrated by the case of Shalom Yankev Abramovitsh (known by his Yiddish penname, Mendele Moykher-Sforim [1836–1917]), one of the founding writers of Hebrew prose. Abramovitsh started out as a Talmudist but became a maskilic Hebrew writer. After his exposure to the utilitarian critique of literature, he began to direct his literary efforts to various "useful" causes. He wrote, for instance, a multivolume Hebrew textbook about zoology (*Toledot ha-teva*, 1862–1872), whose goal was to disseminate scientific knowledge among Jews, however strangely, in the holy tongue. Having confronted the lack of demand for Hebrew, however, he quickly switched to Yiddish, in which he wrote his best and most well-known satirical works and achieved literary fame. Toward the end of the nineteenth century, when utilitarian ideas about literature gave way to new literary approaches and genres, Abramovitsh switched languages once again as he decided to translate his Yiddish works into Hebrew. Overcoming the monumental challenge of Hebrew's lack of vernacular, he ended up inventing his own vernacular Hebrew literary style distinctly drawn from Talmudic Aramaic, which he knew from his yeshiva education.[24]

Despite Jewish writers' commitment to the social good and their desire to break what they saw as the harmful intoxication with the written word, an autotelic textual aesthetic reminiscent of the modes of traditional Jewish learning continued to inspire both Hebrew and Yiddish literatures beginning in the 1860s and onward. The world of Talmudic study—its practices, themes, and language—served as a rich reservoir of expression for writers engaged in the creation of new Hebrew literatures well into the twentieth century.

Chapter Outlines

The chapters of this book describe six distinct stages in the development of Jewish attitudes about the value of the literary pursuit. The first chapter, titled "Men of Letters," begins with the rabbinic world of Talmudic learning. Delving into midrashic Jewish texts and the thought of the founders of the yeshiva movement, the Vilna Gaon and Chaim of Volozhin, the first chapter examines the role that textuality played from within the insular world of Talmudic culture. The chapter analyzes the yeshiva movement's core metaphysical views, in which, contrary to materialist atomism, letters rather than particles were thought to be the building blocks of physical reality. The chapter introduces the concept of Torah lishmah and the textual practices associated with it—such as the culture of debate, letter games and the use of allusion, the quest for innovation, and the play and pleasure of the text—and explains how these textual practices shaped Jewish writers' approach to literature.

The second chapter, "How the Word Became Flesh," investigates the loss of faith in the value of texts and literature that took place in the 1860s among the representatives of the Jewish and Russian religious intelligentsias. Providing the necessary historical and cultural background, the chapter analyzes Russian and Jewish exposés and memoirs that document the growing disappointment of learned elites in the Russian Empire with the institutions of their respective backgrounds. Comparing critiques of such educational institutions as the yeshiva and the Russian Orthodox seminary, as well as of the economic structures of marriage, the chapter explains why Jewish and Russian writers who emerged from their cultures' respective religious intelligentsias can be best understood as kindred spirits whose unexpected cultural affinities led them in similar ideological directions. In particular, the chapter explains the general turn to nihilism, with its rejection of literature in favor of pragmatism, among the Russian intelligentsia and why it was so appealing to Jews.

Chapter 3, "Texts on Trial," documents how the new criteria of literary value based in utility challenged the incipient sphere of Hebrew literature in nineteenth-century Russia. Beginning with an analysis of the texts associated with Russian nihilism that Jewish writers read and debated, such as the novel *Fathers and Sons* (1862) by Ivan Turgenev (1818–1883) and Chernyshevsky's *What Is to Be Done?* (1863), the chapter documents how the Russian critique of literature in the name of utility made its way into Jewish letters. Continuing to examine the writings of the literary critics and the Jewish nihilists Avraham Uri Kovner and his lesser-known brother Yitzhak Aizik Kovner, the chapter explores early debates among Jewish writers concerning the value of Hebrew letters and its relationship to the Judaic textual legacy.

The fourth chapter, "Literary Apostasy," continues to explore Jewish writers' struggle with textuality in one of Hebrew literature's first major works, Lilienblum's *The Sins of Youth* (*Hatot Ne'urim*, 1873). This autobiographical novel documents Lilienblum's escape from his life as a Talmudist into a life of secular literary activity in Odessa, where he subsequently undergoes a materialist "conversion" after discovering the writings of the Russian nihilists. The chapter describes Lilienblum's sharp disillusionment with the value of literature produced by his encounter with the Russian critics. At the same time, the chapter shows that despite his disillusionment, Lilienblum continues to engage with literature in ways that run very much counter to his newfound utilitarian convictions. Lilienblum's uncontrollable attraction to Talmudic literary practices and the Judaic textual tradition emerges, in the chapter's final analysis, to be the lifeline of Hebrew literature.

Chapters 5 and 6 take us into the heart of rabbinic textuality, the Volozhin Yeshiva, as the incubating pod for modern Hebrew letters. Analyzing works by the two most important modern Jewish writers of the late nineteenth century, Bialik and Berdichevsky, who attended the Volozhin Yeshiva before its closure in 1892, these chapters continue to track the development of Hebrew literature into new directions.

The fifth chapter, "Readers' Paradise," describes the exciting and dangerous confrontations of students in the Volozhin Yeshiva with the "forbidden fruit" of secular literature, as told by Hebrew's founding modernist, Berdichevsky. In the latter's literary sketches of students in the Volozhin Yeshiva, which appear in the novella *The World of Nobility* (*Olam ha-atzilut*, 1886), Berdichevsky portrays characters who arduously pore over the Talmud during the day and devote their nights to the even more pleasurable secret consumption of "forbidden books." The chapter follows Berdichevsky's portraits of yeshiva life to observe how the religiously sanctioned worship of textuality inspires the students' transition to secular texts. The yeshiva students' attraction to secular texts, however, takes them further away from their physical lives than the study of Talmud ever did; it ruins their chances of marital happiness, harms their health, and is a harbinger of death. The chapter tracks the development of the idea of a dangerous textuality in Berdichevsky's own life, following him from the Volozhin Yeshiva to Berlin and Bern, and to his intoxication with a new set of texts—this time, by Friedrich Nietzsche (1844–1900).

The sixth and final chapter, "The Talmudic Passion," examines how, at the end of the nineteenth century, Hebrew literature finally transcends the demands of utility by which it had been held captive throughout the century's second half. The chapter illustrates Bialik's aesthetic reconstruction of the modes of rabbinic learning and the passionate devotion to texts at the heart of the rabbinic textual endeavor. Drawing on the trope of the "living dead," which Jewish writers had employed to describe Talmudic scholarship in the nineteenth century, Bialik's first long poem *"Ha-matmid"* ("The Steadfast Student," 1889), cast its protagonist, a young Talmud scholar, as a phantom in a decaying study house. The poet creates beauty, however, where others saw decay. In ways that recall the decadent and religious renaissance taking place in late nineteenth-century Russian and European literature, Bialik's Hebrew verse revels in all aspects of Talmudic culture, establishing it as a source of artistic inspiration. Likewise, the poet Yitzhok Leybush Peretz (1852–1915), writing in Yiddish, endeavors a similar reconstruction of rabbinic culture when he casts a young Talmudic scholar, Monish, as a romantic hero in a scandalous love affair that draws its erotic appeal from none other than his Talmudic passion. Reclaiming Talmudic culture's autotelic approach to texts, Bialik succeeds in transforming the allegedly useless sphere of Hebrew letters into the rich, vibrant, and relevant literature that it continues to be to this day.

Lastly, the book's epilogue, "Reflections on the Value of Literature," asks: What can we learn from the remarkable story of Hebrew literature in the present day? Reflecting on different perspectives on the value of literature and its study in contemporary culture and at the university, the conclusion draws on the story of Hebrew literature to offer a way forward for the study and production of literature and the humanities at large.

Moving through these chapters, one of my book's central aims is to recover the little-understood importance of nineteenth-century Russian intellectual history to the rise of Hebrew letters. The book illuminates the formation of Hebrew literature by reflecting on an equally troubled process among the Jewish writers' contemporaries, the nineteenth-century Russian Orthodox seminarians who became secular writers, critics, and the leaders of a new literary movement in Russia. Like them, yeshiva-educated Jewish writers struggled to define the purpose of a textual engagement whose religious significance had been undermined by the intellectual and social upheavals of modernity. Drawing on Russian cultural and religious history, this book tells a new story of the rise of Hebrew literature in the Russian Empire alongside the development of modern Russian literature, extending the relevance of this story beyond the boundaries of Jewish culture.

No less important, however, is this book's attempt to challenge the ways in which we conceptualize *Jewish* literature. It reconceives the notion of Torah lishmah as a literary practice while offering it as a model for past and current discussions of the value of the study and pursuit of literature. While scholars have paid attention to literary and cultural projects that drew inspiration from Hasidism, folklore, mysticism, and paganism, most of these neglect Jewish writers' productive engagement with the texts of the rabbinic literary tradition and its reading and learning practices, which had a daily and intimate connection to Hebrew writers' lives and works.[25] By recovering the aesthetic influence of rabbinic textual practices on the creation of Hebrew literature in the context of imperial Russia, my book foregrounds the forms and practices of rabbinic textual study and describes them as a set of poetics, which, I demonstrate, shaped the works of modern Hebrew literature in Russia. For this task, my work draws on and contributes to scholarship on Hebrew literature in Russia by a wide variety of works of scholars, such as Tova Cohen, Jeremy Dauber, Shachar Pinsker, Kenneth Moss, Iris

Parush, and others who have written on the culture and textual practices of modern Hebrew writers, as well as the work of the late Benjamin Harshav (1928–2015), which dealt with the origins of modern Hebrew letters.

While the scholarly aim of this book is to present a new account of the emergence of Hebrew literature in the contexts of the Jewish legacy of textual scholarship as well as Russian and Jewish intellectual history, at its heart, this book is devoted to being a serious and open exploration of the multicultural and multigenerational quest for the value and purpose of the literary word. It is my goal and hope that, in telling the story of Hebrew literature in Russia, this book will give readers a new way of thinking about the value of literary texts—be they religious or secular—against the ever-changing economic and ideological backdrops of our world.

Notes

1. Parush, "Another Look," 172.
2. Parush, 206n8.
3. Weinreich, *History of the Yiddish*, 214.
4. See the introduction to Lasman, *Ha-lashon haivrit*.
5. Lilienblum, *Hatot ne'urim*, 215.
6. Lilienblum, 215.
7. Harshav, *Language in Time*, 67, 104–5.
8. From the poem "For Whom Do I Toil" (1870). See Stanislawski, *For Whom*, 104.
9. Introduction to Harshav, *Shirat ha-tehiya ha-ivrit*; Harshav, *Language in Time*, 115–19.
10. Parush, "Another Look," 171.
11. Hever, *Be koakh ha-el*, 7.
12. The narrative of Hebrew's development as the constitution of secular Jewish culture is presented in the following accounts: Moss, *Jewish Renaissance*; Biale, *Not in the Heavens*; Pinsker, *Literary Passports*.
13. A strong argument for the relationship of the Haskalah to European Romanticism is made in Litvak, *Haskalah*.
14. Etkes, "Haskalah."
15. Litvak translates the term *maskil* as a teacher, an instructor, lover of wisdom. Litvak, *Haskalah*, 32.
16. This is the narrative of Yiddish literature found in Miron, *Traveler Disguised*.
17. Etkes, "Haskalah."
18. Litvak, 32–34.
19. Nadler, *Faith of the Mithnagdim*, 151–70.
20. Berdichevsky, *Kitve Mikhah Yosef Berdichevsky (Bin-Goryon)*, 6:34.
21. More recent research has challenged the assumption, however, that there existed no Hebrew women writers until the twentieth century. Magnus, "Sins of Youth," 94.
22. Magnus, 94.

23. One notable exception to the paucity of Hebrew women's writings in the nineteenth century was the Italian maskilic Hebrew poet Rachel Luzzatto Morpurgo (1790–1871), who, raised in the prominent rabbinic and maskilic Luzzatto family, had received an exceptional Jewish education in Talmudic and Kabbalistic texts. Other lesser-known examples include the eastern European novelist Sara Menkin Foner (1854–1936), as well as Yocheved Bat-Miriam (1901–1980), who began writing in the 1920s as Hebrew women's authorship, and Hebrew education, both saw a sharp rise. Zierler, *Rachel Stole the Idols*, 15–39. See also Cohen, "Maskilot."

24. See the author's introduction in Weissman, *Mendele ha-ivri*. Also see Bar Asher, "Mekomah shel ha-aramit ba-ivrit ha-hadashah."

25. Pinsker, *Literary Passports*, 275–304; Biale, *Not in the Heavens*, 15–58.

1

MEN OF LETTERS

Textuality in Eastern European Jewish Culture

SCHOLARS (AND MANY OTHER READERS) OF THE NEW Hebrew literature that emerged in the nineteenth century, because it was a child of modernity, have tended to see it as a secular phenomenon.[1] At the same time, they have often recognized the extent to which the language of modern Hebrew fiction and poetry was laden with echoes, references, and allusions to the sacred Judaic canon and therefore indebted to the tradition of Jewish textual learning.[2] This literature contained the dual qualities of modern and ancient, religious and secular, sacred and profane. Thus, the question of modern Hebrew literature's relationship to the tradition of Jewish textual learning has been central to scholarly efforts to describe and explain it. Most of the accounts of the emergence of Hebrew belles lettres in the modern period are predicated on the idea that Hebrew literature represented a revolt against the Jewish religious tradition and the modes of life that it governed.[3] In the title of his seminal work of Hebrew literary scholarship, the Israeli critic Baruch Kurzweil (1907–1972) posed the question as follows: *Our New Literature: Continuation or Revolution?* Kurzweil described modern Hebrew literature in the early period of its development as a disenchanted pursuit that rejected the divinity of sacred texts and attempted to sever Hebrew writing from the rabbinic monopoly on textual production.[4]

Indeed, in the narratives of Kurzweil and, before him, of such influential Hebrew scholars as Joseph Klausner (1874–1958), the first attempt to create a Jewish literary tradition independent from rabbinic culture had been made already by the Jewish Enlightenment, or Haskalah, movement in the late eighteenth century. Specifically, Mendelssohn and the maskilim who formed around him attempted to rehabilitate the Hebrew Bible and its particular Hebrew language, which the rabbis had long and deliberately sidelined in favor of the Talmud.[5] Klausner and Kurzweil, among others, continued the direction first embarked on by Jewish writers in Russia. These scholars were actively involved in the project of the formation of secular Jewish culture themselves, and the bulk of their scholarship was devoted to describing the break with the rabbinic tradition rather than its continuation.[6] From a historical vantage point, it appears that their efforts were successful. Today, secular Jewish literature and culture and its scholarship thrive. The mechanism by which the tradition of Talmud study in eastern Europe creatively precipitated the formation of modern Hebrew literature, however, has not yet been adequately brought to light.

While the present narrative acknowledges that the emergence of modern Hebrew literature in Russia required nothing short of a revolution to first undermine and then reinvent Jewish literature and culture, I argue that this revolution originated in the world of tradition. Thus, this chapter begins the story of modern Hebrew literature by examining the world of traditional Jewish texts, which provided the intellectual and linguistic context that enabled the formation of modern Hebrew literature in Russia even prior to the popularization of the ideas of the Haskalah.

The study of the Talmud and the entire corpus of traditional Jewish texts has been practiced since antiquity. It was the eighteenth century, however, that brought with it the flourishing of a revitalized rabbinic scholarly culture known as the "yeshiva movement," which revolutionized Jewish culture.[7] Grounded in the thought of the Vilna Gaon and his student Chaim of Volozhin, the movement gradually gained power and social esteem beginning in the late eighteenth century and transformed Jewish culture.[8] The movement was marked by the rise of the new framework of the yeshiva and the figure of the lamdan, or learner—a scholar of Jewish sacred texts. Chaim of Volozhin's founding of the first and most influential yeshiva in Volozhin (located in present-day Belarus) in 1803 set off a chain reaction that gave rise to the Mir Yeshiva in 1815, Reb Mayle's Yeshiva in Vilna in 1831, the Slobodka Yeshiva in 1863, and many other yeshivot until the end of the nineteenth century.[9] Due to the Vilna Gaon's strong opposition to the Hasidim, the adherents of this rabbinic movement became commonly referred to as the "mitnagdim"—the opponents.[10] The yeshiva model was so successful, however, that it was soon adopted by different streams of Hasidim and became the prime model for higher Jewish learning in eastern Europe.

The yeshiva, literally translated as "sitting," housed men of various ages who sat in the study of the classical texts that Jews had been studying for generations. The institutional organization of the yeshiva, however, introduced many new features that were previously not characteristic of the traditional modes of study practiced in earlier periods. Among the most important innovations of the yeshiva was the high status afforded to Talmud study, which was reflected in the learning practices as well as the in the organizational structure of the yeshiva.

While the mitnagdim and the yeshiva movement, as opposed to the Haskalah, were the representatives of orthodox Jewish culture, it would be a mistake to think of the mitnagdim as traditionalists. Although the yeshiva movement placed itself in opposition to the cultural upheavals of the nineteenth century, the movement nonetheless adopted some of the philosophical and social assumptions of the European Enlightenment. Among these was its admiration for reason and for a rationalist methodology applied to the study of Jewish texts, with which it is still identified today. Another Enlightenment idea that the yeshiva movement internalized and enacted in eastern European Jewish life was the separation between public and private spheres.[11] The rise of a new private culture of learning, embodied by the yeshiva, brought with it the erosion of centralized rabbinic power and of the institutions capable of enforcing Jewish law, such as the local synagogue or communal government, while shifting power and cultural capital to the individual pursuit of textual learning.[12] The founding of the Volozhin Yeshiva and the learning frameworks that followed, argues the historian Olga Litvak, created a Jewish counterculture marked by intellectual detachment and elitism—a culture whose values ran against the larger Jewish society, identified with the institution of the synagogue.[13] Whereas the synagogue, as a community institution, still possessed cultural power, it commanded none of the prestige of intellectual brilliance and achievement associated with the yeshiva.[14] In the thought of the mitnagdim, moreover, the synagogue, as a community institution, became associated with boorishness and impiety. This is exemplified in the writings of the Vilna Gaon, who urged his wife to frequent the synagogue "as little as possible," lest she and their daughters succumb to "jealousies, folly, and libelous speech."[15] The yeshiva movement's deliberate distancing from the synagogue and from the Jewish community at large signified its movement toward elitism and resulted in the separation of religious textual learning from all other spheres of Jewish life and practice.

The modern institution of the yeshiva in Europe was unprecedented both in size and scope, raising new challenges regarding its financing.[16] An important characteristic of the new structures of the Lithuanian yeshivas (true to a lesser extent of smaller learning frameworks, such as the *kloyz* or the *beit midrash*) was their independence from the central Jewish synagogues and community. Large yeshivas were often located in small towns, isolated from large Jewish centers to safeguard the elitism and aloofness of the mitnagdim from the interference of Jewish society. Yeshivas supported themselves by funds from itinerant emissaries reaching out to distant and international patrons.[17] This allowed the yeshiva to be mostly autonomous in its intellectual pursuits, with the local Jewish community having no control over the yeshiva's governance. The Volozhin Yeshiva, for instance, was supported by a system of independent patronage, somewhat akin to the patronage of art. A portion of these funds were distributed to students as small weekly stipends in order that they no longer be obliged to rely entirely on charity or the support of community members. Under this new system of autonomy, as the historian Eliyahu Stern observes, the students of the yeshiva were "no longer beholden to parents, rabbis," or part of a larger Jewish community; rather, they regarded themselves first and foremost as the "children of the yeshiva."[18]

The intellectual character of the yeshiva can be encapsulated in the idea of Torah lishmah, that is, the study of Torah—a term inclusive of all sacred Jewish texts—"for its own sake." Originating in Tannaitic texts, the term *Torah lishmah* underwent a radical transformation in the works of Chaim of Volozhin, who established this activity as the ultimate end to which Jews should strive. The unprecedented importance that the leaders of the mitnagdim assigned to Torah study not only elevated it above the practical needs of society, such as employment and livelihood, but also placed it, at times, above the basic principles of piety and even the observance of the other commandments.[19] Chaim of Volozhin designed the Volozhin Yeshiva to be the embodiment of this ideal—a place of never-ending study, where students were expected to learn all day and all night without engaging in any extraneous activities. Although the Russian authorities believed it to be a rabbinical training school, the yeshiva did not aim to ordain rabbis; nor was its aim to establish any *pesak*, a practical legal "decision."[20] Instead, the study of the practical applications of Jewish law became secondary to the study of the most obscure sections of the Talmud. It was a place entirely devoted to the ideal of Torah lishmah, the pursuit of Torah knowledge for its own sake, whose utter impracticality was exalted by its adherents as the highest attainable form of freedom and pleasure.[21]

This milieu of the rabbinic world—its values, practices, and institutions—composed the traditional system in which all the central writers of Hebrew literature in nineteenth-century Russia had been educated. I will refer to this milieu, its practices, and its institutions as *Talmudic culture*, treating it as a franchise of transferable practices pertaining to Jewish writers' attitudes about textuality.

Textuality in Rabbinic Thought

The theological status of Torah study within Talmudic culture is based in idealist metaphysics that date back to the earliest strata of Jewish texts. The very first words of Midrash Genesis Rabbah, commenting on the first verse of Genesis, encapsulate the idealist approach:

> Rabbi Hoshaya opened [with the verse in Proverbs 8:30]: "I [the Torah, or Wisdom] was to Him an *amon*; I was his delight each day." *Amon* means "pedagogue," *amon* means "covered," *amon* means "hidden," and some say, *amon* means "great." . . . Alternatively, *amon* means "artisan." The Torah said: "I was God's artisan's tool." . . . When a mortal king builds a castle, he does not do so from his own knowledge but consults an architect, and the architect does not build it from his own knowledge but from scrolls and blueprints in order to know how to make rooms and doorways. So too, God looked into the Torah and created the world. (Genesis Rabbah 1:1)

The midrash here is not only interested in the clarification of scripture but in answering fundamental metaphysical questions about the nature of the universe and about God. Drawing on the verse from Proverbs, the midrash develops the idea that the Torah was God's "pedagogue," a sort of an architectural plan at which God looked to create the world. Using its characteristic playful method, the midrash carries out a counterintuitive reversal of the conventional view of God as an almighty creator in favor of one where God is the student, and the Torah—the blueprint behind the physical world—is the teacher.

The sages of the midrash feared that the conception of the Torah as the master plan of creation might lead one to doubt God's omnipotence and notion of creation ex nihilo. Thus, the midrash immediately anticipated the objection of its philosophical rivals with the following story: "A philosopher once asked Rabban Gamliel and said to him: 'Your God is a great craftsman because he found great materials to help him with creation: *tohu* and *vohu*, darkness, wind, water, and void'" (Genesis Rabbah 1:9).

The invocation of the "philosopher" indicates that the midrash is waging a polemic against early materialist thinkers with whose ideas the rabbis came into contact. The philosopher argues the position of the Greek and Roman materialists, in particular the school of Epicurus, whose name and philosophy became used in rabbinic culture as a synonym for heresy. The philosopher's literal reading of the first verses of the creation story in Genesis points out that the Torah itself seems to support the idea that the basic forms of matter—such as *tohu* and *vohu*, darkness, wind, water, and void—were eternally present, and God, who is a "craftsman" in this view, had only to put all of the primal materials together. This position reflects that of Lucretius, the student of Epicurean philosophy, who argued that everything is created from preexisting particles and that matter and void—*tohu va-vohu*—are at the basis of all things.[22] Rabban Gamliel, for his part, objects by bringing proof texts to document the creation of each of these elements from the primordial *nihil* with the act of speech, namely, that God "commanded, and there was" (Amos 4:13 in Genesis Rabbah 1:9). In other words, the polemic waged by the sages of the midrash against the ancient Greek materialist viewpoint is that God is not an artisan but rather an Author, in the most radical sense of the word.

This idealist conception of textuality as the substrate of the physical world, found in the midrash and other Tannaitic sources, became central to the thought of the Vilna Gaon, the yeshiva movement's founder. Arriving at an idealist metaphysics from Jewish sources, the Gaon's ideas were in conversation with the famed Enlightenment philosopher Gottfried Wilhelm Leibniz (1646–1712), in which both the rabbi and philosopher were involved in an Enlightenment quest for the "theory of everything," to locate a " universally valid coherent system that could be justified and contained within a first and absolute Idea."[23] Drawing on the texts of the Kabbalah, the Gaon perceived nature as a "divine mathematics" whose code was written with Hebrew letters.

The idea of the world as a code—a mathematical matrix consisting of the letters of the Hebrew alphabet and their corresponding digits according to *gematria*, Hebrew numerology—was introduced by *Sefer Yetzirah* (*The Book of Creation*), which is one of the earliest Hebrew works, dating to the second century BCE. In succinct and poetically captivating Hebrew poetry, the first chapter of this mystical work describes the universe as composed of Hebrew letters: "With thirty-two wondrous paths of wisdom did Yah, the Lord of Hosts, . . . engrave his name, and created his universe by the three *sefarim*: with *sefer* [text or code], *sfar* [count/number], and *sippur* [telling/speech]" (Sefer Yetzirah 1:1).

Describing the creation of the world with the twenty-three letters of the Hebrew alphabet and the ten digits, which together make up the "thirty-two wonderous paths of wisdom," this early Kabbalistic text participates in the rabbinic conception of a textual universe. The root of *se-f-r*, which is also the word for "book," is taken apart to distill the three primary functions of texts—as code, as number and count, and as a form of verbal communication—which are all the ways with which Talmudic culture and its hermeneutical system interpret sacred texts. The notion of viewing nature as the "book superior to all books" was not unique to Jewish culture; it was an established trope of European literature from the Middle Ages in writers from Galileo to Rousseau.[24] Contrary to the Western symbolic conception of "nature as scripture," however, in the Jewish context, this idea is not to be interpreted metaphorically, argues Eliot Wolfson, but rather literally, where the Torah as "a prototype of all books, the hypertext," informs us about the semantic character of nature.[25]

The rabbinic idea that reality, at its most basic level, is composed of sacred texts (be it the Torah, the names of God, or the letters of the Hebrew alphabet) implied, then, that it was possible to transform reality through the manipulation of its constituent text. Like a coder rewriting the script of a program, the practical Kabbalist, a practitioner of esoteric teachings, was attributed the power of animating inanimate objects, reviving the dead, creating a golem, and more, all through the manipulation of Hebrew letters.[26] Practical magic aside, the Vilna Gaon was involved in the perpetual study and emendation of rabbinic texts, working with the assumption that the act of emending the texts is directly tied to the creation of a divine order and the redemption of the world from a state of chaos.[27] And all this, he believed, could be accomplished by the textual endeavor alone—without ever needing to leave the confines of his study.

There is another central component to the mitnagdim's textual theology, explored by the Midrash Rabbah on Genesis, worth noting—namely, the pleasure of the textual endeavor. Alongside the Torah's sublime place as God's blueprint for the world, it is also described by the concept of *sha'ashu'im*—play and delight. The Torah, God's partner in creation, is depicted in rabbinic thought as both a lover and child—whose playfulness is incompatible with the Christian conception of the logos.[28] In fact, God himself is often depicted in the Talmud as studying the Torah with great pleasure, reciting the words of his favorite students, playing and listening to the study of little children—in all of these images, the activity of Torah study is characterized as sha'ashu'im, a pleasurable and nonteleological activity synonymous with play.

Torah for Its Own Sake

In a culture that viewed the Torah as God's partner in creation and pleasure, its study, both in practice and in principle, was held to be the apex of worldly experience. That is, partially, why its study required no external justification. The concept of Torah lishmah, the study of the Torah for its own sake, is interpreted in several Talmudic passages as a negative injunction rather than a positive one. That is, it was understood that Torah study should not be instrumentalized for financial gain nor for personal aggrandizement as summed up by the rabbinic injunction "do not make the Torah a crown to exalt yourself nor a spade to dig with" (Mishnah Avot 4:7). In other words, the study of the Torah was only to be done in the service and pleasure of God. This idea was further developed in Hasidic thought, where the proper end of Torah study was to achieve *dveikut*, or cleaving—an ecstatic state of closeness to God.

The theology advanced by the mitnagdim, however, ushered in a radical transformation of the notion of Torah lishmah, one that was unprecedented in Jewish intellectual history.[29] In his theological magnum opus *Nefesh Ha-Hayim* (redacted 1780–1820), Chaim of Volozhin undermined the Hasidic conception of dveikut with a radical new stance. "The truth of the matter," he wrote, "is that *Torah for its own sake* means, for the sake of the Torah."[30] In other words, the study of the Torah has no end other than the Torah itself.[31]

But what does it mean to study Torah for the Torah itself? Chaim of Volozhin's radical tautology, the idea of study for the sake of study—a notion that is surprisingly akin to the French art slogan "art for art's sake"—transformed the mitnagdim's approach to study into what I describe here as the worship of textuality. Once the teleological targets of dveikut (closeness to God) and piety are removed from the conceptual framework of this age-old Jewish principle, the object of devotion became the text, in the broadest sense. However strange it may seem, in the culture of the yeshiva, the focus on God was so effectively replaced or, at best, mediated by the focus on textual scholarship that "mere faith was considered not as much wrong as it was vulgar."[32] Moving into the nineteenth century, the result of this radical redefinition of Torah lishmah was its gradual secularization, consisting of the transference of the initially religious devotion to Torah study to Hebrew literature and, later, to other fields of textual art and scholarship beyond the world of Jewish tradition. Torah lishmah, as we shall soon see, became literature for its own sake.

The transference of religious devotion from the sacred texts of the Judaic canon to textuality at large was also accompanied by the transference of the hermeneutic and textual practices that were endemic to the yeshiva framework onto secular Hebrew literature, as to any texts that Jewish writers brought up in Talmudic culture wrote, read, or studied. The phenomenon of the transference of the textual practices of the yeshiva and the beit midrash into the works of nineteenth-century Jewish writers has been widely observed by scholars regardless of the fact that most of these writers had long left Jewish observance and undergone secular transformations.[33] Describing the textual practices of maskilic writers in late imperial Russia, Jeffrey Veidlinger observes that

> books were studied rather than read. Many reported reading the same book over and over again, striving even for complete memorization of the text, much as yeshiva students memorized extensive passages of the Talmud. Those new to secular reading likely took the written word for truth, just as they had been taught to understand the biblical text with which they were most familiar. . . . Maskilim brought with them the methods of *pilpul* learned in the yeshivas to the literature they read. Memoirs describe readers summarizing the arguments of books they had just absorbed, challenging minute points in those works, and seeking some type of a dialectical resolution before moving on to the next book. . . . Maskilic books were sacralized on the model of rabbinic texts.[34]

In what follows, I will outline and conceptualize the central categories that characterize the textual practices and attitudes that Jewish writers, trained in the frameworks of Torah lishmah, imported into nineteenth-century Jewish literature written in Russia. My purpose here is twofold. First, it is to foreground how these textual practices and attitudes derive from the metaphysical framework of Torah learning in Jewish culture, which we have already described. The second purpose is to explain the clash between the metaphysical assumptions about textuality held by the mitnagdim and the notions of utility imported into Jewish literature from the Russian context, which challenged and undermined Jewish writers' faith in the value of the literary endeavor.

Transferable Textual Practices

The Text as the Basis of Physical Reality

Because of the understanding of nature as a scriptural text, the events and objects described in books acquired, for the learners of the Talmud, the ontological status of real events, and oftentimes, the book and the events in it appeared even "more real than the physical and external circumstance."[35] Tovah Cohen explains that, since the lamdan spent most of his time with books, books constituted his physical world. Thus, "the debates between former and latter authorities over the interpretation of scripture or a Talmudic passage were as vivid as arguments that he himself had witnessed."[36] The fact that these Talmudic disputes bore no relation to reality and that there was nothing more at stake in them "than the minutiae of exegeses" was of no consequence.[37]

Jewish writers with a yeshiva education who left the world of learning in favor of a new materialist outlook on life devoted much of their time to satirizing the treatment of texts as physical reality, sometimes with the depiction of their younger selves as naive readers or with the help of fictional characters. Despite satirizing the Jewish attitude toward texts in works of Hebrew fiction, Jewish writers did not stop themselves from engaging in the very practices they sought to criticize. This circularity appears most prominently in the work of Moykher-Sforim, for whom the idea of the entrapment in textuality, produced by the culture of Talmudic learning, served as the springboard for satire throughout his oeuvre. In his novella *Di klyatshe* (*The Nag*, 1873), a young Talmudic scholar called Isrulik decides to acquire a useful profession and sets out to study medicine. To pass the Russian qualifying exams, however, he is required to master Russian literature and folklore. But when he starts reading classic Russian folktales about the old witch Baba Yaga and the immortal sorcerer Kaschei the Deathless, fiction and reality merge, both for the protagonist and for Abramovitsh's text. Assisting in this conflation, Abramovitsh arranges a meeting between the young Talmudist and the Russian sorcerer, and this is how Isrulik recounts their acquaintance: "I lengthily recounted to him my knowledge of all his exploits, as they were written. I derided and slung mud at Baba Yaga along with the other sorcerers and stargazers, arguing how they all fell short of his prowess and could not hold a candle to him—all in the manner of a learned Talmud scholar."[38]

Abramovitsh's satirical insight in this passage is that even in his communication with a fictional character from Russian folklore, Isrulik cannot help but to recount to Kaschei all that he has read of him "as [it] was written." The "manner of the learned Talmud scholar"—as a textual practice, a mode of thinking, a communication style, and a genre—is a condition that generally plagues the characters of Abramovitsh's oeuvre. As the novella progresses, so does Abramovitsh's damning critique of Jewish textuality. In the novella's final section, Isrulik meets Satan himself, who takes him on a celestial flight above eastern Europe. As they fly over yeshivot, study houses, children's *hedarim*, and Jewish publishing houses—all institutions involved in the dissemination of texts and textuality—Satan reveals, in a sinister punch line, that they are all, in fact, working for him.

In a later novella, *The Abridged Travels of Benjamin the Third* (1878), likewise originally written in Yiddish but translated by Abramovitsh into Hebrew in the 1890s, Abramovitsh uses the motif of Don Quixote to advance his critique of Jewish culture's entrapment in texts. The novella describes the adventures of Binyomin, who like Cervantes's famous hero, is blind to the harsh realities of his life in the Russian Empire and builds all his goals and aspirations on stories from eclectic religious texts and folktales. Binyomin together with his accomplice Senderl, who is modeled on Sancho Panza, are so egregiously ill suited for the real world that they are expelled from the Russian military due to their sheer uselessness. As the following episode demonstrates, however, the condition of confusing reality with fiction is not a malady that Abramovitsh assigned uniquely to them but one that extends to their entire town of Tuneyadevka, or "Loafersville": "Once, it so happened, someone arrived in Tuneyadevka with a date. You should have seen the town come running to look at it. A Bible was brought to prove that the very same little fruit grew in the Holy Land. The harder the Tuneyadavkens stared at it, the more they saw before their eyes the River Jordan, the Cave of the Patriarchs, the Tomb of Mother Rachel and the Wailing Wall."[39]

This satirical vignette depicts the practice of bringing proof texts from scripture to prove the existence of an already-existing physical object. Although comical and absurd, this scene was nevertheless intended to reflect the epistemology of Talmudic culture. Once it is established that the fruit in question is indeed a date as described in the Bible, the characters' imagination takes flight, and all of the geographical reality surrounding them begins to transform into the imagined geography of the Holy Land as dictated by the texts of tradition. Benjamin Harshav theorizes that Jewish society in eastern Europe was not rooted "in a geographical area of its own—a physical here and now." But in their everyday awareness, Jews were connected to "a fictional world outside of history and geography, based in a library of texts and their interpretations."[40] To say that this description applies to all members of Jewish society would, of course, be a misrepresentation. Textual idealism was prevalent enough within Jewish culture, however, to merit Abramovitsh's satire. In many of Abramovitsh's works, as in this passage, the depiction of the Jews' disconnectedness from reality is a tactical element of his realist critique, which insisted that books must be dictated by reality, not the other way around.

Torah as Literature and Literature as Torah

Seemingly antithetical to the understanding of the Torah as the basis of physical reality stands the notion that the Torah is a work of literature. Jay Harris explains that in rabbinic Jewish culture, the divine speech of the Torah, which is identified as "song" in Kabbalistic literature, "must be appreciated as if it were 'poetry' filled with the many tropes to which the poetic soul resorts."[41] The Midrash and Talmud, as we saw, conceived of a universe that was created with divine speech and that the material world was brought into existence by God's ten "sayings" in the creation story in Genesis (Mishnah Avot 5:1). Literature, understood as the divine voice embodied by the text of the Torah, thus became itself sacralized as the divinely elected medium for God's communication with human beings.

Emerging from this understanding of the Torah as literature is a hermeneutical system characterized by an omnisignificant approach to the meaning of sacred texts. In rabbinic literature, it is associated particularly with the second-century Tannaitic sage Rabbi Akiva, who is able to "extrapolate reams upon reams of Halakhah upon each tip of a *yud*," considering the letters themselves even down to the calligraphic particularities of the written text (Talmud Bavli Menahot 29a). In nineteenth-century Hebrew literature, Y. L. Gordon's maskilic poem "The Tip of the Yud" (1873) famously satirized the attention to the tip of the letter *yud* as a small-minded and gratuitously stringent exegetical tactic of rabbi authorities in his day.

The hermeneutic practices of the lomdim attributed meaning to each detail of the scriptural text, from the outermost layer to the innermost one. This approach became known as *pardes* exegesis. The pardes, "the orchard" (a cognate of "paradise"), symbolizes the mystical orchard of sacred texts to which Talmudic sages and students venture—often at their own peril—in the hopes of gleaning a deeper understanding of the Torah and, thus, the universe. In rabbinic literature, the term *pardes* became an acronym that stands for the four layers of scriptural interpretation: *peshat*, "the simple (or contextual) meaning," the most literal commonsense interpretation; *remez*, "hint," the allegorical interpretation of the text; *derash*, "exegesis" and interpretation; and lastly, *sod*, "secret," the esoteric interpretation of scripture and of reality.

The consequence of regarding Torah as literature was a blurring of boundaries between texts that fell under the umbrella of Torah and secular literary texts. The overlap between sacred and secular texts became an established trope in the lives of the lomdim who became Hebrew writers in Russia, as well as in their literary protagonists. According to the personal accounts of Jewish such writers as Lilienblum, Bialik, and Berdichevsky (subjects of the following chapters), when they first encountered secular Hebrew poetry and literature, usually in tattered and outdated maskilic journals passed among students in the beit midrash, they pored over it with the same diligence and passion with which they had previously studied the Talmud. When a secular text found its way into the pile of Talmudic tomes that the lomdim were studying in the beit midrash, it was usually "adopted" by the learners as another exciting text to be studied. In the exact same way, when aspiring Jewish writers discovered the ideas emerging from the Russian intelligentsia, such as nihilism and materialism, for instance, these new ideas were conveyed to them by a new set of texts that came to replace the truth-defining status that sacred Jewish texts previously held. Thus, while the content and even language of the literature consumed by yeshiva-trained Jewish intellectuals drastically changed over the course of the nineteenth century, their approach to it remained fundamentally "yeshivish."

The Torah as an Intertextual System

The lomdim's notion of Torah did not end with the Pentateuch and prophets but included the Mishnah, the Talmud, and the multitude of midrashic and mystical texts as well as their later interpretations. It was a growing system perpetually made larger by the efforts of each generation of students and interpreters until it eventually came to include modern Hebrew letters.[42]

Since the time of the Midrash, the term *Torah* had already been defined in the broadest sense: "Scripture, Mishnah, laws, Talmud, *toseftot, aggadot,* and even what a seasoned student is bound to say to his teacher, all were said to Moses at Sinai" (Exodus Rabbah 47:1). The surprising factor here, of course, is the latter clause, which suggests that "what a seasoned student is bound to say to his teacher" *in some future time* can also be understood as Torah. Talmudic culture's view of a continual, ongoing divine revelation mediated though textual study and production, as it was developed by the mitnagdim, was one that greatly encouraged ingenuity. The ability to innovate and to create a *hiddush*—an innovation that transforms and renews the matrix of sacred texts, which is essentially the world itself—was considered an act of cosmic significance and one that brings God great pleasure.[43] Despite the dialogical nature of scriptural interpretation conceptualized by the early rabbis, however, the permissible boundaries of interpretation were circumscribed by strict principles of hermeneutics and, of course, by tradition. This was true especially with respect to the interpretation of Jewish law, which operated on the principle of seniority in which interpreters of later generations could not undermine earlier ones. Thus, with the passage of time, the intertextual universe of sacred Jewish texts was growing more and more static, and a true hiddush was becoming less likely to come by.

Characteristic of the lomdim's engagement with this intertextual universe of sacred texts was a nonlinear and multigenerational study of texts. When studying a Talmudic passage, the Torah lishmah practitioner envisioned an almost endless intertextual universe of Jewish texts on which he could draw to shed light on a local interpretation. The more sources he could engage, the better he could showcase his Talmudic prowess to his peers or teachers. Tova Cohen writes that "no page of Talmud was ever studied in a linear fashion."[44] The study of the Talmud involved constant textual acrobatics that included consulting various rabbinic commentaries and glosses, looking up references and allusions to scripture, comparing pages of different Talmudic tractates, comparing differences in versions of the same Talmudic debate or story between the Babylonian and Jerusalem Talmuds, and, for more advanced scholars, taking into account manuscript variants.

The very layout of the classical Jewish book encouraged this intertextual engagement. In most religious Jewish texts, with the primary example being the Talmud, the main text occupies only a small space on the page; it never stands in isolation but is always surrounded by a myriad of commentaries and glosses. The form and layout of a traditional text also served as an inspiration for modern Hebrew literature. Moshe Leib Lilienblum composed, for instance, a modern-day Mishnah written in the traditional style, surrounded by his commentaries, dealing with questions of labor and Jewish economic productivity. An additional feature of the intertextual nature of Talmud study, furthermore, resulted in a blurring of all distinctions between the past and present. For instance, in Bialik's poem "Ha-matmid," the diligent Talmud student repeatedly chants to himself the words, "Rava said that Abbayye said," repeating the words of long-dead Talmudic sages who are as real to him as if they were alive in the present.

Alongside their scholasticism, the lomdim were well attuned to the play and pleasure of textual learning. Rabbinic and early Hebrew writing attests to its writers' fondness for word and letter games. A fascinating example of this is the rabbinic practice of numerology (gematria), using the traditional correspondence of each letter in the Hebrew alphabet to a numerical value. The premise of rabbinic numerological exegesis is that an equivalence or correspondence in the numeric value between words reveals the semantic connections among them. Extending this practice to modern Hebrew letters, Lilienblum signed his autobiography with the pen name Tzelofchad bar Hushim ha-Toheh, which translates as "fear's shadow, son of the senses, the confused." This strange and comical symbolic name, in addition to being the numerological equivalent of his real name, is one example of how Jewish writers continued to practice and enjoy rabbinic textual practices in secular contexts, even if there was no utility to be derived from them. Other letter games played by modern Hebrew writers included acrostics, anagrams, mnemonics, and alphabetical poetry. The letter acrobatics characteristic of rabbinic hermeneutical play and other textual practices, which constitute the notion of *melitza*, or poetic embellishment, were ubiquitous in the writings of the older generation of maskilim, who were not yet touched by nihilism's scorn for allegedly useless literary practices. These playful literary devices also appeared in the writings of Jewish nihilists, however, who were categorically opposed to such "useless" aesthetic embellishments as, for instance, the alphabetical poem of archaic Hebrew curses that Avraham Uri Kovner directed at his rival in his early work of Hebrew literary criticism.[45]

The intertextual practices of the lomdim who became Jewish writers made their writing opaque to outsiders and limited their reading public to only those who could understand them—a likewise learned intertextual community of educated male readers. Cohen explains that writers who were exposed to the traditional system of Jewish education shared similar reading strategies because they were always taught to read several texts simultaneously—the Torah and its commentaries, the Hebrew text and its Yiddish translation, or two similar passages from the Talmud.[46] Maskilic writers with these shared reading strategies formed an "interpretative community," as per Stanley Fish.[47] Even when these writers transitioned to secular works, their interpretive community remained narrowly limited to yeshiva-educated males. Although Jewish writers began, in the 1850s, to fight for a Hebrew literature that would speak to the masses, this transformation did not happen until the twentieth century—both because of the absence of a colloquial Hebrew and because, as I suggest, due to scholarly hubris and group insularity, they enjoyed writing in coded and subversive ways.

The Culture of Talmudic Debate

The culture of debate served as an important part of the educational frameworks of the lomdim. Among yeshiva students, learning was carried out in study-partner pairs (*havruta*), whose goal was for each partner to challenge the other's interpretations and engage in ongoing dialectics. One's sharpness was often assessed by how well one performed in these debates by finding a contradiction and reconciling it. Memoirs of Volozhin students depict the heads of the yeshiva, Naftali Tzvi Berlin and Yosef Ber Soloveichik, to have encouraged students to find a contradiction in their interpretations of Talmudic passages.[48] Deliberately finding a contradiction in the teacher's argument was not viewed as an affront, as it would be in most other contexts, but, rather, earned the student more respect from his teachers and peers for having achieved a higher level in his learning.

In the educational frameworks of the lomdim, where no women were admitted, Talmud learning was a homosocial activity.[49] It was conducted in the greatest hall of the yeshiva, or a big room, where men of various ages (some as young as ten) would debate interpretation and struggle with their learning partners waging the sacred "war of the Torah." This mode of study-hall learning was often described to have extravagant physical manifestations. It was common, for instance, to read, to recite, or to chant the text aloud; to walk around or to sway back and forth; and to gesticulate with one's hand. Even someone who was sitting by himself would not stay still. He would likely be seen moving back and forth in the same place, a movement that usually signified that he was working on the memorization of passages (an important practice to establish Talmudic expertise) or on an internal dialectical study of the text.

The vibrant physical atmosphere of debate in the study hall found a strong expression in the works of lomdim turned Hebrew writers, on whom it had left variable impressions. Abramovitsh, in his memoir, described the beit midrash atmosphere in carnivalesque terms. He writes that, on the day that his father first took him to the study house, "[he] was like a man who had come for the first time to a great market on market day." He compares the debates and negotiations between the studying pairs to "people engaged in [the] buying and selling of strange goods, wares, and rare valuables." He describes how he was struck mute by the "commotion, noise, and tumult of the market place, which could be heard from each side and corner: running and pushing, shouting, asking, mumbling, winking their eyes, stomping their feet . . . gripped by lust for the trade." Bewildered at first, Abramovitsh writes how this "strange scene eventually became dear to his heart" and served as a source of aesthetic inspiration.[50] These practices were also a source of shame, however, for such writers as the nihilist Avraham Uri Kovner, who, in a denunciation to the Russian government, wrote that "the practice of studying in pairs 'leads to noise and cries, accompanied by grimaces, movements of the hands, head and the whole body, such that if a passerby accidentally entered . . . and saw this picture, he would think that he had come not to an educational institution but to a mad house.'"[51]

As with individual study of the Talmud, the culture of debate that was a defining feature of the textual practices of the lomdim was likewise "for its own sake," and not aimed at producing a solution. That is to say, the debate itself, rather than its reconciliation, was the end goal. The rabbinic approach to the interpretation of text, which permeated the yeshiva, was marked by the appreciation for contradiction and intellectual sparring, the belief in omnisignificance, and a tolerance of polysemy, or the truth of multiple meanings.[52] Describing the exegetical approach of *Ha'emek Davar*, by Naftali Tzvi Berlin, who was the head of the Volozhin Yeshiva in the latter half of the nineteenth century, Jay Harris explains, "No speech is reducible to a single accepted significance," and "the unanswerable question was more favored to the resolution of a contradiction."[53]

Hebrew and Aramaic as Living Languages

Finally, by constantly engaging with sacred Jewish texts, the lomdim developed an intimate relationship with the languages of these texts—namely, Hebrew and Aramaic. While these languages may have seemed "dead" or outdated to the average Jew, among the Talmud-learning elite this was far from the case. In fact, for the lomdim, these were the languages in which they spent the major (and most pleasurable) part of their day, and to them Hebrew and Aramaic were, thus, very much "living" languages.[54] Hebrew and Aramaic were the languages of ideas, intellectual engagement, poetry, and aesthetics, as well as the languages in which the lomdim communicated with the dead sages of the Talmud, who were their daily interlocutors.

In fact, Hebrew and Aramaic were so vital within Talmudic culture that they served to transform the colloquial use of Yiddish of both learned and lay members of Jewish society. Max Weinreich has classically described the cultural nexus of the world of Talmud study—involving such functions as language, expressions, and argumentation logic—as "the way of the *Shas*," where the term *Shas* is a rabbinic acronym for the Shishah Sedarim, the six orders of the Mishnah at the base of the Talmudic system.[55] Jordan Finkin has further argued that the vernacular Yiddish spoken not only by the learners but by the rest of Jewish society was likewise permeated by the language of Talmud study, and "even people who had never as much as seen a page of Talmud derived their words and expressions from the 'way of the Shas' that integrated and shaped their Yiddish."[56]

The languages of Talmudic culture permeated each part of the lomdim's lives, from intellectual study to the domestic use of Yiddish in the home and synagogue. Most importantly to the rise of Hebrew literature in Russia, however, the adaptation of terms and expressions from the world of Torah learning and its languages into the realm of colloquial speech was what enabled Jewish writers to invent a literary form of Hebrew colloquial speech that was hitherto nonexistent. This new literary colloquial language—a hybrid of biblical Hebrew and Aramaic and their Yiddish transformations, also known as the *nusach*—became the new language of modern Hebrew literature in Russia.

Conclusion

Through its autotelic valuation of literature and its preservation of Hebrew and Aramaic languages, among many other factors, the rich world of Talmud study laid the groundwork for the creation of modern Hebrew literature in Russia by its defected members. The freedom to engage with Jewish texts and ideas without any exterior motive, along with the pursuit of knowledge for its own sake, was, arguably, the greatest contribution of the rabbinic world to Hebrew letters and to Jewish intellectual achievement more broadly. It also exacted a high price, however, from its practitioners and their surrounding culture. As the next chapter will illustrate, the cultural institutions set in place for the maintenance of the Torah lishmah ideal adversely affected many aspects of the learners' lives, their families, and finances and led to a growing number of defectors, who soon turned against the idea of autotelic textuality and came to blame the yeshiva and all of the rabbinic institutions associated with it, for both their personal troubles and those afflicting Jewish society in Russia.

Notes

1. Hever, *Be koakh ha-el*, 7.
2. Hever, 8.
3. The Israeli literary critic Baruch Kurzweil was among the first to bring the discussion of Hebrew literature's relationship to its religious tradition to the foreground of Hebrew literary scholarship. The debate regarding the nature of secular Jewish literature and identity—the question of whether we should see Hebrew literature as a new creation that only draws inspiration from traditional tropes, as per Kurzweil, or rather a direct continuation and reframing of the Jewish tradition—continues to be explored by contemporary Jewish historians, such as Shmuel Feiner and David Biale. See Kurzweil, *Sifrutenu ha-hadashah*; Biale, *Not in the Heavens*; Feiner, *Milhemet tarbut*; Shaked, *New Tradition*.
4. Kurzweil, 16, 46.
5. Parush, "Another Look," 174.
6. Shachar Pinsker addresses the important engagement of Hebrew modernists with rabbinic textual practices but not during the early years of Hebrew literature's beginnings. S. Pinsker, "Intertextuality, Rabbinic Literature."
7. Jewish Lithuania, referred to commonly as "Lita," refers to a region that "constituted the Duchy of Lithuania when the Polish-Lithuanian Commonwealth was established in 1564 and also areas which later became parts of Poland, Belarus, and the neighboring Baltic states." Stampfer, *Lithuanian Yeshivas*, 2.
8. For historical and social accounts of the mitnagdim, see Nadler, *Faith of the Mithnagdim*; Stampfer.
9. The Volozhin Yeshiva was preceded by the beit midrash of the Gaon in Vilna and by the Yeshiva of Eyshishok founded in 1790. Yeshivot that were founded later included Reb Mayle's Yeshiva in Vilna in 1831, Slobodke in 1863, Radin in 1869, Kelem in 1872, Telz in 1882, and Slutsk in 1897. For dates and geographical locations, see Katz, *Lithuanian Jewish Culture*, 150–51.
10. Stampfer, *Lithuanian Yeshivas*, 2.

11. E. Stern, *Genius*, 141.

12. E. Stern, 137.

13. Litvak, "Revolt of the Study," 28.

14. Litvak, 29.

15. Cited in Litvak, 29.

16. Stampfer, *Lithuanian Yeshivas*, 3, 35.

17. Stampfer, 3.

18. E. Stern, *Genius*, 138.

19. The radical notion that Torah study supersedes and suspends other religious obligations, such as prayer and procreation, appears in the theological treatises of the Vilna Gaon and his student Chaim of Volozhin. Lamm, *Torah lishmah*, 100.

20. Stampfer, *Lithuanian Yeshivas*, 3, 35.

21. Mishnah Avot 6:2, cited in Volozhiner, *Nefesh Ha-Hayim*, 4:43.

22. Lucretius, *Nature of Things*, 15.

23. E. Stern, *Genius*, 37.

24. Curtius, *European Literature*, 324.

25. Wolfson, *Language, Eros, Being*, 202. Cited in E. Stern, *Genius*, 198n22.

26. On the origins of the "golem," see Scholem, *Origins of the Kabbalah*, 102–22.

27. E. Stern, *Genius*, 53–62.

28. D. Stern, *Midrash and Theory*, 15–38; Boyarin, "Gospel of the Memra," 287.

29. Nadler, *Faith of the Mithnagdim*, 152.

30. Volozhiner, *Nefesh Ha-Hayyim*, 25.

31. Lamm, *Torah lishmah*, 137. See also Volozhiner, *Nefesh Ha-Hayyim*, 4:7.

32. Litvak, "Revolt of the Study," 29.

33. Cohen, "Maskil as Lamdan," 63.

34. Veidlinger, *Jewish Public Culture*, 71–73.

35. Cohen, "Maskil as Lamdan," 64.

36. Cohen, 65.

37. Cohen, 65.

38. Mendele Moykher-Sforim, *Nag*, 94.

39. Mendele Moykher-Sforim, *Tales of Mendele*, 307.

40. Harshav, *Language in Time*, 2.

41. Harris, *How Do We Know*, 241.

42. Benjamin Harshav uses Itamar Even Zohar's notion of a "polysystem" to describe this "reservoir" of interconnected and ever increasing texts of the Jewish tradition. Harshav, *Language in Time*, 34.

43. "Each individual word that is innovated by a person—God kisses it and crowns it." Volozhiner, *Nefesh Ha-Hayyim*, 31.

44. Cohen, "Maskil as Lamdan," 70.

45. Murav, *Identity Theft*, 51.

46. Cohen, "Maskil as Lamdan," 61–65.

47. Dauber, *Antonio's Devils*, 47.

48. This depiction appears in several of the Volozhin memoirs. See Etkes and Tikochinski, *Yeshivot Lita*.

49. Boyarin, *Unheroic Conduct*, 133.

50. "Reshimot letoledotai," in Mendele Moykher-Sforim, *Kol Kitvei*.

51. Murav, *Identity Theft*, 22.
52. D. Stern, *Midrash and Theory*, 18.
53. Harris, *How Do We Know*, 244.
54. Cohen, "Maskil as Lamdan," 67.
55. Weinreich, *History*, 214.
56. Finkin, *Rhetorical Conversation*, 2.

2

HOW THE WORD BECAME FLESH

The Loss of Faith in Literature in the Russian Empire

IN THE 1850S, UNDER THE AEGIS OF THE Haskalah, Hebrew finally began to thrive in the Russian Empire. The unexpected success of the first modern Hebrew novel, Avraham Mapu's *Love of Zion* (1853), heralded to the maskilim that their dream of reviving Hebrew literature might be coming to fruition.[1] By the late 1860s, however, the bourgeoning sphere of Hebrew letters was in danger of disintegrating once again into centuries-old oblivion. The threat this time came from young Jewish intellectuals with yeshiva backgrounds. Jewish men of letters who had aspired to become poets and writers of Hebrew began to turn their backs on the literary efforts of the Haskalah; they no longer saw Hebrew as useful. "My brothers, the enlightened ones," wrote the maskilic poet Y. L. Gordon in 1870, "have scorned the aged mother and her cutch / abandoned the language whose hour has passed / abandoned its literature, so awkward and bland / They say 'leave her for the language of the land!'"[2]

What prompted Jewish writers to abandon the project of Hebrew literature that they had worked so hard to cultivate only a decade earlier? Was the idea of leaving Hebrew for "the language of the land" the result of growing assimilation, or was there another reason for this stark shift in attitudes held by Jewish writers? This chapter shows that the encounter of Jewish writers with Russian nihilism led them to develop an insider critique of Jewish textuality that, in their view, undermined the Hebrew literary pursuit. Many of the founding writers of Hebrew literature, such as Avraham Uri Kovner, Abramovitsh, and Lilienblum, among others, began as Talmud learners who dabbled in Hebrew poetry and prose while still in the yeshiva. After leaving the protected bounds of a society that had reserved an esteemed place for them as Talmud learners and literati, however, they were confronted with an economic order in which they found themselves to be completely disenfranchised. A destructive blow to these writers' dreams of reinventing themselves as modern Hebrew writers stemmed from their growing conviction that their attraction to texts, cultivated by years of Talmudic learning, was responsible for their personal and economic failings, as well as for Jewish society's undesirable backward state in Russia.

Moved by the theories of philosophical materialism and by the anti-aesthetic notions of the Russian nihilists, who had risen to prominence in the 1860s, Jewish writers came to reject the Haskalah's romantic faith in literature as a means of sentimental and aesthetic refinement. Operating within a new materialist paradigm of utility, they argued that literature must provide Jewish society with tangible social and economic benefits that could affect people's material conditions. Armed with these new ideas, they dared challenge the Haskalah's most prized ideal—the revival of the Hebrew language, arguing that Hebrew should be replaced with more "useful" spoken languages, such as Yiddish or Russian. Kovner indeed switched from Hebrew to Russian, and Abramovitsh, as is well known, began his literary career in Hebrew, then switched to Yiddish, and in the late 1890s returned to Hebrew.

The growing disillusionment with the written word and with the literary pursuit as a whole among Jewish intellectuals was part of a larger shift that had been taking place among the Russian intelligentsia. The deep discord between the exclusive devotion to texts and the pressures of the material world was not unique to Jewish writers but was one shared by men of religious learning who were coming of age in mid-nineteenth-century Russia. This was the case particularly among the sons of Russian Orthodox priests, known as the *popovichi*, who belonged to a highly literate, religious group and whose representatives played a key role in the Russian Empire's intellectual development and radicalization. The members of this group were the first to experience and articulate their disillusionment with their religious textual education and with the redemptive promises of sacred texts and secular literature. Their invention of nihilism, with its rejection of belles lettres and its associated pleasures, was a reaction to what they perceived as the unchecked power afforded to textuality and its unregulated production. Taking their case against literature to the pages of Russian literary journals, their story and arguments served as a powerful model for Jewish writers' emulation. Examining the pivotal shift in attitudes toward textuality that took place in the mid-nineteenth-century Russian Empire, as depicted in the writings of Russian and Jewish religious literary elites, this chapter documents how the discontents of religious textual culture led both of these groups to embrace a philosophy that rejected the sanctity of the word in favor of a putatively more productive engagement with the material world.

Priests, Rabbis, and Radicals

While the Russian Orthodox clergy and the Jewish learning elite rarely occupy the pages of the same book unless the subject is historical hostility, the comparison between these two literate groups that shared an esteem for religious learning and literature sheds light on the evolution of both Russian and Jewish literatures in this period. Having already dealt with the world of Talmud learners and their institutions in the previous chapter, let us now present an overview of the Russian Orthodox clergy.

Viewed from within Russian society, the priestly class constituted Russia's educated religious elite, much like Talmud scholars in Jewish society. Priests occupied the highest rank of the clergy, above deacons, sacristans, and other clerical positions. Like Jews, they composed a visible minority distinguished by their social and learning institutions.[3] The popovichi, literally "of the priests," were the sons of priests in rural towns in the Russian Empire. Most priests' sons did not themselves assume pulpit positions—either by choice or due to a paucity of positions. Thus, there was a floating surplus of educated individuals who could not easily find an occupation. Their movement outside the closed clerical estate, however, was highly restricted, similarly to that of the Jews. They were not permitted to leave the clerical estate, intermarry, or to assume extraclerical positions.[4] Marriages, too, were tied to the profession. Priests' sons would pass through the clergy's educational system, and—somewhat similarly to young Talmud learners limited by stipulations in their marriage contracts—they were expected to secure their position and livelihood through marriage to a priest's daughter.

The identity of the popovichi as religious elites was solidified though their formal educational institutions, specifically the Russian Orthodox seminary. Theological seminaries had become the formal educational institution of the clergy as a result of Peter the Great's church reforms in the early eighteenth century. Like yeshivas, theological seminaries in Russia were new institutions that underwent reform and exponential growth in the modern period, reaching 61,798 students by the middle of the nineteenth century.[5] When seminary enrollments radically outgrew the clergy's resources, the government began opening the way for priests' sons to leave the clerical estate as part of an effort by the Russian state to dismantle its estate-based society during the Great Reforms of the 1860s.[6] In the brief window during the late 1840s to 1850s leading up to Russia's reforms, Russian seminarians, Jews, and people of various ranks began to enter the universities. There, they embarked on a process of secularization in which they gradually shed most layers of their religious faith and practice. Despite the government's temporary opening of class mobility, integration proved difficult and largely impossible. Priests' sons encountered many of the same challenges as did Jews and other minorities.[7] The economic and social hardship that priests' sons encountered during their university years made them, like the Jews, prone to political radicalization—a fact that undoubtedly contributed to the reason both of these groups are overrepresented in Russian revolutionary movements.[8] The Russian clerical class produced many individuals who had an immense impact on Russian letters—prime examples of this being Chernyshevsky and Dobrolyubov, who were writers, critics, and the creators of Russian nihilism. This connection between the Russian clergy and nihilism was cemented even further by Russian fiction, with such important fictional portrayals as Turgenev's Bazarov (in *Fathers and Sons*, 1862) and Dostoevsky's Rakitin (in *The Brothers Karamazov*, 1879), among many others.

As a unique class distinguished by its literacy, priests' sons had a special relationship to texts. The popovichi children who later became distinguished as writers and nihilists, as in the case of Chernyshevsky and Dobrolyubov, were recognized to manifest "genius" or extraordinary literary talents at a young age and described themselves as "bibliophiles." Childhood textual virtuosity, especially the ability to memorize large bodies of text, was a trope shared with Hebrew writers, who, like Lilienblum, for instance, described themselves as having memorized entire tractates of the Talmud at a young age. Another shared experience was one of textual absorption. Like the many Jewish writers who recall their love for textuality as having begun with the rich world of the Midrash and Jewish folktales, popovichi memoirists recall reading tales about the lives of saints and the deep influence of this reading on their characters.[9] Chernyshevsky, for instance, claimed that his first experience of literary pleasure came while reading *Chet'i Minei* (*Monthly Readings*), the sixteenth-century hagiographic collection of stories about saints' lives compiled at the turn of the eighteenth century by Dimitry of Rostov.[10] One of the stories was the famous tale "Life of Alexei, Man of God," who abandoned his family and his bride on her wedding night to live a life of poverty while disguised as a beggar.[11]

Similar narratives of asceticism figured for the lomdim in stories about the ascetic lifestyle of the Vilna Gaon. A common reading for young lomdim was the story collection *Aliyot Eliyahu* (*The Ascents of Elijah*), which described how the Gaon spurned "food, drink, and sleep" and preached the complete abdication of reality and material needs, even if it meant subjecting one's family to poverty and starvation, having himself allegedly allowed his wife and children to suffer from hunger.[12] Jewish saint stories were also a popular genre among the Hasidim in which legends of the Ba'al Shem Tov made up an early religious literature written in Hebrew. In writings of later Hebrew authors, such as Bialik and Berdichevsky, the theme of asceticism and world denial inspired such literary characters as the *matmid*, the diligent Talmud student who fasts and deprives himself of sleep and all worldly pleasure.

Overall, the early lives of both the popovichi and Jewish writers revolved around an intimate and sentimental relationship to texts, sacred and secular. Dobrolyubov, reflecting on his younger self from the disillusioned vantage point of a nihilist, recalled how deeply he was affected by reading and how he often wept when reading a sad story.[13] Lilienblum recounts a similar emotional reaction to literature and how reading Mapu's Hebrew novels had acted like a love potion between him and his love interest (see chap. 4). In addition, both Jewish and Russian religious intellectuals were perpetually engaged in acts of writing. While many lomdim penned Hebrew poems, acrostics, and commentaries to traditional Judaic texts, the popovichi were avid writers of diaries, which served as "secular confessionals" through which they mediated their lived experiences and kept track of their moral and spiritual development.[14] The practices of reading and engaging with texts would never disappear and would inconspicuously continue to inform writers from these backgrounds after their turn to nihilism.

The highly involved relationship with textuality—which mediated the lived experience of Russian religious elites as the texts of the Jewish tradition did for the Jews—predisposed the popovichi to diagnose themselves as Don Quixote–like dreamers and to attribute their later difficulties of adjusting to secular life to their textual education.[15] The belief in the truth of texts and in their sacred value—attitudes and practices that we shall see as prominent themes in the works of Jewish writers who attended yeshivas—entrapped the popovichi in a fictional or, as they later concluded, "illusory" world from which they tried to extricate themselves with great pain.

The Yeshiva versus the Seminary

Unlike the yeshiva, which was depicted as a place of intellectual challenge and growth, the seminary was ubiquitously described in memoirs as a place of intense adversity, where its students embarked on their first steps to disillusionment and subsequent radicalization. Here, Russian students of the sacred word usually described themselves as having experienced a religious crisis, where feelings of social injustice in the wake of the corruption of their childhood ideals by the seminary administration undermined their faith in traditional authority. This generally traumatic experience of the seminary years was also a time of the crystallization of a collective identity that led seminarians to gravitate toward one another once they entered secular culture.[16]

Outsider depictions of the seminary had been a long-standing trope in Russian fiction since the 1850s; however, with a growing sense of dissatisfaction, these depictions began emerging onto the literary scene from within the clergy itself. For instance, I. S. Belliustin (1819–1890), a popovichi memoirist and reformer, published a bitter exposé of the educational and social institutions of the Russian Orthodox clergy. The exposé first appeared in 1858 in France and quickly spread among Russian intellectuals. In it, he blamed the corruption of the clergy on its educational institutions:

> It is sad and painful to see how degraded and demoralized the clergy has become. It is even sadder to see that the clergy is itself partially responsible for this state of affairs and does not even have the right to console itself by saying that we suffer everything for Christ's sake. It does not behave in a manner that would arouse in others the veneration that is always vital for its service, so elevated and sacred. Wherein lies the evil? We shall follow the life of a rural priest from the years of his childhood and see that what has so profoundly denigrated the rural clergymen is the inevitable result of its education.[17]

Describing the path of a priest's son from childhood to adulthood through clerical institutions—beginning with seminary life and ending with an arranged marriage to a priest's daughter—Belliustin argues that the church institutions eventually destroyed the boy's character morally and physically.

The grievances of the popovichi toward their educational system can be compared to Jewish writers' critiques of traditional Jewish education in the 1860s and onward. A grievance that popovichi and yeshiva-educated writers shared and that became a focal point of the materialist critique they later advanced was the dissatisfaction with a solely textual, and hence "useless," education. The popovichi directed this complaint toward the seminary curriculum. They experienced their learning of Greek and Latin as "dead languages as useful in real life as Sanskrit."[18] They complained that the seminary curriculum, which consisted of subjects like philosophy, theology, and rhetoric, was an irrelevant and poorly taught mix of scholastic obscurantism. A similar sentiment of the harm inflicted on society and the individual by a religious textual education and its "useless" curriculum appears most strongly in Lilienblum's memoir novel *The Sins of Youth*, where he writes:

> The education is the cause of the dreadful, dark folly that haunts my townsfolk to this day. Robbed of childhood, I was imprisoned in my study room all day, not allowed to enjoy the pleasant days of youth . . . my strength, not nurtured in freedom and childish games, deprived of all knowledge of any subject not connected with Talmud study. . . . My head was clouded with awful nonsense . . . filled with corrosive poison. . . . They did not even teach me the letters of the gentiles' alphabets. . . . I did not even know how to distinguish Russian from Polish print.[19]

Not only does Lilienblum bemoan not being prepared by his education to confront the world outside of the yeshiva by being taught Russian, or math, for instance, but viewing all of his Talmudic learning as "nonsense," he has lost appreciation for the only thing for the sake of which he was deprived of all the pleasures of youthful life.

The theme of religious textual learning as a form of life denial was also articulated widely by the popovichi. Belliustin was critical of the fact the education of the young was entrusted to a rector who was always a monk—"a learned man," but one who was "dead to all that is alive."[20] The lack of a curriculum that adequately engaged with practical matters, combined with an ethos of asceticism and the hateful practice of rote memorization, according to Belliustin, crushed the seminarian's spirit, made him inactive and numb to the world, and transformed him into a living-dead creature like his rector. The seminary student exists in "a state of total inertness, physical and spiritual."[21] The striking resemblance of this image of the seminary student to Jewish writers' depictions of Talmud students as living-dead beings—evident in copious examples, from Lilienblum's image of the Hebrew writer as the "eternal dead of the Babylonian Talmud" to Bialik's later depiction of the Talmud student as a living-dead creature—coveys the

shared idea held by Russian and Jewish men of letters that the textual occupation was lacking a solid link to what was real in a material sense.[22]

Examining the experience of study in the seminary more closely, we
find another overlapping feature of religious textual study that popovichi
and yeshiva students shared and similarly derided—namely, disputations
on circular or supernatural subjects. Nikolai Pomyalovsky, another popovichi memoirist who later became a nihilist writer, describes such debates
in his autobiographical novella *Seminary Sketches* (1863). He writes that
seminary students enjoyed engaging in dialectics and circular questions,
such as "what comes first, faith before love or love before faith, is original
sin contained in the embryo, can the devil commit sin, etc. The 'brains'
[the smart students] triumphantly orated the pro and contra of the same
proposition, depending on the orders of their supervisors, and put to use
all one hundred rhetorical devices as well as every known trick of sophistry
and parabolism."[23]

This picture of seminary students engaging in abstract debates "using
all one hundred tricks of sophistry and parabolism" closely resembles Jewish writers' depictions of yeshiva students' debates and *pilpulim* (sophistic
arguments) in the 1800s. Dialectical argumentation as a means to compli-
cate an argument rather than to solve it was a central feature of Talmudic
education in the yeshiva, where it occupied a central role. For the popovichi in seminaries, however, disputations were a small luxury in the sea of
rote learning, capriciously enforced by corporal punishment (which, while
widespread in early Jewish educational frameworks like the *heder*, was in-
stitutionally absent from the yeshiva).[24]

The more significant complaint of the Russian clerical class, however,
extended beyond the curriculum. Jewish writers who had been educated in
the yeshiva, as well as the Russian popovichi, blamed their religious leadership for hypocritically promoting the lofty ideals of textual study while dis-
regarding the worldly price that the guardians of these ideals—along with
society as a whole—had to pay to sustain them. In memoirs and diaries,
popovichi described their painful perception of the moral discrepancies
and injustices present in the infrastructure of their educational and social
institutions. By their own accounts, the future nihilists' disregard for authority began with life under the seminary administration: "What did he
[the seminary pupil] see in the school authorities and teachers? Evil and
cruel hirelings whose sole aim was bold, unchecked, unpunished plunder.
He saw that his teacher (who was often drunk) recognized neither law nor

justice, and administered punishment or pardon to students in the most capricious ways."[25] In response to the tyranny of the seminary administration, seminarians developed brotherhoods that rebelled against their superiors even when it entailed punishment for all, and such small acts of rebellion were a feature of yeshiva life as well.[26]

Descriptions of the seminary experience reveal a growing sense of incongruity between the spiritual ideals advocated by the clergy and the material conditions under which these ideals were supposed to be carried out. Belliustin describes the seminarians' living arrangements in the homes of townsfolk as steeped in "loathsome poverty, invariably accompanied by filth, by rudeness that borders on bestiality, by the most abominable vices that they do not even bother to conceal." The biggest offense, according to Belliustin, is that even a basic material dignity is absent from the institutions responsible for upholding the "exalted and sacred" mission of religious learning. And when that mission becomes physically and morally corrupted by "filth" and "abominable vices," the seminarian's soul is dragged down by the gross materiality of existence and becomes "ruined in him forever."[27]

The pioneering Hebrew writer Avraham Uri Kovner articulated an analogous critique in 1869 in an exposé of the yeshiva entitled "Yeshibotnaia Bursa" ("The yeshiva's bursa"), published in the Russian-language Jewish paper *Den* (The day). The title—an amalgam of the yeshiva and the *bursa* (the seminary dormitories)—suggests the link that Kovner is making between the economic and social woes of the students of religious texts in Russia. He writes that the yeshiva, "which Jewish law requires to be a place of pristine cleanliness and holiness," is mired in filth, grease, and foul odors, and, moreover, the "yeshiva student, nearly without exception, will have skin diseases, various boils [*puzyri*], rashes, and sores [*yazvy*], and, if a new student comes to the yeshiva, from the close contact with others, in a short time, he will get the same sores as well. It is obvious that—in quarters shared by so many young men of various temperaments and inclinations—the morality of students suffers terribly, and various vices develop among them in the crudest form."[28]

The underlying reason for the critique of the yeshiva, argues the historian Eliyahu Stern, is the result of their physically passive lifestyle and economic unproductivity.[29] Avraham Uri Kovner presents here an almost identical description of the "abominable vices" and skin conditions as in Belliustin's exposé, which he had likely read. The driving grievance behind both exposés is that the ideal of the religious textual endeavor can never be redemptive as long as it exists without a functional economic framework that could sustain it.

A Marriage Made in Hell

The discrepancy between reality and the ideal was especially pronounced in the sphere of marriage—a sphere that underwent a radical reinvention in nihilist writings. The ideal of marriage as a spiritual union was a central feature of the young seminarians' initial romanticism; they dreamed of finding in their spouse both an ideal woman and a best friend for life.[30] Instead, an arranged marriage to a priest's daughter was the prerequisite for acquiring a position. Like the ubiquitous dissatisfaction with arranged marriages among the lomdim, for popovichi, such an arranged marriage entailed a legitimized form of degradation for both parties. Pomyalovsky writes, "Nowhere is the sanctity of marriage more violated than among seminarians. In the seminary the desecration of marriage and its perversion are legalized and hallowed by tradition. In the course of fourteen years a seminarian is flogged perhaps four hundred times, he is humiliated and corrupted morally intellectually and physically, only so that he can marry an assigned bride and take her father's position."[31] Building the life of a young couple on such close financial and physical ties to the bride's parents would often result in marital troubles as the disagreements would always start with the "terms of the marriage contract."[32]

The financial structure that governed marriages among the lomdim, in particular the practice known as *kest*, was a sore subject that received much attention in Hebrew writings by maskilim and materialist Jewish writers. Kest, Yiddish for "room and board" or "sustenance," also rendered using the Hebrew *mezonot*, referred to a marriage agreement provision designed to finance the impractical pursuit of learning. The historian Immanuel Etkes explains that the rise of the yeshiva and the lomdim's need for independence raised the question of how to support them.[33] One solution was to put off marriage, but this would have been unacceptable by Jewish law and generally viewed as undesirable in Jewish society. Instead, marriage itself was transformed into an institution that would finance the learning ambitions of male scholars. What resulted was the practice of a contractual arrangement, by which the parents of the bride committed to financially supporting the young couple for a number of years after their marriage so that a scholarly groom could devote himself to full-time study. After the promised years of parental support expired, the wife would often take over the burden of financial responsibility while the husband would continue to study.

This arrangement emerged as a traumatic rite of passage for lomdim in their transition to becoming Jewish writers and remained a tragic milestone in the biographies of almost all early Jewish writers, including Avraham Ber Gottlober (1811–1899), Lilienblum, Kovner, Abramovitsh, Berdichevsky, and Bialik. As described in countless memoirs of lomdim who became writers, the financial, emotional, and physical drawbacks of a kest marriage far outweighed the ideals and benefits of the scholarly freedom afforded to them by Torah lishmah and, in some cases, doomed all their future attempts to become financially independent.

Although the ideal of learning required aloofness from social pressures, the practice of kest effectively denigrated the ideal of Torah lishmah into a business transaction subjecting it to community market forces. In *The Marriage Plot*, Naomi Seidman observes that "unlike the balanced mutuality of a love match (in its ideal form), the financial aspect of arranged marriage encouraged competitiveness from the outset, with each side attempting to gain an advantage through maneuvers that bore an unseemly resemblance to marketplace bargaining." Combining this with Alan Mintz's observation that an arranged marriage was "a set of transactions in which each family tries to maximize its three basic sources of 'capital': learning, ancestry, and money," we can begin to understand how economic factors were, in fact, highly involved in what was intended to be an economically disinterested pursuit of learning.[34]

Men's scholarliness and intellectual strength were ranked as the highest priorities on the marriage market. An affluent Jewish father, who was not learned himself, yearned for a scholarly son-in-law.[35] The more talented the groom, the higher was his value. Having rabbinic ancestry also mattered for both men and women, but in the case of the groom, ancestry could be overlooked in favor of extraordinary scholarly ingenuity. If a match had been made, the negotiations of the kest would begin with extensive and contentious prenuptial bargaining. The duration and amount of economic support after marriage was determined by the groom's scholarly lineage and personal talents in learning, and often the prospective groom would be subjected to examination of his Torah knowledge at the initiative of the bride's father before the agreement was signed. Following marriage, the groom, usually a boy of thirteen to eighteen, was forced to leave his parental home—a separation that created great suffering as described in many personal accounts—and would move to the household of his wife's parents. He had to adjust both to the intimate bonds of matrimony and to his wife's parents' ways of life—all factors that contributed to marital strife and the disgust that defectors often experienced over the "dark side" of Torah lishmah.

In households living under the kest arrangement, Jewish women were often the providers for the family, working in shops and taverns, while also raising children and fulfilling domestic duties. Yet the added load of financial responsibility served only to reinforce the association between women and crude materiality, which further widened the insurmountable gap between the real woman and an imagined "ideal woman" found in literature. The gender structures the kest reinforced were thus heavily criticized by Hebrew writers, with one central grievance being the reversal of gender roles. While the working woman was depicted as crude, masculine, and unattractive, the Jewish scholar was depicted as feminine and weak, as well as idle and socially parasitic.[36] This stark reversal of gender roles in Jewish culture was humorously caricatured by Abramovitsh in the novel *The Brief Travels of Benjamin the Third*, where both of his male characters, Benjamin and Sendrel (who figure as Jewish satirical representations of Don Quixote and Sancho Panza), are beaten by their wives and expelled from the Russian military after their conscription because they cause more trouble than they are worth.[37]

In response to the discontents of the structures of the Jewish marriage and gender norms, Y. L. Gordon composed his long poem "Kotso shel yud" (1875) as a maskilic defense of the Jewish woman. The poem features Bat Shu'a, the heroine, who is a young woman endowed with all the graces of Victorian womanhood, and quickly paints her deterioration at the hands of rabbinic culture, which has subjected her to servitude and labor while depriving her of access to any higher spiritual matters. In a direct assault on the values of Talmudic culture, her husband is described as a good-for-nothing idler whose only expertise is "to uproot mountains in the ethereal ways (or fables) of Abaye and Rabba" and who later abandons her as a chained wife, an *agunah*, with two children and not a penny to spare.[38]

The dissatisfactions of family life under rabbinic culture in Russia, as many Hebrew writers described, contributed likewise to the disintegration of the Jewish family unit among rabbinic elites toward the nineteenth century. As in the cases of Ginzburg, Gottlober, Kovner, Lilienblum, and

Berdichevsky, among many others, the first or second arranged marriage always ended tragically, as most of these men either divorced or abandoned their wives and children. Another common trope for the disintegration of the Talmud learner's marriage was the discovery that the groom was a heretic, as was the case with Gottlober, Lilienblum, and Berdichevsky. In two of these three cases, the wife's family not only cut off financial support but forced the defected learner into exile, leaving his children behind. Even if the couple remained married, as in the case of Bialik and his wife, the discontents of such arranged financial relationships continued to resonate in Hebrew writers' works of modern Hebrew fiction until the early twentieth century.[39]

The Path to Disenchantment

The personal stories of Chernyshevsky and Dobrolyubov illustrate how disenchantment with the value of texts and literature took place in the lives of nihilism's founders and loudest voices, who were widely read and regarded by Jews. Chernyshevsky and Dobrolyubov were the sons of well-educated rural priests from Saratov and Nizhny Novgorod and received the best education available to members of their position. "Latin, Greek, Biblical history, Holy Writ, Biblical Hermeneutics, Dogmatic Theology, Philosophy, Orthodox History and Church Liturgy" were some of the exams they passed with high marks.[40] Toward the end of their seminary years, they began to seek new intellectual horizons beyond the clergy. They both dreamed of obtaining a university education and began to pursue this goal against their fathers' wishes. Chernyshevsky taught himself French and German and was accepted to the historical-philological faculty at the University of St. Petersburg. Dobrolyubov, whose father strictly prohibited him from enrolling in a university, traveled to St. Petersburg with the assumed intent of joining the Theological Academy. He enrolled, instead, at St. Petersburg's Main Pedagogical Institute.[41] The two met in 1856 and, instantly recognizing each other as ex-seminarians, began forming an intellectual alliance.

For Chernyshevsky and Dobrolyubov, writes Irina Paperno, "the confrontation with the real world of independent life in the capital proved a cruel and painful experience."[42] In their diaries, they complain of suffering from poverty and material hardships, as from difficulties integrating into society. Unlike noblemen, or even *raznochintsy* (members of various lower ranks) who sometimes attended the gymnasium schools, seminarians were ignorant of social graces, music, art, and athletics, and, as a result, they felt humiliated and belittled at the university.[43] Painfully aware of their own inadequacy, their diaries often expressed a strong dissatisfaction with themselves and a desire to transcend their background. Chernyshevsky and Dobrolyubov "began to view their theological training as a burden—a body of knowledge that was inculcated in them without their consent," not only because it did not prepare them for life in secular society but also because they felt that it limited their intellectual growth.[44] The move to the university, then, was a step toward taking charge of their intellectual development.

Long before formulating their hostile attitudes toward aesthetic literature, the nihilist critics were its eager consumers. Chernyshevsky was an avid reader of Russian, German, and French literary journals and kept a meticulous record of all his readings in his diary. He eagerly consumed poetry and the prose of Mikhail Lermontov (1814–1841) and Nikolai Gogol (1809–1852) and could recite passages from Goethe's *Faust* in the original German.[45] This voracious reading was what first exposed Chernyshevsky and Dobrolyubov to *The Essence of Christianity* (1841) by the German philosopher (and ex-theologian) Ludwig Feuerbach (1804–1872), something that Chernyshevsky recorded in his diary on March 10, 1849.[46]

The invention of Russian nihilism by the sons of priests was the result of a gradual process of disillusionment that began with seminary life and continued through the difficulty of the university years. Disillusionment came to Chernyshevsky and Dobrolyubov from multiple directions at once—from the perceived failures in their religious backgrounds, from the hostility and hardship of their new lives in the capital, and, worst of all, from their own sense of inadequacy—giving them the impression that they were unfit for existence in the real world. They found both the explanation and cure for their self-diagnosed maladjustment to reality in their reading of Feuerbach. Feuerbach explained, "Faith is the power of the imagination, which makes the real unreal and the unreal real: in direct contradiction with the truth of the senses and with the truth of reason."[47] This idea that God is the great illusion of a human imagination in need of comfort and fulfillment, which appeared some fifteen years prior to Marx's famous pronouncement that religion is the soporific opiate of the people, provided these ex-seminarians with an instantly gratifying explanation of their experience of maladjustment to secular life. The removal of the "grand illusion of God" paved the way to undermining the smaller illusions that people hold dear in their everyday lives. Dobrolyubov argued, for instance, that the Russian people, reared on superstitions and old wives' tales, were ignorant of the world and in denial about their lives. These fictions, he argued, cultivated an overactive imagination that caused "passivity, inactivity and disconnection from the world of action" in adult life.[48] As people who spent their early lives educated in the clergy, both he and Chernyshevsky saw themselves as firsthand victims of an overactive imagination. These realizations set the purging of religion and other harmful illusions as the goal of Chernyshevsky's and Dobrolyubov's personal transformations as well as of their journalistic work with which they hoped to waken Russian society from its slumber.

The texts of the materialist scientists Ludwig Büchner (1824–1899), Jacob Moleschott (1822–1893), and Carl Vogt (1817–1895), as well as the social-utopian thinkers John Stuart Mill (1806–1873) and Charles Fourier (1772–1837), provided the substance with which Chernyshevsky and Dobrolyubov would fill their new world devoid of "illusions." The embrace of materialism for these former men of religious texts, resulted in what Max Weber termed the "disenchantment of the world"—a demystification of all intangible or nonphysical concepts and experiences and their philosophical reduction to physical causes.[49] Materialism's credo was that all that exists in the universe consists of matter and its transformations. Nothing else can be said to exist unless it can be perceived by the senses or measured by the instruments of science, even if only in principle, as in the later negative formulation of the critic Dmitry Pisarev (1840–1868) that "the impossibility of evident manifestation excludes any reality of existence."[50]

In this view, the mind, devoid of the illusion of "soul," was thought to be a physical substance, like all other things in nature. Consequently, human consciousness with all of its passions was reduced to the physiological processes of the nervous system. Extending materialist philosophy to the arts, the nihilists, as disillusioned men of faith and letters, began to shun forms of expressions that could seduce people with the false hope of transcendence.

Conclusion

What nihilist Russian literary critics had in common with the writers of Hebrew literature in the nineteenth century was an upbringing among highly literary religious intelligentsias and the subsequent rejection of these cultures. These formative cross-cultural identities implicated Russian and

Jewish writers in similar performative contradictions that manifested in their relationship to texts. For instance, the Russian nihilists argued that the pursuit of literature was infinitely inferior to such practical occupations as medicine and physical labor, yet they devoted their entire lives to literature, often risking economic ruin and imprisonment. Similarly, they argued that the written word needed to be detached from religion and mysticism. Yet, as the next chapter will show, the nihilist writers reproduced the practices of Russian Orthodox hermeneutics in their works, eliciting precisely the type of religious veneration they had scorned in their religious upbringings. These inconsistencies were soon to be replicated in the lives of yeshiva-trained writers who found inspiration in the nihilists' call for utility but, likewise, continued to reproduce the allegedly useless practices of rabbinic hermeneutics in Hebrew fiction and literary criticism.

Notes

1. On the importance and popularity of Mapu's novel *Love of Zion* see Seidman, *Marriage Plot*, 21–70.

2. From the poem "For Whom Do I Toil" (1870). Stanislawski, *For Whom*, 104.

3. Frede, *Doubt, Atheism*, 121.

4. Nathans, *Beyond the Pale*, 25–27; Brower, *Training the Nihilists*, 62.

5. Freeze, *Parish Clergy*, 103; Freeze, "Introduction," 20.

6. Manchester, *Holy Fathers, Secular Sons*, 4.

7. Frede, *Doubt, Atheism*, 120.

8. Manchester, *Holy Fathers, Secular Sons*, 4.

9. Manchester, 121.

10. Paperno, *Chernyshevsky*, 208.

11. Rzhevsky, "Life of Alexis."

12. Nadler, *Faith of the Mithnagdim*, 88. See also Levin and Luria, *Sefer Aliyyot Eliyyahu*, 1:34.

13. Manchester, *Holy Fathers, Secular Sons*, 177.

14. While autobiography writing has long been linked by scholars to Rousseau and his influence on the rise of the "autobiographical habit" in Russian literature, for popovichi, diary keeping had a religious function. The priests were encouraged to keep a diary for this purpose. Manchester, 180–81.

15. Turgenev, "Hamlet and Don Quixote."

16. Manchester, *Holy Fathers, Secular Sons*, 126.

17. Belliustin, *Description of the Clergy*, 65.

18. Belliustin, 78.

19. Cited in Cohen, "Maskilot," 103.

20. Belliustin, *Description of the Clergy*, 88.

21. Belliustin, 84.

22. See discussion in the introduction to this volume.

23. Pomyalovsky, *Seminary Sketches*, 47.

24. For the disparagement of the heder by writers of the Jewish Enlightenment, see Zipperstein, "Transforming the Heder."

25. Belliustin, *Description of the Clergy*, 86.

26. For memoir descriptions of student life in the yeshiva, for instance, the account of the student rebellion in Volozhin (by Moshe Eliezer Aizenshtat), see Etkes and Tikochinski, *Yeshivot Lita*, 119.

27. Belliustin, *Description of the Clergy*, 66–68.

28. Kovner, "Yeshibotnaia Bursa."

29. E. Stern, *Jewish Materialism*, 65.

30. Manchester, *Holy Fathers, Secular Sons*, 192.

31. Pomyalovsky, *Seminary Sketches*, 103.

32. Belliustin, *Description of the Clergy*, 111, 113.

33. Etkes, "Marriage and Torah Study," 155.

34. Seidman, *Marriage Plot*, 118.

35. Etkes, "Marriage and Torah Study," 156.

36. Gluzman, *Ha-guf ha-tsioni*, 105–30.

37. Mendele Moykher-Sforim, *Tales of Mendele*, 301–91.

38. Gordon, "Kotso shel yud," 136.

39. See the fascinating narrative of Bialik's decade-long affair with the painter Ira Jan in Holtzman, *Hayim Nahman Bialik*, 104–13.

40. Frede, *Doubt, Atheism*, 121.

41. Frede, 122.

42. Paperno, *Chernyshevsky*, 39. For descriptions of poverty and social hardships that popovichi and other nonnobles had to face in university, see Brower, *Training the Nihilists*, 101–4.

43. Frede, *Doubt, Atheism*, 77–78.

44. Frede, 124.

45. Frede, 125.

46. Chernyshevsky and Alekseev, *Dnevnik*, 265.

47. Feuerbach, *Essence of Christianity*, 242.

48. See Dobrolyubov's article "What Is Oblomovshchina?" English translation available in Dobrolyubov, "What Is Oblomovism?," 174–217. See also Frede, *Doubt, Atheism*, 138.

49. For Max Weber, the powerful effects of the disenchantment of the world result from "intellectualization," which entails the elimination of magic and supernatural forces from the human understanding of the universe. The natural sciences, which are at the forefront of intellectualization, ensure that "all things can be mastered by calculation" and "one no longer needs to have recourse to magical means or to implore the sprits." Weber, *From Max Weber*, 139.

50. See Pisarev's essay titled "Nineteenth-Century Scholasticism" in Pisarev, *Selected Philosophical*, 104.

3

TEXTS ON TRIAL

Utility and the New Criteria for Literary Value

Taking Russian and Jewish intellectual circles by storm, the nihilists' materialist worldview raised new questions regarding literature. How can literature effectively serve as an instrument of social benefit? And if a literary text has no such beneficial potential, or worse, if it appears to advocate against what is considered "social progress," does is still deserve to be read? More generally, by what criteria are some texts considered "good" and others "harmful"? With these questions the new critics of literature began to explore their new relationship to texts in the wake of their break with religion. Through a close reading of Jewish and Russian nihilist texts and the ways in which they attempted to satisfy the demands of utility—as well as the ways in which they often failed to do so—this chapter explores the pressures exerted on the nascent sphere of Hebrew literature by the new criteria of literary value. Examining the writings of Avraham Uri Kovner, the founder of Hebrew literary criticism and a scandalous writer described in his day as a Jewish nihilist,in conversation with his literary allies and opponents, the chapter describes how the change in literary ideology brought Jewish writers to reject the legacy of Talmud study and Hebrew literature as one unit.

The Trouble with Fiction

Using the scientific and social theories they had at their disposal, the three leading voices of Russian nihilism, Chernyshevsky, Dobrolyubov, and Pisarev, sought to invalidate the belief in supernatural phenomena rampant among the deeply devout Russian folk—from normative religious concepts such as God and the soul to the myriad mythological creatures of Russian folktales. With a similar empiricist worldview, the nihilists assailed literary fiction. The problem with literary fiction, for these literary critics, lay precisely in its fictional nature. The claim of factuality had indeed occupied writers from Cervantes (1574–1616) to Emily Brontë (1818–1848), who, using their rhetorical and imaginative skill, continued to insist that their stories were "entirely true," or hailed from a true source. Jean-Jacques Rousseau (1712–1778), for example, found no shame in his contradictory insistence that his epistolary novel *Julie* (1761) was "not a novel."[1] This problem of authenticity, which had long occupied writers of fiction, resurfaced once again in the 1860s in the writings of the Russian nihilists.[2] The issue is this: regardless of whether it is sacred or secular, literature often refers to beings, things, and events that do not exist in tangible reality and are thus, in a sense, false. And while, unlike religion, fiction does not require a strict adherence to its claims, the nihilists nonetheless saw a great danger in it. They argued that literature, fictional as it may be, had an enormous power over its readers akin to that of religion and could thus pose a threat to social progress. Literature's unchecked ability to make false claims about the world was responsible, they claimed, for the passivity, backwardness, and existential naiveté plaguing nineteenth-century Russians. For literature to be of any positive significance, it needed, first of all, to be useful.

One of the ways in which the nihilists envisioned literature's power being harnessed for social progress was through the notion of realism. If a literary work was restrained by a strict resemblance to reality, its verisimilitude, they argued, ought to be exploited for modeling practical ways and behaviors of achieving social change. The notion of realism in literature had been developed a decade prior by Vissarion Belinsky (1811–1848), who hailed from the nonnoble intelligentsia and rose to prominence as Russia's first professional literary critic.[3] Belinsky's works and his notions of realism, scholars have shown, were profoundly influenced by Russian Orthodox hermeneutics, in particular, the doctrine of anagogy, or spiritual ascent through engagement with sacred texts.[4] Applying this doctrine to the works of Alexander Pushkin (1799–1837) and Gogol, Belinsky believed that engagement with certain works of literature could bring the critic closer to truth or reality "as it really is"—and he termed the power of literary works to do so "realism."[5] Chernyshevsky, who developed these ideas further in his dissertation "On the Aesthetic Relation between Art and Reality" (1855), argued that the degree to which the literary work reflected the objects of reality should be the determining measure of its value.

Although the nihilists' attachment to the notion of realism was an effort to bring literature closer to scientific truth according to the reigning empirical conceptions of the time, the theological structures underlying their approach to literary texts led them to define reality in philosophically idealist terms. The result was that the nihilists' notion of literary realism seemed to commingle reality and fiction. According to Paperno, realist aesthetics assigned a dual role to literature vis-à-vis the world: "On the one hand, the intention of realism (as proclaimed by radical critics) was the direct and precise representation of social reality, as close to the empirical object, or as true to life as possible. (Truth, *is-tinnost'* or authenticity of representation, became the central aesthetic category, more important than beauty.) On the other hand, realism clearly had a didactic intent and wished to have a direct impact on reality."[6] The two contradictory functions of realism—one, to reflect reality as closely as possible, and two, to inform it—thus became the nihilists' new guidelines for Russian literature.

Chernyshevsky and Dobrolyubov, joined by Pisarev, their young disciple and influential critic in his own right, surveyed Russian literature and censured works that did not satisfy their new criteria. The first crusade was against literary works that favored aesthetics over the representation of reality or social utility. In "The Abolition of Aesthetics" (1865), Pisarev delivered a diatribe against certain writers whom he viewed as "aesthetes" and "priests of pure art," depicting them as "charlatans" and "social parasites."[7] The nihilist critics continued to direct their assault on the protagonists of Russian fiction in whom they found traces of aestheticism, passivity, and decadence. In "What Is Oblomovism?" Dobrolyubov made a negative example of Oblomov (from the 1859 novel of the same name by Ivan Goncharov, 1812–1891), a genteel landlord who could not raise himself from his couch without the help of his serf butler. Following Dobrolyubov's lead, in "Pushkin and Belinsky," Pisarev mocked Pushkin's protagonist Eugene Onegin (of the eponymous 1833 novel) for having no greater concern than the beauty of his nails.[8] The argument that all literary texts must serve a useful function was so convincing, or so it seemed, that a writer's esteem could not save him from the nihilists' scorn. Russia's beloved Pushkin was thus dethroned as national poet and cast by the nihilist critics as a decadent worshipper of art for art's sake. Such articles penned by Chernyshevsky, Dobrolyubov, and Pisarev from 1859–1865 in the Russian journal *The Contemporary* (*Sovremennik*) transformed it into "Russia's mouthpiece for radical social criticism" as well as an influential source of new ideas for radicalizing post-yeshiva writers, who would often refer to it.[9]

The nihilist critics' criteria for evaluating literature and art were met with intense opposition from the camp of conservative writers. The debate about aesthetics that broke out among Russian writers is best illustrated by the appearance of two very different but equally influential novels: Turgenev's *Fathers and Sons* in 1862 and Chernyshevsky's *What Is to Be Done?* in 1863. *Fathers and Sons* describes the clash between the patriarchs of the Russian nobility and their freethinking children, who, after having encountered radical thought at the universities, were beginning to reject their aristocratic upbringings for the values of the "new people," who were rational, unsentimental, antiauthoritarian individuals.[10] Turgenev's novel tries to paint a realist depiction of such a "new person" in the character of Bazarov, whom he calls a "nihilist" in the text. Bazarov's clerical origins are one generation removed. He is a *raznochinets*—a son of a doctor but the grandson of a priest. An unsentimental student of medicine and natural science with a strong penchant for the dissection of frogs, Bazarov is a staunch materialist. He argues that the empirically knowable world is the only legitimate source of knowledge and speaks of his dissected frogs as symbols for human insignificance in the face of a material universe. Ironically, Bazarov ultimately dies after cutting himself with an infected dissection knife, as he is practicing his dissection skills on a dead human body.

In the novel, Arkady, a recent graduate from the University of Petersburg returns to his father's small estate in the provinces, with his new friend Bazarov in tow. Back at home, Arkady introduces Bazarov to his liberal aristocratic father, Nikolai, and old-fashioned uncle Pavel as follows:

> "He's a nihilist," repeated Arkady.
>
> "A nihilist," said Nikolai Petrovitch, "that's from the Latin *nihil*, nothing, as far as I understand, the word means a man . . . who accepts nothing?"
>
> "Say, who *respects* nothing," put in Pavel Petrovich. . . .
>
> "Who regards everything from a critical point of view," observed Arkady.
>
> "Isn't that the same thing?" inquired Pavel Petrovich.
>
> "No, it's not the same thing. A nihilist is a man who does not bow down before any authority, who does not take any principle on faith whatever reverence that principle may be enshrined in."[11]

Taking an interest in the character and the philosophical positions of nihilists, embodied in Bazarov, Turgenev's novel inspired a debate about the meaning and moral status of Bazarov's nihilism in the Russian journalistic press. The debate was about whether Bazarov is a paragon of intellectual honesty—a hero who bravely faces the somber truths of science or, rather, a villain, who holds his convictions in order to legitimize his base nature, devoid of any aesthetic and moral refinement. In the novel, Bazarov is portrayed as insolent—insulting and disrespectful to those who treat him kindly, unsympathetic and even cruel to his elderly parents. Bazarov is also a misogynist who treats women as the objects of his carnal urges. The writers of *The Contemporary* thus refused to be identified with Bazarov, seeing him as a malicious caricature of Dobrolyubov and the young radicals.[12]

Pisarev, the protégé of Chernyshevsky and Dobrolyubov, however, reappropriated the character of Bazarov and the term *nihilist* as positive characterizations of self-styled "new people." Recognizing himself and his intellectual allies in Bazarov, in an 1862 article entitled "Bazarov," Pisarev recast the former's "savageness" as stemming from a heroic intellectual honesty:

> As an empiricist, Bazarov acknowledges only what can be felt with the hands, seen with the eyes, tasted by the tongue. . . . All other human feelings he reduces to the activity of the nervous system. Consequently, the enjoyment of the beauty of nature, of music, or painting, poetry, and the love of a woman, do not seem to him to be any loftier and purer than the enjoyment of a copious dinner or a bottle of good wine. What rapturous youths call an "ideal" does not exist for Bazarov. He calls all this "romanticism" and sometimes instead of romanticism he uses the word "nonsense."[13]

In recontextualizing Bazarov, Pisarev found it necessary to supply allegedly omitted missing details of Bazarov's life and provide psychological motivations for Bazarov's actions in the novel. Pisarev explained, for instance, that "Bazarov had naturally been led to his radical persuasion by his experiences as a poor plebeian at the university" and that "behind Bazarov's cruelty to his parents was his painful realization of the inevitable alienation from them."[14] Thus transformed, even those negative characteristics of Turgenev's character that had so offended the staff of *The Contemporary*—his rudeness and insolence, cruelty and disdain for emotion, rejection of art, and lack of aesthetic sentiment—were reevaluated positively as the signs of a brave new social and philosophical position.

Pisarev's re-creation of Bazarov in his own image of a nihilist returns us to the formative contradiction of the nihilists' relationship to literature—namely, the confusion between reality and art. On the one hand, the nihilists believed that literature was an imperfect mirror that could never equal the representation of its object in reality. On the other hand, literature was somehow expected not only to reflect reality accurately but to extrapolate it.

That is, literature's goal was not only to portray characters who allegedly resemble real types of people in the world but also to project or to "return" the corrected image back to reality.[15] The result was that, in the attempt to make fictional literature realistic, the nihilist critics would often confuse reality with fiction.

Indeed, not unlike the Don Quixote–like Jewish characters caricatured by Abramovitsh's novels, the nihilist critics sometimes treated literary characters as if they were real people. Pisarev, for instance, was so impressed with the "truthfulness" of Turgenev's *Fathers and Sons* that he claimed that the character of Bazarov was based on a "'correct' understanding of the 'astonishingly accurate' real 'type' of person."[16] But then, instead of remaining true to Turgenev's actual text, in his attempted realist reading of *Fathers and Sons*, Pisarev flattened and simplified Bazarov. Pisarev reduced Turgenev's complex character by wiping out the human weaknesses that had so convincingly made him resemble a real person. Pisarev wishfully saw Bazarov as a man who "needs no one, fears no one, loves no one, spares no one, and lives according to the guiding principle of calculation."[17] Turgenev's Bazarov, however, was far from this description. He was often melancholic, afflicted by anxiety about his social status. He desired to distinguish himself and to be loved but lacked the confidence to pursue either love or his own success. His insolence is often portrayed as a defense mechanism against his class anxiety, and behind his cold empiricism hides the need and desire for transcendence. It was after all Bazarov, who—even before the character of Konstantin Levin in the 1878 novel *Anna Karenina* by Leo Tolstoy (1828–1910)—romantically mused on a haystack under the stars about humanity's purpose in the universe: "Here I lie under a haystack. . . . This tiny space I occupy is so infinitely small in comparison with the rest of space, in which I am not, and which has nothing to do with me; and the period of time in which it is my lot to live is so petty beside the eternity in which I have not been, and shall not be . . . and in this atom, this mathematical point, the blood is circulating, the brain is working and wanting something. Isn't it loathsome? Isn't it petty?"[18]

According to Turgenev, certain empirically untenable assumptions, such as the belief in a soul that enables humans to act as free moral agents, may constitute an indispensable part of the human need for meaning. Even a character as antisentimental as Bazarov could not, it appears, make peace with a purely materialist view of the universe. But how could Pisarev, a critic who placed so much emphasis on "the truth as it really is," not take note of Bazarov's desire for transcendence? Coincidentally, the lives of the real Pisarev and the fictional Bazarov did merge, but only in their tragic ends—Pisarev drowns and Bazarov, in an instance of poetic justice, dies after an infection sustained from his careless handling of a dissection knife on a human cadaver. Turgenev's novel leaves open the possibility that Bazarov committed suicide.

Despite their rejection of the traditional frameworks of Russian culture and religion, the nihilists and the new philosophical frameworks they had erected for themselves were no less steeped in illusion and idealism. The circuitous return of the nihilists' ideas to those of their religious origins is best demonstrated by Chernyshevsky's novel *What Is to Be Done?* Written during the author's confinement for revolutionary activity, the novel was published in 1863 by accident, after being mistakenly overlooked by the censor. Subtitled "Stories about the New People," Chernyshevsky's radical novel was intended as a guidebook for aspiring nihilists but was received as the secular gospel of a new creed that significantly affected life in Russia.

In *What Is to Be Done?*, Lopukhov, a medical student of nonnoble origins with materialistic convictions, rescues Vera Pavlovna from an arranged marriage to a nobleman, by proposing a fictitious marriage between her and Lopukhov himself. Chernyshevsky describes their marriage as guided by the principles of gender equality and rational egotism. They sleep in separate bedrooms (without consummating their marriage for some time) and practice "freedom of the heart," which allows them to love anyone they please. When Vera Pavlovna falls in love with Lopukhov's best friend, Lopukhov harbors no hard feelings. Thinking "rationally" about the situation, he steps aside and fakes his own death so that the new couple can live happily together without him. Presenting new ideas concerning marriage, labor, human emotions, and spirituality, the novel offers readers a literary model of Chernyshevsky's nihilist utopia.

Chernyshevsky begins the novel with a realist credo, arguing that the novel's aesthetic limitations are of no consequence in light of the novel's more important virtues of "truthfulness" and "usefulness":

> I have not a shred of artistic talent. I barely even grasp the language—but these are of no consequence. Read on, dear public! And this reading shall not be without profit. Truth is a goodly thing. Truth compensates for the faults of the author who heeds her. Therefore I say unto you: If I would have not warned you, perhaps you would think that my story is written artistically,

that the author possesses great poetic talent. But I did warn you that talent
I lack, and now you shall know that all the merits of my story lie only in its
truthfulness.[19]

In this preface, the radical Chernyshevsky returns to his priestly roots by
assuming the tone of a preacher, a prophet, and a guide—perhaps a vesti-
gial habit of his clerical background. Taking the place of the literary aestheticism and embellishments, which Chernyshevsky praised his work for
avoiding, is an abundance of allusions to the New Testament and mystical
Christian references. The very title of Chernyshevsky's novel is an allusion
to the episode of the baptism in Luke (3:10–14) where the multitude that
came forth to be baptized asked of John: "What shall we do?" Its subtitle,
"Stories about the New People," too, is an allusion to the Pauline notion
of history beginning anew with Jesus as the "New Adam." Alternatively,
as Paperno argues, the "New People" to whom the novel is dedicated are
to be viewed as the "apostles of a new creed" with Chernyshevsky as their
new prophet.[20] Apocalyptic symbolism also heavily figures in the novel in
Vera Pavlovna's four visions of the "Kingdom of Heaven," which prophesy
a new heaven on earth—a utopian messianic age that will come after the
revolution.[21]

Scholars have long observed that a secular version of religious asceticism pervades the works of the Russian nihilists.[22] The mysterious figure
of Rakhmetov, for example, in Chernyshevsky's novel seems to be modeled
on "The Life of Aleksei, the Man of God," from the hagiographic collection
Chet'i Minei (*Monthly Readings*), which Chernyshevsky enjoyed reading as
a child. The story of "The Life of Alexei, Man of God" ("Zhitio Aleksiea
cheloveka bozhiia") appears in the monthly readings of the lives of Russian
saints under the month of March. It portrays a wealthy young man who
gives away his property, abandons worldly success and the love of a woman,
and dedicates his life to faith, subjecting himself to self-mortification. Rakhmetov, like Aleksei, leads an ascetic lifestyle, utters mystical hints about
the revolution, and sleeps on a bed of nails to build up his endurance for the
coming of the "end of days."

Despite, or perhaps because of, its neomessianic vision of a secular utopia, Chernyshevsky's novel was a literary hit whose popularity overshad-
owed aesthetically inclined and established writers such as Pushkin and
Gogol.[23] Though the book was banned soon after its publication, young
people found ways of disseminating it, reading it from old journals, and
transcribing it by hand. *What Is to Be Done?* acquired the status of a new

bible among university students, and its ideas and characters became objects of emulation among aspiring young radicals to the point of alarming the authorities. A review of the novel's impact on Russian society by the Ministry of Internal Affairs reported real cases of daughters running away, wives leaving husbands, and fictitious marriages that were allegedly inspired by Chernyshevsky's novel.[24] The novel's influence on young Jewish men and women was similarly observed, often out of proportion, and depicted by Jewish writers well into the twentieth century.

The Jewish Nihilists

To understand how nihilist texts and ideas entered Jewish culture and the sphere of Hebrew letters, let us examine the story of the three Kovner brothers, who were all Jewish and Russian writers in the 1860s. Most scholars of Russian Jewish literature and history are familiar with Avraham Uri Kovner (1842–1905), the "villain" of Jewish literary criticism who first introduced nihilist ideas to a Jewish audience.[25] What is less known, however, is that this Kovner also had two older brothers, Shaul "Savelii" Kovner (1837–1896) and Yitzhak Aizik Kovner (1840–1891), each of whom, having encountered nihilist thought, followed it along different paths, leaving their smaller marks on Jewish and Russian intellectual life.

The Kovners were born into a scholarly and impoverished family of impressive rabbinic lineage.[26] Their father, a Talmud scholar, was barely able to support the family of eleven children, two of whom did not survive infancy, by working as a teacher of young children (*melamed*) and a cantor.[27] The oldest son, Shaul (Savelii, in Russian), distinguished himself from childhood by his studiousness and talent for learning. He attended a state-sponsored rabbinical seminary. Not recognized as such by most orthodox Jews in Russia, these institutions were part of the Russian government's program of reforming the empire's Jews and focused mainly on secular subjects. Eventually, the state seminaries produced graduates who could become "rabbis according to the state" (*rabanim mita'am ha-medinah*). The schools were often staffed by prominent maskilic writers, and the graduates of these schools could eventually enroll in the Russian universities. The reason why a devout mitnagdic family would send their son to such a school was likely financial (they were unable to afford a regular yeshiva) rather than a sign of secularization.[28]

Upon graduating with the highest of grades from the state-run rabbinical seminary in Vilna, Shaul became eligible to take the gymnasium's finishing exams and successfully enrolled in the medical school of Kiev University. This was in the early 1860s, when the Russian nihilist writers were especially active, publishing articles popularizing science and materialism. Shaul likewise began to work and to write about medicine and the natural sciences. Alongside his medical training, he published articles that popularized medicine and science in Russian and Hebrew; among his writings, he produced the Russian book *Spinoza, His Life and Works* as well as the Hebrew articles "Maimonides as a Physician" and "Do We Know What Leprosy Is?"[29] Shaul's successful integration into the Russian intelligentsia was a powerful source of influence for Avraham Uri, who would soon join him in Kiev.

Around the age of ten, following a brief stint at the elementary-school level of the state-run rabbinic seminary, Avraham Uri Kovner, enrolled in the Mir Yeshiva, the second-most important yeshiva in Lithuania after the Volozhin Yeshiva. At the Mir Yeshiva, Klausner writes, "Kovner first acquired a taste for forbidden books"—which were books of Hebrew grammar, medieval Hebrew poetry, works by the Kabbalist (and author of the first Hebrew drama) Moshe Chaim Luzzatto (1707–1746), and journals of the Haskalah.[30] Around this time, Avraham Uri Kovner began his first forays into producing literature; he tried his hand at poetry and even began writing a novel. Kovner's time at the Mir Yeshiva was brief. Kovner claims to have received "a public punishment" of being slapped on the face by the head of the yeshiva in front of the other students. Murav suggests that the experience of public shaming at the hands of the yeshiva authority and similar experiences that he witnessed during that time raised his awareness of the injustice and corruption of the rabbinic leadership of Jewish society.[31] After the Mir Yeshiva, Avraham Uri continued to study in different mitnagdic yeshivas, including at Stolbtsy, a Musar yeshiva, and various study houses in Vilna and Kovno. At eighteen, he entered a marriage with a kest contract (see chap. 2). That is, he was expected to study Talmud full-time under the "watchful eye of his father-in-law, who wanted him to become a scholar," while his wife and in-laws supported him.[32] But instead of devoting himself to the Talmud, he indulged in literature, following in the footsteps of maskilic writers before him.

While we know little about the life of the middle brother, Yitzhak Aizik, it likely followed the traditional trajectory for a man from a Jewish scholarly background. The exact yeshiva he attended is unknown, but his Hebrew prose and facility with rabbinic texts attest to him having received a mitnagdic education in either a yeshiva or a beit midrash. At seventeen, he too was married into a kest arrangement and delighted in "forbidden books." The demands of material reality, however, quickly put an end to the indulgence of the young yeshiva student. In need of money, Yitzhak Aizik became a grain merchant, who would travel through the towns of Jewish Lithuania, where he, in turn, witnessed the material plight facing many Jewish communities. Yitzhak Aizik then started publishing articles in a column titled News from Vilna, appearing in the maskilic Hebrew journal *Ha-Melitz*. *Ha-Melitz* was edited by Aleksander Zederbaum (1816–1893), an editor and publicist of Jewish and Yiddish journals and a moderate maskil, who also published Avraham Uri Kovner's first articles and then feuded with him over their radical and offensive content.

Yitzhak Aizik Kovner's articles drew attention to some of the Jewish community's most pressing social issues, such as the cholera epidemic in Vilna in 1866 and the deaths of two Jewish women in a factory gas leak. His articles often criticized the rabbinic authorities for failing the Jewish community at a time of economic strife, for instance, by not overriding the extralegal prohibition of the consumption of legumes (*kitniyot*) on Passover during the famine of 1868.[33] A deliberate focus on "usefulness" and the concern for material well-being thus became the moral imperatives of Yitzhak Aizik Kovner's literary activity.

In the case of the Kovner brothers, a direct source of nihilist and materialist ideas was the university, which was a known site of radical recruitment.[34] Once the oldest brother, Shaul, had established himself as a student at the university in Kiev, he corresponded with his brothers until he eventually invited Avraham Uri to come stay with him. Avraham Uri then traveled to Kiev for the purpose of improving his Russian and learning subjects that would be useful to leading an integrated life in Russia, but, ironically, he found financial support for himself by working as a private tutor teaching Hebrew and, likely, Talmud, a common occupation for yeshiva-educated men. Avraham Uri spent four years (1861–1865) in Kiev, where he studied Russian, German, and some French. He was not a formal student at the university (he had not passed the gymnasium exams), but he audited classes and was nonetheless part of a circle of Jewish intellectuals at Kiev University in the 1860—at the height of the influence of the nihilists.[35] Avraham Uri Kovner's writings also attest to his familiarity with the materialist thinkers Ludwig Feuerbach, Ludwig Büchner, and John Stuart Mill, who helped shape the nihilist worldview.

Fathers and Sons

The young generation of Jewish writers who came of age after the Great Reforms of the 1860s began to wage a war against their literary "fathers," just as the Russian nihilists had done a decade earlier. They cast the moderate maskilim as the "old generation" of sentimental romantics—whereas the younger generation aligned themselves with the nihilist critics. Armed with their newly discovered materialist and utilitarian notions, the so-called Jewish nihilists voiced their contempt for literary activity that is detached from life and argued that the material and social plight of the Jews in imperial Russia could be alleviated only by a structural economic transformation rather than by a panacea of lyrical poetry, which they accused the old generation of promoting.

Avraham Uri Kovner was the first Jewish writer to present a nihilist critique of Hebrew literature in the Jewish journalistic press in a series of attacks on Jewish writers. His first attack was a brief essay titled "Davar el sofrei yisra'el" (A word to the writers of Israel), published in *Ha-Melitz* in 1864. In it, Kovner reworked Chernyshevsky's formulation of Feuerbach's "critique of the imagination" for a Jewish audience. The "Critique of the Imagination" in Ludwig Feuerbach's *The Essence of Christianity* (1841) provided a simple psychological explanation for the human need for religion and transcendence, arguing that God was an illusion of a human imagination desperate for comfort and fulfillment. Kovner accused Hebrew poets of "soaring on the wings of their imagination" to "sing with the angels up high" while ignoring the material demands of society on the ground. Like Dobrolyubov, he argued that maskilic writers irresponsibly delighted readers with textual ornamentation (melitza) and fantastic reveries that encourage them to escape from the troubles of the real world. But once they awaken from the comforts of aesthetic fiction, "melancholy and depression" are bound to set in. Kovner further argued, like Pisarev, that poetry was not an effective medium for inducing social change. Novels, on the other hand, he argued, were better suited to address social problems because their content was more realistic and their language more easily understandable.[36] Echoing Pisarev's ideas in "The Destruction of Aesthetics" ("Razrushenie estetiki," 1865) and Chernyshevsky more broadly, Kovner argued that unrealistic art was harmful because it fostered a dissatisfaction with reality.[37]

Avraham Uri Kovner's second critical attack, titled "Heker Davar" ("An Investigation of the Matter [or the Word]") (1865), was a diatribe against maskilic Hebrew periodicals (specifically, *Ha-Magid* and *Ha-Karmel*) and their editors.[38] Kovner opens it with a declaration that, unlike maskilic writers, he does not resort to useless aestheticisms: "I shall not pour out my heart here with lyricisms like the rest of the writers in order to find favor with the reading public; their regard for me is irrelevant. If they are wise, they will recognize the truthfulness of my composition—even without lofty and loud ornaments—and if not, even a thousand prefaces would not avail."[39] Kovner is reacting here against the maskilic penchant for elaborate prefaces where it was common for the author to showcase his textual prowess with wordplay, acrostics, and other elements of rabbinic textuality. More importantly, however, Kovner's declaration is a direct homage to Chernyshevsky's preface in *What Is to Be Done?*, where the latter proudly declared that he has not a "shred of artistic talent" and that the only virtue of his work is its "truthfulness."[40]

Kovner began his collection of critical essays by chastising maskilic Jewish writers for their lack of critical social engagement. He complained that the editors of Jewish journals and newspapers devoted large sections to allegedly useless literary activity, such as poetry, exegesis of Jewish texts, or celebratory communal events like the inauguration of a new Torah scroll, writing that "in a week's time the journal could not find a worthier topic than all this nonsense!"[41] Then, following Dobrolyubov's example, Kovner turned to lambasting the style and reputations of the esteemed writers of his time. He could not resist, however, engaging with Hebrew letters in the exact same ways as the writers he criticized. For his own part, he composed witty rabbinic acrostics to the name of the writers he wished to denounce.[42]

Increasing his provocations, Kovner attacked the Hebrew language, arguing that "Hebrew, like all other languages, is written in dead letters that have no sanctity in themselves," and called on Jewish writers to produce a "living" literature in either Yiddish or, preferably, "the language of the state."[43] After invoking nihilist ideas to challenge the maskilim's investment in Hebrew literature, and after leveling personal attacks and insults at prominent writers and editors of Jewish journals, Kovner finally succeeded in drawing attention to himself by inciting the wrath of the Jewish literary establishment.

Kovner's lead opponent was Gottlober, likewise a post-yeshiva writer and an established maskilic Hebrew poet. Gottlober was outraged by Kovner's assault on the Hebrew language and maskilic literature at large. Gottlober saw himself as a loyal civil official. He was a teacher at the state-run Jewish school in Zhitomir that was run almost exclusively by maskilim. Gottlober was thus threatened by the appearance of dissident and nihilist ideas in the maskilic journals he represented. To dissociate Kovner from the maskilim, Gottlober tactically accused Kovner of being a freethinker and political radical, linking him, as Murav suggests, to Chernyshevsky, who had been imprisoned in 1862.[44] Gottlober's attack on Kovner was obscurely titled "A Letter on Animal Suffering" and verbosely subtitled "A letter to those who grieve over the lifelessness of Hebrew literature and a reflection on the pernicious influence of nihilism and its grievous consequences" (1865). This elaborate title contains a pun on the Hebrew term for animals, *ba'alei hayim*, which literally denotes "owners of life." Gottlober turned this compound into a sarcastic reference to the nihilists, "the alleged owners of life," who are actually "animals" and are, thus, a cause of nuisance and suffering to the public. He writes:

> Know, dear reader, of the plague called "nihilism" so you may guard yourself from it. Do not bother responding to those *nig'ei listim* ["plagued robbers," in Hebrew, a homophonic pun on "nihilists" in Russian] because *peshuto kemashma'o* ["their plain meaning is exactly as it sounds"], zero and null. A nihilist is someone who believes in nothing and only relies on his senses. He rejects tradition and undermines the authority of the Tsar. The nihilist thinks himself wiser than the "seven pillars of wisdom" and accepts no one but himself as the "true judge and ruler." And this so-called "Kav-naor" [a homophonic pun on Kovner's name, denoting "vessel of folly"], that son of cattle, insults our righteous Tsar Alexander. . . . But we should thank this Kove-ner [pun, *koveh ner*, "may his candle be extinguished"], who mimics these nig'ei listim [nihilists], due to his evil spirit which he calls "the spirit of life," for warning us of their true intentions.[45]

Interpreting this strange passage, we must first observe that Gottlober's writing style and means of communication, saturated with word games, puns, double meanings, citations from scripture, and rabbinic expressions, represent the importation of rabbinic hermeneutics into secular Hebrew prose. The scholastic obscurantism of this passage, along with its playful air of Talmudism, is precisely what the nihilists' utilitarian critique of literature finds objectionable.

Also interesting is that Gottlober is a fan of Ivan Turgenev. He is clearly familiar with *Fathers and Sons*, whose protagonist is the nihilist archetype

Bazarov. Gottlober's definition of nihilism echoes the debate that Turgenev's characters had regarding Bazarov, in which the old guard of the gentry gave him a rather negative interpretation: the nihilist, in the words of the character Pavel Petrovich, is one "who respects nothing."[46]

Echoing the derogatory definition of nihilist as "zero and null," Gottlober participates in Turgenev's fictional debate, aligning himself with the generation of the "fathers." Turgenev himself was an opponent of nihilism, and so the reading of *Fathers and Sons* helped Gottlober buttress his position. When Gottlober tries to contend with Chernyshevsky's novel *What Is to Be Done?*, however, he is driven to the verge of paranoia: "Yes, women, too, applaud nihilism; they chop off all their hair, remove their crinolines, don round hats, and cover their hearts with abominations. There are those who copy Rakhmetov, and others Kirsanov of Chernyshevsky, and yet others choose to copy the 'genius' Bazarov. Each chooses according to his or her tastes. Go out into the great city and behold exactly what is written in those books: the black dresses, chopped hair, and round hats of the female nihilists—how many Vera Pavlovnas and Kukshinas there are in the marketplace!"[47] The defining image of this passage features the multiplication of fictional characters onto reality, specifically, the image of female nihilists taking to the streets of Russia. More than being Gottlober's horror fantasy, this passage indicates an unintentional philosophical alignment between the nihilists' notion of literary realism and the Jewish approach to text, concerning the idea that texts reflect and even predict reality.

What is crucial in understanding this letter is that—for Gottlober, a former Talmudist—the fact that people would want to imitate and "live out" a text is not at all troubling; it is almost second nature to him. Instead, his problem is that people are in danger of being absorbed by the *wrong* texts—texts that Gottlober sees as undermining the edifying literary agenda of the Haskalah. And he had good reason to fear. As Jeffrey Veidlinger's research into Jewish library data shows, the interest in nihilist works by Chernyshevsky and Pisarev far outweighed any interest in Hebrew literature, let alone religious learning.[48]

Kovner's provocation and Gottlober's response began a duel about the meaning and moral status of nihilism in the Jewish press that was modeled on the debate about the essay "Bazarov" in the Russian journals. Though loud and outspoken, the Jewish nihilists were in the minority. Avraham Uri Kovner was joined by his middle brother, Yitzhak Aizik, who had been known for his journalistic work until then. Angered and likewise threatened

by the accusation of freethinking and its association with political terrorism, Yitzhak Aizik Kovner, in his book *Sefer ha-matzref* (*The Crucible*), de-
fended the nihilists against such accusations and, at the same time, carried
out a comprehensive critique of Jewish literature and society. By the time he
wrote this work, nihilism had become even more strongly associated with
political terrorism due to the attempted assassination Tsar Alexander II by
Dimitry Karakozov in 1866.[49] *Sefer ha-matzref*, which was barred by the
censor in 1868, is a valuable document of literature and intellectual history
that provides access to the thoughts, concerns, and knowledge of a Jewish
nihilist. One of its highlights is that, similarly to Pisarev's reconfiguration
of Bazarov, Yitzhak Aizik Kovner reconfigures the Jewish nihilist by renaming him a "teleologist":

> The author of "A Letter on Animal Suffering" [Gottlober] defined "nihilist"
> as a person who thinks that all is null and useless and thus sets out to destroy
> everything and to undermine all authorities. However, dear reader, I have
> studied the term in various German dictionaries and can assure you that the
> term denotes a *useless man* who is unsuccessful at what he does, who cannot
> harm himself or his surroundings. How could a useless man possibly present
> a danger to the Tsar's rule and be a destructive force? In truth, a nihilist is a
> man without use and power. As it says in 1 Samuel 12:21: "Do not chase after
> the idols, for they are zero and null." Rather, a man who has talents and wishes
> to benefit his people should be called a "teleologist." The meaning of the word
> "teleology" in German denotes the study of purpose. Therefore, our devoted
> literary critics who only wish to benefit the people are the complete opposite
> [of Gottlober's accusation] and should be called "teleologists."[50]

In a passage that very much resembles the style of a rabbinic debate
about a term in scripture, Yitzhak Aizik Kovner attempts to rehabilitate the
nihilists by changing their name to one that he found more representative of
their true intentions: teleologists, those who desire to serve a beneficial purpose. Like Gottlober, Kovner uses a writing style characteristic of rabbinic
textual practices. He carries out an exegesis of the word *nihilist*, changes its
meaning, and proposes various definitions based on German dictionaries.
He even brings in a Hebrew scriptural proof text to clarify a Latin term.
Nevertheless, Yitzhak Aizik Kovner was blind to the persistence of rabbinic
textual habits in his own writing as he continued to apply the critique in the
name of utility to other maskilic works. Kovner did not spare even the most
prominent and best loved Jewish writer of the Haskalah, Mapu, the author
of *The Love of Zion*, whose novels he accused of favoring beauty over utility
and for lacking in realist depiction.[51]

The Writer as a Social Parasite

A striking feature of the application of the utilitarian critique of literature to Hebrew letters is the equation between the notion of Torah lishmah and literary aestheticism made by Jewish nihilist writers. While previously the notion of Torah lishmah had been limited to the sphere of religious study, the Jewish nihilists observed that an autotelic and self-pleasing quality, which they attributed to traditional Talmud study, pervaded all the literary endeavors of their contemporaries. For these young writers who emerged from yeshiva backgrounds, the strongest opposition to the Hebrew literature of the Haskalah movement was that it was steeped in the textual practices of Talmud study and rabbinic hermeneutics. Lilienblum, a self-pronounced "half-nihilist," complained in his diary that "while the intellectual world of the Russians is rattled by the fresh ideas of Chernyshevsky and Pisarev, our respected writers are sitting, their hands covered in ink, trying to shock the world with a banal clarification of scripture, poring over an ancient book that is already falling apart—both its binding and its ideas. . . . Give us bread! Give us the air of life!"[52] For Lilienblum, as for his contemporaries, the charge that all Hebrew writers' literary efforts consisted of the same "poring over ancient books" and getting their hands dirty with ink instead of "life" posed an existential threat to Hebrew literature and called for a serious reassessment of the role of textuality within Jewish culture.

Seeing a great danger in the unrestrained resources that Jewish culture allocated to the textual endeavor, the Jewish nihilists sought to purge modern Jewish literature of what they saw as its art for art's sake ethos, cultivated by the textual practices of the yeshiva, and to transform it into a strict vehicle for social service. Tellingly, Yitzhak Aizik Kovner's explanation for why Hebrew literature fell short of the demands of teleology and usefulness was that Hebrew literature was steeped in the Torah lishmah ethos of rabbinic textual practices:

> "Teleology," the study of purpose [*torat ha-takhlitiyut*], shows us that purpose and meaning have long been absent from the writers in our midst because not one of them thinks about the benefit of society. . . . Their only wish and desire is to write more and more books to no end, which satisfy only their love of themselves. . . . This especially applies to Talmudic compositions that build castles in the air . . . and accumulate various laws and *aggadot*, sophistry and hermeneutics, interpretations and contemplations [*halakhot ve'aggadot, pilpulim udrushim, peirushim ve-hagahot*] one onto the other. . . . They build their compositions on air and on a love of nonsense. They lack all important substance, and there is no point to any of them.[53]

It is revealing here to compare the language Kovner used in this passage to Pisarev's critique of poetry in his essay "Flowers of Harmless Humor" ("Tsvety nevinnovo yumora," 1865), where the latter similarly writes:

> If it is not quite clear to readers why our lyric poets represent a complete absence of ideas and should be included in the list of parasites that despoil the ideas of others, I will at once set them straight. Our lyric poets feed their destitution on the tiniest grains of thought and feeling that are the common possession of all men . . . but the lyricists have turned this well-known sentiment to their advantage and begun to elicit an income from it, thanks to their ability to create something out of nothing and to clothe the intangible dust of feelings in the thin woven garments of iambs, trochees, anapests, dactyls, and amphibrachs. . . . All of these writers write for the process of writing, and the public reads it just for the process of reading. This produces mutual pleasure.[54]

Like Pisarev, Yitzhak Aizik Kovner charges Jewish poets (*sofrim*), "allusion crafters" (*melitzim*), and "interpreters" (*darshanim*) with the socially harmful proliferation of "useless" writings that "lack purpose" and "ideas." This useless writing is built on "air," "dust," and "nonsense." Pisarev's "iambics, trochees, anapests, dactyls, and amphibrach" of aesthetic poetry become, for Kovner, the "laws [and] sharp literary maneuvers and hermeneutics and interpretations" of Talmud study. Poets and Talmudists write for "the love of the process," "to produce more and more books" and for a selfish "love of themselves" and for the sake of the "process," while the benighted public consumes their useless and harmful products with "mutual pleasure."

This comparison highlights the way in which Yitzhak Aizik Kovner mapped the critique of aesthetic literature onto the practices of Talmud study and onto Jewish literature at large. An identical argument is advanced by Avraham Uri Kovner, who wrote in a Russian-language Jewish paper that "Jews do not study Talmud in order to comprehend the numerous subjects in it, but rather for the sake of the process of study, which is itself considered pleasing to God, and according to several scholarly authorities, preferable even to prayer."[55]

Of course, Pisarev's and Kovner's critiques of aesthetics are also socioeconomic. Pisarev portrays aesthetic writers as social parasites who take advantage of "feelings that are the possession of all men" and make a profit from them. For Yitzhak Aizik, the practitioners of Torah lishmah are also social parasites but for the opposite reason: as long as the study house provides a "sanctuary for their idleness," they feel justified not to engage in any useful labor. He thus writes that "it is an obligation incumbent upon each community in their city to shut down the study-houses, for had they not been a sanctuary [for the idle], each person would have long found how to apply themselves."[56]

Identifying the root of the problem with the Torah lishmah theology of the mitnagdim, in his nihilist critique of Jewish life in *Sefer ha-matzref,* Yitzhak Aizik Kovner tore down the icon of the mitnagdim, the revered Gaon of Vilna, for neglecting the worldly needs of society in favor of all-consuming textual study. "Weren't all forms of wisdom revealed to him?" Kovner asked rhetorically. "Why, then, did he not leave us at least one book with the principles of some wisdom, science, or philosophy? Something to guide us on how to properly conduct our nation with the state, on how to lead a moral and natural life?" Striking at the core of the holy of holies—Torah scholarship—Kovner asked irreverently, "For what did he merit such great respect? For sitting locked up in his room for more than forty years . . . and learning for twenty hours a day? Why couldn't he learn for ten hours and devote a little time for the benefit of society?"[57] Yitzhak Aizik Kovner's fast-paced and blithe tone in these lines conveys his profound disappointment that the prized ideal of Torah lishmah was an illusion, never capable of redeeming Jewish life in eastern Europe. He sees the Gaon's excessive emphasis on textual learning as a misplaced priority that exacerbated the material plight of the Jewish community. From his new and disillusioned vantage point as a Jewish nihilist, Kovner claimed to have realized the true cost of the intellectual idealism of Torah lishmah: a life of poverty, worldly detachment, an arranged marriage, and social and economic impotence.

Conclusion

The discovery of nihilism and the intellectual crisis that it provoked was the experience of a generation of yeshiva-educated writers who launched their literary careers in late-imperial Russia. Aside from Avraham Uri Kovner, these writers were Lilienblum, who, born in 1842 in Kaidan, Kovno province, attended the yeshiva of Vilkomir, and Abramovitsh, who, born in 1836 in Kapolya, Minsk Province, attended the yeshivot of Slutsk and Tomkovich and the beit midrash of the GRA in Vilna. Other Jewish writers often associated with the Jewish nihilists included Peretz Smolenskin (1842–1885) and Avraham Ya'akov Paperna (1840–1919). Their intellectual development followed a similar trajectory that began with intense study of religious texts and moved from there to the Haskalah and, finally, to an encounter with the ideas of the Russian nihilist critics, which led to their disenchantment with Hebrew literature altogether. The nihilists' program of subjecting literary works to the crucible of utility was greatly productive for Russian literature, generating a new wave of satirical and realist works from the 1870s onward. The ways in which the utilitarian critique of literature affected Hebrew letters, however, was less predictable and was continually mitigated by Jewish writers' reluctant attraction to "uselessness." Hebrew writers who found a meaningful social calling, as it happened at times, lost their poetic voice—as was the case with Lilienblum, the subject of the next chapter. Although nihilist ideas had an immense impact on Hebrew literature, the demands for usefulness were never fully realized. At every point, Hebrew writers broke free of its constraints and returned to the aesthetic model of Torah lishmah and to inspirations from the world that produced it.

Notes

1. Darnton, "Readers Respond to Rousseau," 229.
2. On the problem of authenticity in fiction, see Hartman, *Scars of the Spirit*, 3–40.
3. McLean, "Realism."
4. Smith, "Anagogical Exegesis," 204–9.
5. The nihilists' version of realism was directly opposed to German romanticism, where reality was transformed into an object of art through its contact with the sublime or sacred. By contrast, the imperative of realist aesthetics was for art to reflect an unaltered version of reality "as it really is." McLean, "Realism," 364.
6. Paperno, *Chernyshevsky*, 8–9.
7. Pisarev, *Kritika Literaturnaia*, 285–86, 330.
8. See Dobrolyubov, "What Is Oblomovism?" ("Chto takoe oblomovshhina?"). Pushkin's and Goncharov's novels had artistically done the work of criticizing the same flaws of their characters that the nihilists pointed out. The nihilists, however, had deliberately conflated the characters' flaws with the preferences of the authors (who were landowners) in order to advocate the revolutionary abolition of the nobility. Terras, *History of Russian Literature*, 298.
9. Frede, *Doubt, Atheism*, 135.
10. Frede, 146.
11. Translation adapted from Turgenev, *Fathers and Sons*, 24–25.
12. For the feud between Dobrolyubov and Turgenev, see Lampert, *Sons against Fathers*, 238.
13. Pisarev, "Bazarov," 2000. Translation available in Pisarev, "Bazarov," 1996.
14. Paperno, *Chernyshevsky*, 14.
15. Paperno, 9.
16. Cited in Paperno, 14.
17. Pisarev, "Bazarov," 2000.

18. Turgenev, *Otcy i deti*, 118. Translation adapted from Turgenev, *Fathers and Sons*, 150.

19. Chernyshevsky, *Chto Delat'*, 9. Translation adapted from Chernyshevsky, *What Is*, 9–10.

20. Paperno, *Chernyshevsky*, 198.

21. Paperno argues that Chernyshevsky's novel belongs to a long tradition of translating Christianity into utopian social system, such as, for instance, the French utopian Charles Fourier, from whom Chernyshevsky heavily borrowed, and even Feuerbach himself can be said to belong to this group. Russia, however, was a novice participant in that tradition because the other European countries had undergone the struggle with their religious traditions earlier. Paperno, 196.

22. Berdyaev, *Origin of Russian Communism*, 46.

23. Paperno, *Chernyshevsky*, 28.

24. For the reception history of Chernyshevsky's novel, see Paperno, 27–31. It is fascinating that the novel's reception as a kind of secular gospel that had a tangible impact on people's lives was reported and feared, in Jewish literature, as the next chapter illustrates.

25. Avraham Uri Kovner's reputation as a "villain" derives from his infamous bank note forgery (which he attempted to justify with the principles of nihilism in a letter he wrote to Dostoyevsky) and from his subsequent arrest, followed by an equally dramatic conversion to Russian Orthodoxy. Recently, Svetlana Natkovich's research into Kovner's diaries revealed that he was a perpetrator of rape and sexual abuse. Murav, *Identity Theft*; Natkovich, *Ḳazanovah mi-Vilnah*.

26. Klausner, *Historiyah shel*, 4:141.

27. Kovner emphasizes the harrowing effects of poverty on his family, recalling in his autobiography that upon learning of the death of a newborn child, his father was relieved that there would be fewer mouths to feed. For Kovner's biography, see Klausner, 4:140–43.

28. Nathans, *Beyond the Pale*, 32–37.

29. Klausner, *Historiyah shel*, 4:143.

30. Klausner, 4:141.

31. Murav, *Identity Theft*, 22.

32. Murav, 24.

33. Feiner, "Introduction," 17–18.

34. In the 1860s, Russian imperial universities played a key role in the incubation and spread of nihilism and revolutionary ideologies. The time when the Kovner brothers would have been at Kiev University was a time of the transition after the Great Reforms, and there were still relatively few Jews attending any university, but their numbers significantly increased in the two following decades. See Nathans, *Beyond the Pale*, 206–9; Brower, *Training the Nihilists*, 98–99.

35. On Kiev as an epicenter for Jewish nihilists, see Meir, *Kiev, Jewish Metropolis*, 33.

36. A. Kovner, *Kol kitvei*, 207.

37. Pisarev, *Kritika Literaturnaia*, 330.

38. The original was published as a pamphlet that included Kovner's translation of a section from Buchner's *Force and Matter* into Hebrew. Murav, *Identity Theft*, 41.

39. A. Kovner, *Kol kitvei*, 6–7.

40. Chernyshevsky, *Chto Delat'*, 13; Chernyshevsky, *What Is*, 9–10.

41. A. Kovner, *Kol kitvei*, 7.

42. Murav, *Identity Theft*, 51.

43. Murav, 43.

44. Murav, 46.

45. Gottlober, *Igeret tsa'ar ba'alei hayim*, 13, 16, 18.

46. Turgenev, *Fathers and Sons*, 24–25.

47. Gottlober, *Igeret tsa'ar ba'alei hayim*, 16.

48. Veidlinger, *Jewish Public Culture*, 75–77.

49. Verhoeven, *Odd Man Karakozov*, 47.

50. I. Kovner, *Sefer ha-matzref*, 254.

51. I. Kovner, 106–7.

52. My translation. Lilienblum, *Ktavim otobiografiyim*, 3:110.

53. Abridged translation of Hebrew text in I. Kovner, *Sefer ha-matzref*, 62–63, 65.

54. Pisarev, *Kritika Literaturnaia*, 292. Translation adapted from Weiner, *Anthology of Russian Literature*, 2:386.

55. A. Kovner, "Yeshibotnaia Bursa."

56. I. Kovner, *Sefer ha-matzref*, 228–29.

57. I. Kovner, 149.

4

LITERARY APOSTASY

The Rejection of Textuality and the New Hebrew Writer

THE CRITIQUE OF LITERATURE IN THE NAME OF utility had the sobering effect of leading Jewish writers to reflect on their attraction to the textual endeavor and to question whether their preoccupation with the written word was something they could justify. For Hebrew writers especially, finding this justification was no easy task. The flowery romanticism of the *Love of Zion* in 1853 thus gave way to the self-critical and philosophical prose of Lilienblum, whose autobiographical novel *The Sins of Youth* (*Hatot Ne'urim*) appeared in Odessa in 1876. Crafted from diary entries, letters, pastiches of rabbinic texts, and creative retellings of his life, the novel is a psychological investigation into the loss of faith in literature and the textual endeavor. At the same time, the novel is itself a stark example of the cognitive dissonance experienced by the pioneering Hebrew writer who cannot bring himself to stop engaging in an activity he no longer sees as valuable.

Considered one of the first works of modern Hebrew fiction, *The Sins of Youth* is widely regarded by scholars as a maskilic narrative about the loss of faith in God and the break from the Jewish religious tradition—crises that result in the production of secular Jewish literature, in particular the autobiography.[1] Lilienblum is a small-town Talmudist who becomes involved with forbidden books and is excommunicated as a result of it. He then moves to Odessa, where he discovers the writings of the Russian nihilist critics, a discovery that indeed leads to his rejection of the Judaic textual tradition. Although the rift with tradition occupies a central part of the novel's plot, the break from Jewish observance and from the Orthodox community had surprisingly little effect on the writer. Instead, this chapter shows, the great drama at the center of this Hebrew novel is Lilienblum's loss of faith in texts and in the value of the literary pursuit, engendered by his conversion to nihilism and its utilitarian view of literature.

The distinction between the loss of religious faith, as previously conceived by scholars, and the loss of faith in texts, as I argue here, is far from trivial. The theological distinction between religious observance and the practices of Torah learning was an inherent feature of the mitnagdic worldview on which Lilienblum, as a Talmudist, was reared. Even after Lilienblum had rejected normative faith and observance, he nonetheless retained an attraction to the practices of Talmud study for which there was no longer a place in his modern, disenchanted reality. The autobiography represents Lilienblum's reluctant eulogy to his Talmudism and the lingering nostalgia for the "world of contemplation," which remains the disillusioned writer's sole source of pleasure.[2] Lilienblum's continual longing for the autotelic engagement with Judaic texts thus emerges as a creative force that gives rise to the Hebrew novel.

A Double Life

Lilienblum was born in 1843 in the Lithuanian town of Kaidan (Kėdainiai in Lithuanian). He was the only son of a mother who descended from a line of important rabbis from among the mitnagdim. His father, not distinguished by scholastic achievements, worked as a barrel maker but was nonetheless well versed in classical Jewish texts. Lilienblum recalls that his father loved the stories of the Aggadah and would often read them to his son. Lilienblum's aptitude for learning showed great promise, and his family hoped he would perpetuate its honorable lineage by becoming a great rabbi and scholar of the Talmud.[3]

He began to study the Talmud and its commentaries at the age of seven. At twelve, he joined a small local yeshiva. Alongside the Talmud, he studied the Hebrew epistolary arts and traditional books on Hebrew grammar written by religious commentators and poets. Lilienblum mentions his particular fondness for Avraham ben Meir ibn Ezra (1089–1164), a medieval commentator known for his attention to the plain meaning of the text (peshat) as well as the commentaries of the more contemporary philosophically inclined Meir Leibush ben Yehiel Mikhael Weisser (known as Malbim, 1809–1879).[4] The young Lilienblum fancied himself a *melitz*, a wordsmith and poet. He enjoyed playing with Hebrew words, composing gematrias, anagrams, and witty rhymes to entertain himself and his friends. By thirteen, he was already considered a Talmudic prodigy. Lilienblum was unwillingly betrothed, in accordance with the widespread custom of kest (see chap. 2), to an eleven-year-old girl from a relatively wealthy family, who promised the considerable dowry of three hundred rubles and six years of financial support so that Lilienblum could devote himself entirely to Talmud study. By the age of eighteen, residing now in Vilkomir, Kovno Province, in the house of his in-laws, Lilienblum, who was already a father of several children, claimed to have mastered all thirty-seven tractates of the Babylonian Talmud and was reviewing them for a second time. He reports, with a self-critical sense of the intensity of his diligence, studying at a rate that sometimes reached fifty folio pages of Talmud per day.[5] Soon, the young Lilienblum had large parts of the Talmud committed to memory together with its classical and more recent commentators.[6] Recognized for his scholarly accomplishments, he became the head of two small yeshivas in Vilkomir.

When the young Talmudist needed a break from the dry Talmudic passages, he would shift his attention to stories, parables, mystical texts, liturgical poetry and dirges, and folklore of the rabbinic world. Just as the young Russian Orthodox seminarians were inspired by hagiographic literature, Lilienblum writes that, as a young Talmud student, he found his life's passion in stories and tales from the Jewish tradition.[7] Texts often elicited in Lilienblum intense emotional reactions. As in Dobrolyubov's diary account, Lilienblum recalls crying in front of his peers when he heard a sad story from his teacher.[8] Sentimentality and the investment in the fictional world described in texts—a common experience among Jewish and Russian writers in the nineteenth century—both gave Lilienblum immense pleasure and, at the same time, constituted a habit of world denial, which, as he later learned, was difficult to break.

The novel recounts one especially poignant example of Lilienblum's young literary imaginativeness. In the anxious period of Lilienblum's unwanted betrothal, he was reading Aggadic collections and listening to folkloric tales told by his uncle, in which he discovered the colorful Jewish folk villains of Samael, appearing as the primordial serpent or Satan, and Lilith, his female consort who delights in deceiving young scholars. On the eve of Yom Kippur, the holiest day of the Jewish calendar, after reciting a central prayer (*ha-vidui ha-gadol*, "the great confession," which is also the subtitle of his novel) Lilienblum recalls falling asleep and, upon waking, realizing that he had had a nocturnal emission. This "spilling of the seed" is considered a violation of rabbinic law, so, naturally, Lilienblum is filled with dread, and the following scenarios start taking shape in his mind: "Lilith and her demonic crew were hovering all over the world all night seeking out Jewish boys to make them stumble. . . . My heart melted and my stomach turned inside out. . . . Those she-demons found me and started torturing me, and as a result of this I made pure and noble souls imbued with God's own glory into lost wanderers because I delivered them as booty to the dark forces, God have mercy on us!"[9] Palpable dread overwhelmed Lilienblum. He imagined that the female demons had captured his soul, and he felt guilt and compassion for the unborn "pure souls" that he "wasted" and delivered to the demonic forces. Of course, Lilienblum tells this story with critical distance, mocking his younger self for his uncritical approach toward this folkloric text. Despite his having gained this self-knowledge, however, texts continued to haunt Lilienblum and inform the reality of his life.

Lilienblum's first exposure to secular literature happened inconspicuously and was a natural outgrowth of his Torah learning. Secular books and periodicals made their way harmoniously into the mix of religious literature that Lilienblum was studying. It all occurred in the study house, which often figures in subsequent works of Hebrew writers as a place for the dissemination of new ideas and the exchange of books and secular knowledge. In the study house, Lilienblum was approached by a fellow learner who saw a Jewish philosophy book in his hand. "What books do you have in there," asked the fellow, "and do they have any Haskalah in them?" Lilienblum did not yet fully understand what Haskalah meant. The fellow learner pushed an old copy of the Hebrew journal *Ha-Maggid* into Lilienblum's hand, and thus began Lilienblum's preoccupation with Hebrew literature and the Jewish Enlightenment.[10]

What Lilienblum found in Hebrew journals was not heretical, per se, or different in *form* from the kinds of materials that Lilienblum would read in religious books. The maskilic Hebrew journals that Lilienblum read, *Ha-Magid*, *Ha-Melitz*, and *Ha-Karmel*, contained Hebrew poetry, translations of German Jewish scholars, Hebrew dramas, modern commentaries on traditional Jewish texts, and even local community news. The journals also often contained Hebrew and Yiddish translations of European works. Lilienblum's first encounters with European literature were rather eclectic. They included works like a historical account of Napoleon's wars translated into Hebrew, *Don Quixote*, the novel *The Mysteries of Paris* (*Les Mystères de Paris*, 1843) by Eugène Sue (1804–1857), and others.[11] His discovery of the

Haskalah journals further cultivated Lilienblum's passion for texts and his dream of becoming a Hebrew poet. It was during this time that Lilienblum first tasted some of the ideas of Russian materialist philosophy through the articles of Avraham Uri Kovner, whose ideas Lilienblum dismissed at the time as negatively biased toward the Talmud, only to reconsider them a few years later.

His exposure to the maskilic Hebrew journals heightened Lilienblum's growing sense of oppression among the simple and devout people of his town. For instance, Lilienblum had long been bothered by the supernatural or irrational elements of religious faith and practice. Lilienblum's reading of the German Jewish and Galician scholars linked to the *Wissenschaft des Judentums* movement (academy study of Judaism), such as Heinrich Graetz (1819–1871) and Nachman Krochmal (1785–1840), gave him the intellectual tools to reject the "irrational practices" of his Jewish townsfolk. According to the Hebrew literary scholar Alan Mintz, the Haskalah gave Lilienblum "a new body of scriptures in the writings of Mendelssohn, Krochmal, and the late maskilim, as a new eschatology in a vision of a society of enlightened manners and productive activity, in addition to a framework of social explanations which provided a comprehensive critique for Jewish society."[12] This new set of scriptures, however, did not yet displace the old. Finding support for the rationalist ideas of the Haskalah in traditional Jewish commentaries, such as Maimonides and the Gaon of Vilna, Lilienblum's first aspiration as a newly made freethinker was to unite the Talmudists with the maskilim in a war against an easy common target—the supernatural and superstitious elements of extralegal Jewish tradition and belief. The intellectual flourishing that the Haskalah stirred in Lilienblum inspired him to try his pen in a series of poems mocking the belief in demons.

His early twenties were an intellectual heyday for Lilienblum, who was delving into Jewish texts that he studied alongside maskilic texts. In *The Sins of Youth*, he describes many of the books he read in this period. Among those that made a strong impression on him during his transition to the Haskalah, Lilienblum listed the *Guide for the Perplexed* by the medieval philosopher Maimonides, as well as many works that commented on and sometimes disputed *Shulchan Arukh*, the canonical law code by Yosef Karo, such as those by Yehezkel Landau (1713–1793), Avraham Danzig (1748–1820), and Shlomo Eiger (1786–1852). Lilienblum seemed to have devoured every maskilic text that came his way with the same diligence that he applied to the Talmud. Lilienblum found himself a study partner (*havruta*), a similarly minded companion from his yeshiva. Together, they would read Hebrew poetry and fiction and study the Song of Songs; they would apply the examples of historical criticism that they had encountered in the Haskalah periodicals to examine the composition of the Mishnah, coming up with their own theories that differed from the accepted accounts of the traditional commentaries.[13] The hermeneutic practices with which rabbinic learning combined with his exposure to the ideas of secular historical thinking sowed the seeds of the poetic license Lilienblum would use to integrate and rewrite traditional Jewish texts into Hebrew fiction.

For the entire duration of his time in Vilkomir, however, Lilienblum was leading a double life. His life was not divided, however, between religious and secular texts, but rather, as characteristic of mitnagdic dualist theology, the discord that he experienced was between the life of the mind and the life of the body, in which the latter was nothing but a constant cause of displeasure. Lilienblum describes how his father arranged his kest marriage agreement to a girl from a wealthy family. Being a young scholar, he was forced to submit to the authority of his in-laws and wife, and naturally, problems ensued. Mitnagdic mind-body dualism was, in fact, at the very core of the kest arrangement, which institutionalized the division of intellectual and spiritual labor from physical labor. Thus, the kest contributed to a divide between Torah learning and all other demands of practical life from which the Talmud scholar was exempt because such activities were derided as *bitul zeman*—a waste of precious time that should be devoted to the study of Torah.[14]

The kest was disparaged as one of the greatest vices in Jewish culture by Lilienblum's autobiographical predecessors. The combined efforts of the autobiographies Salomon Maimon (1754–1800), Mordecai Ginzburg (1795–1846), and Lilienblum turned life under the kest arrangement into a familiar trope. A young scholar ends up in the uneducated household of his wife. He is disturbed by the unexpected physical demands of his unwanted early marriage, which the young boy would be unable or unwilling to consummate, and which would result in unwanted sexual reactions, as we have seen from Lilienblum's nocturnal emission scene. Added to this were the crude financial disputes about the paying out of the kest financial agreement, which the in-laws would often break. In autobiographical accounts, the parents-in-law often exaggerated the amount of financial support or simply broke their promises. Once the young family would run out of financial support, the choices of occupation for a groom who was unaccustomed and unwilling to do anything other than study the Torah would be limited. Being a melamed, a teacher of young children (as was the case with Avraham Uri Kovner's father), provided too little income to support a family. Alternatively, teaching the Talmud to advanced students, as in the case of Lilienblum, was a temporary measure resorted to by scholars whose in-laws were no longer able or willing to support them but who had not established themselves in any other work.

Aside from the wife, who, proscribed from studying the Talmud, epitomized gross physicality, the mother-in-law featured as an established villain in these maskilic accounts. In memorable depictions, Maimon describes how his mother-in-law beat him, whereas Ginzburg, in his Hebrew autobiography *Aviezer* (1863), humorously recounts how his mother-in-law almost poisoned him to death with a magic potion intended to alleviate his sexual impotence.[15] Lilienblum likewise devotes pages to descriptions of what he had to endure from the superstitions and whims of "that wretched woman." Lilienblum often fought his mother-in-law's insistence on extralegal superstitious practices. For instance, he militantly resisted her putting a cat into the newborn's cradle for good luck. The episode even inspired Lilienblum to write a playful poem about the nonexistence of demons.[16] In Lilienblum's reworking and toward the latter part of the nineteenth century, however, the critique of kest became less of a personal grievance than a call to a materialist revision of Jewish culture in which men must assume financial responsibility.

Lilienblum's descriptions of his married life are filled with shame and self-deprecation because, in his view, his lack of a practical vocation forced him to be dependent on his simple-minded and superstitious small-town environment. His situation only worsened in the aftermath of his becoming the town's heretic. His in-laws stopped supporting him, yet he could not manage on his own. His wife's business suffered terribly, which only contributed to domestic strife. It was only in the world of texts, among religious books and secular journals, that Lilienblum was able to find refuge from his material troubles and to feel truly alive.

A Martyr of the Enlightenment

What put an eventual end to his life under religious coercion but not to his unhappiness was the ordeal of Lilienblum's excommunication. The story began when Lilienblum decided to organize a literary group among his colleagues in the study house, an idea that inspired the creation of a similar secret club at the Volozhin Yeshiva during the time of Berdichevsky and Bialik. The club was devoted to collecting and reading religious and secular (specifically Haskalah) books, which Lilienblum was gathering into a small library. Among the books he acquired were a Hebrew concordance, valuable religious commentaries, translations of German Jewish scholars, Hebrew literature, and, of course, many maskilic journals. Due to the unfortunate result of the vigilant religious zealotry of one yeshiva student, however, news of Lilienblum's plans and efforts reached the town's rabbi.

Scholars have shed light on the literary construction of many highly stylized episodes in this autobiography and on their divergence from depictions of the same events in his personal correspondence.[17] Hence, the fact that the following events strongly resemble an episode from *Don Quixote* should come as no surprise. The devout supporters of this traitor to Lilienblum's secrets found him guilty of the possession of forbidden books. They locked Lilienblum in his room, seized all the rare and expensive books from his library, and took them to the town's rabbi to be burned.[18] The rabbi first pleaded with Lilienblum to give up his intoxication with forbidden books. But Lilienblum, who insisted on the separation between study and religious practice, argued in his own defense that, as long as he maintained his observance of Jewish law, he could read and study whatever he pleased. After a mock trial, the community ostracized Lilienblum as a heretic and labeled him a "Berliner"—a follower of the freethinking Berlin maskilim. The townspeople began to harass him and his family. He writes that his wife was insulted in the streets and that his children were beaten at school. And, as a common retaliation tactic against religious heretics, the community even threatened to deliver him to the Russian authorities as a freethinker and a traitor to the tsar.

Strangely, despite the threats and denunciations of the Vilkomir community, Lilienblum exhibited no sign of an existential crisis regarding his excommunication. On the contrary, this small-town melodrama energized him, and Lilienblum began to fancy himself a "holy-martyr for the enlightenment."[19] While his family was being boycotted and threatened by the community, Lilienblum reveled in the texts of the Haskalah and wholeheartedly believed in the exalted value of literature, knowledge, and enlightenment. It was on this high note that Lilienblum embarked on his next journey to Odessa—a journey that would shatter his faith in texts forever.

The Defense of the Talmud

While still living with his in-laws in Vilkomir, Lilienblum made his first official foray into the Hebrew literary milieu with the publication of "Ways of the Talmud" ("Orhot ha-Talmud," 1868) in *Ha-Melitz*. The article that begins Lilienblum's literary career is none other than a defense of the Talmud. In it, Lilienblum defends Talmudic literature from the maskilim, who dismiss it as benighted; he defends it from the radical Jewish nihilists, who deem it "useless" and even evil; and lastly, he defends it from the established rabbinic authority of his time, which, he claims, has corrupted the law and stifled the continuation of the legislative process. In other words, in this literary debut, it was Lilienblum against the world.

The article reads like an impressive pastiche of proof texts from rabbinic literature. Lilienblum himself later acknowledged that the article contains "little critique but much Talmudic expertise."[20] Lilienblum, who is a master interpreter of rabbinic texts, proves to his readers that he could summon, manipulate, catalog, and interpret rabbinic literature at will from the very first lines, which begin thus: "In recent times, writers of little understanding began piling complaints against the Talmud, seeing in its stories nothing but folly and in its legislative practices a dangerous burden for the Jewish people. But I shall test my strength here to be the defender of this lofty book, ancient of days, whose words were the fountain of living waters to the seed of Jeshurun [Israel] from the day of their exile to this very day."[21] Lilienblum sets out to defend the Talmud against "writers of little understanding"—a denunciation directed particularly at Avraham Uri Kovner and at the moderate maskilim, who fail to appreciate the Talmud's positive value as a "fountain of living waters" that allegedly preserved the Jewish nation in exile. With this statement, Lilienblum's article already sets itself apart from the secular Hebrew writers of his time and maskilim in general, who almost universally favored the Hebrew Bible over the Talmud and saw Talmudic literary narratives (Aggadot) as harmful tales that instilled belief in the supernatural.

Acting as a literary critic of Jewish texts, Lilienblum finds himself engaging in rabbinic hermeneutical practices as he creatively reinvents the Talmud's literary and legislative features in the style of a traditional commentary filled with proof texts and allusions. His interpretations, however, already deviate from tradition as they are historical and interested in realism. In all his arguments in this essay, one notices a claim to social utility;

the Aggadot, if read properly, he argues, can be seen to serve a positive national purpose, and the Talmud's liberal legislative spirit tries to establish laws that are "beneficial to life."

Arguing against the maskilim's accusation that Talmudic literature is "filled with nonsense," Lilienblum reinterprets more than thirty Aggadic texts as he attempts to prove that they have brought the Jews utility rather than harm. Lilienblum not only insists that the miraculous tales are fictional—a statement that provoked the ire of the Orthodox factions—but Lilienblum also subverts the tradition from within by arguing that great Talmud scholars themselves never believed in the literal truth of such tales. According to Lilienblum, "These agadot were not harmful in the slightest because the wise never believed them [to be literally true]." The superstitions derided by the maskilim, he argues, are not from the Talmud but are inventions of uneducated laypeople. For this category of person, Lilienblum uses the common epithet *am ha'aretz*, ignoramus or boor, that recurs throughout rabbinic literature. He tries to support his argument using the example of Russian peasants who are illiterate and believe in superstitions. Lilienblum writes, "Likewise, among our women and multitudes we find harmful beliefs that are laughable but also pain my heart, which have no mention in any book."[22] Lilienblum proceeds with a historical reading of a midrash about the fall of Beitar. He argues that the miraculous tales of the revival of the dead, found in Talmudic Aggadot about Beitar, albeit fictional, served to uphold the national morale at a time of hardship. Without these Aggadot, "children of the rabbis' imagination," the Jewish people might have perished long ago. In this defense of the Talmud, Lilienblum imputes Jewish survival in the Diaspora to the products of rabbinic literary creativity. The notion of Talmudic literature as a national literary treasure that sustains the Jewish people served as a source of inspiration for later Jewish writers such as Bialik and Ravnitsky in their work on the project of "the ingathering of the agadah" (*kinus ha-agadah*).[23]

Following the defense of Talmudic literature, Lilienblum proceeds to the defense of Talmudic legislation, or more precisely, the spirit of Talmudic legislation. Bringing in examples in which the Talmud seems to attenuate (a literal reading of) biblical law—such as in the case of capital punishment, *lex talionis* ("an eye for an eye"), punishments of a suspected adulteress (*sotah*), and the wayward and rebellious son (*ben sorer u-moreh*)—he argues that the original spirit of Talmudic legislation was geared toward improving earthly life. This included looking for lenient rulings and legislating "useful rulings" (*takanot mo'ilot*) that help society. Lilienblum faulted Orthodox rabbinic legislators of Jewish law or more recent generations, who had made religious life intolerable. The liberal and life-affirming spirit of scholarship in the Talmud had been shackled by later rabbinic leaders' adherence to the *Shulchan Arukh*, the sixteenth-century code of law compiled by Yosef Karo that became regarded as authoritative and immutable. Lilienblum thus absolved the Talmud of blame for present conditions in Jewish life. According to the historian Olga Litvak, Lilienblum's counterintuitive argument here was that "the proliferation of stringencies [*humrot*] among the orthodox in Eastern Europe signifies the abdication of Talmudic principle to dubious spiritual considerations," specifically, spiritual considerations and superstitions that appealed to a less intellectually inclined laity. With characteristic mitnagdic hubris, Lilienblum concludes by calling on the combined efforts of the learned elite and Jewish intellectuals (maskilim) to purge Jewish law of the traces of mysticism, superstition, and communal traditions accepted as law and to return to the Talmudic spirit of useful rulings.[24]

In "Ways of the Talmud," we find Lilienblum in transition. He rejects rabbinic authority, yet he still has faith in the Talmud and the canon of the Jewish tradition as a textual system that holds the key to the improvement of Jewish life. It is evident that the concern with utility is one that informs Lilienblum's view of literature and of rabbinic texts. When Lilienblum discovered the writings of the Russian critics in a subsequent phase of his struggle with textuality, his faith in the usefulness of rabbinic literary endeavors vanished almost entirely.

The Talmudist and the City

The crisis that undermined Lilienblum's faith in literature occurred in Odessa. Like Chernyshevsky, for whom "the confrontation with the real world in the capital proved a cruel and painful experience," Lilienblum was extremely disillusioned by Odessa because he soon learned that the real world did not care about literature or ideas but only about material pleasures.[25] Here are some of Lilienblum's first impressions of Odessa:

> The city known for its enlightenment and tolerance contains neither. Its enlightenment bears an air of cool freedom, borne of commerce and hedonism, and is founded in self-deception rather than inner enlightenment, produced by deep reflection. Its tolerance is the child of loneliness. Left to himself, each man does whatever he pleases, and thus charlatans abound. . . .

Hebrew literature is dead here; or better—it was never born. While Hebrew journals flourish and Hebrew books are sold by the thousands, most of the people do not know a word of Hebrew—and the self-styled maskilim despise it with deep-rooted hatred. . . .

The cause of all these sights is that the Talmud never affected the inhabitants of this land. While free of its heavy burden, they are not free from the spirit of folly, which people heed more diligently here than in our small town.[26]

Lilienblum's first impression of Odessa deems it anti-intellectual and driven by money, folly, and base desires in a way more egregious than the traditional society from which he had fled. A world free of the "heavy burden" of Jewish law appears to be no less ruled by irrational and ignoble urges. For Lilienblum, the Talmud remains a guiding beacon of nobility in the sea of hedonistic freedom. Indeed, Lilienblum was first appalled by his observation of the liberal sexual conduct of wealthy Jewish merchants and others who visited brothels in Odessa.[27] Of course, for Chernyshevsky, as for Lilienblum, even in the absence of religion, a life of hedonism was a priori out of the question. Lilienblum's dreams of becoming a Hebrew writer were quickly shattered when he came to Odessa and realized that no one in the big city cared about it. "The city did a terrible thing to me," he recalled. "I am a man of contemplation and feeling and the life of action is foreign to me. Now I am in the midst of the world of action, from which I am so distant. Haskalah and Hebrew literature have no value here and all those who study it are looked down upon by the multitudes who live in the world of action and of commerce."[28]

He was further convinced of this conclusion when the recommendation letter that he took to Zederbaum, founder and editor of *Ha-Melitz*, did not succeed in securing him a position in the Hebrew journal. Within only a few days of his arrival, he was already reminiscing about his old town and the "little yeshiva boys who ran after him and called him an *epikores* [heretic]."[29] The dangerous heretic of Vilkomir was irrelevant in Odessa, whose world, he painfully learned, revolved not around ideas but gross materialism—and not in the philosophical sense.

Soon, however, his reading of Russian radical critics clarified his confusion between philosophical materialism and people who were simply materialistic. He learned to read Russian well and could soon work through Chernyshevsky's *What Is to Be Done?*, Turgenev's *Fathers and Sons*, and a seven-volume collection of the works of Pisarev.[30] The scientific explanation of the world that the nihilists' works advocated improved Lilienblum's opinion about the material world, convincing him that the material world could not, by definition, be evil or inferior, in contrast to what his traditional education had taught him to believe. The bold arguments of Pisarev and Chernyshevsky about literature beguiled Lilienblum into becoming a loyal follower of a philosophy that held that "Shakespeare is less valuable than a good pair of boots."[31] He recalled the impression that reading *What Is to Be Done?* made on him as follows:

> In January, I acquired *What Is to Be Done?* by Mr. Chernyshevsky; its valuable ideas made a great impression on me and gave me pleasure. The ideas that I found in this book (many of which were not new to me) filled the emptiness in my brain because they stood for something that I saw as positive: the [right to] happiness, the fulfillment of each individual, the necessity of labor for each person, regardless of the situation; freedom of feelings [presumably, Chernyshevsky's notion of "freedom of the heart"]; knowledge of the true benefit, *to'elet*. I also read other books that uphold this system of thought, and I almost became intoxicated with them.[32]

Lilienblum's reading of Russian materialist critics exposed him to a new, exciting world of ideas that, unlike those of the Haskalah, he believed, offered him a foothold in the real world of Odessa. Once again, however, he could not restrain himself. His reading—and more precisely, his intoxication with yet another set of texts—threw him back into a new all-consuming textual whirlwind, akin to his engrossment with the works of the Haskalah, the Talmud, and Aggadot when he was younger. Ironic as it may be, this new episode of textual intoxication ultimately led him to reject literature, his previous raison d'être: "In this first year here I saw that there is no place anywhere for imagination, visions, passions and dreams. . . . The great machine that is the universe runs its course under the laws of nature; the predetermined will come to pass, and that which was never meant to be will never be. This terrible crisis that overcame me continued into its second year. I lost my imagination; I lost literature; I lost my sense of safety. My heart melted in tears but to no avail."[33]

The ideas of Pisarev and Chernyshevsky led Lilienblum to a dead end. On one hand, a world in which science was the sole authority—"the great machine that is the universe"—might have appeared more intellectually honest, or at least free from illusions that cause people unnecessary harm to society. On the other hand, this vision of the world was all-consuming and denied the ontological legitimacy of anything other than the material. What previously gave meaning to Lilienblum's life were texts, and they were what fired his imagination, passions, and dreams. Having no function in the material world other than to deceive the mind, imaginative literature became a liability. The materialist worldview of the Russian writers not only explained to Lilienblum the reality of life in Odessa but also warned him of the inevitability of his failure as a man of texts and scholasticism to affect the material world. In acquiring "a materialist view of life" (*mabat gashmi al ha-hayim*), Lilienblum lost the only thing that gave his life meaning: the pleasure of the text. What ensued was a crisis that drove Lilienblum to despair.

The most important consequence of Lilienblum's exposure to the thought of Russian critics was Lilienblum's changed valuation of his identity as a writer. According to the Haskalah ideology, "the Hebrew writer and poet were . . . thought to occupy a kind of priestly role superior in moral authority to political or religious leaders." With his loss of faith in the Haskalah, according to Mintz, Lilienblum "denied himself this last means of transcendence; the only thing he was good at and was rewarded for became a conspicuous form of contemplation [*iyun*]."[34] Here is the moment when Lilienblum comes to this crucial realization: "The treasure that I had inside my brain, my only possession that I accumulated in my head during the days of my life became null. Literature, which constitutes our theology, because is not a practical matter, became a burden. I was like a philosopher who lost his way, I found myself lonely and lost in the world of life, my mind was emptied, and my soul shuddered."[35] Lilienblum, a former Talmudist well trained in the mitnagdic system, finally realized the cause of his crisis—namely, that since engagement with literature was the central object of worship for the mitnagdim, in losing faith in texts, he was losing everything that formerly had meaning.

Indeed, Lilienblum's exposure to the texts of Russian materialist critics engendered a reversal in his values: according to the ideology of the mitnagdim, Torah lishmah was the ultimate end while any engagement with the material world was considered a waste (*bitul*). But in the new materialistic worldview, textual study and literature were the waste—or worse, they were embodiments of self-indulgence. No textual occupation could compare to being, for instance, a doctor, a natural scientist, or a physical laborer. Lilienblum's "soul shuddered" both from the loss of his beloved Talmudism but also in horror that his life had been one great waste.

Waste or wastefulness (connoted by the term *batalah*), as the antithesis of utility, was a crucial focal point in Lilienblum's text. Perhaps the strongest articulation of the idea that fiction was similar to the Talmud in its impracticality is found in the title of Lilienblum's autobiography, *The Sins of Youth*. Lilienblum enumerates three particular "sins" that led to his failure at living in the real word: his lack of a practical vocation, early arranged marriage, and a futile obsession with a woman whom he loved but did not want to marry. As is characteristic of rabbinic hermeneutics, however, the title also has a hidden, subversive meaning. It is a rabbinic euphemism for masturbation, another form of this waste. The title evokes the episode of Lilienblum's nocturnal emission, an inadvertent wasteful spilling of seed but one connected to the category described as *hotza'at shikhvat zera le-vattalah*, the (deliberate) wasteful emission of seed (semen) outside of potentially reproductive and approved sexual context.

By effectively titling his autobiography *Masturbation*, Lilienblum labeled his own attempt at writing and also the literary endeavor at large as a wasteful practice akin to the idea of spilling of the seed wastefully. Though Lilienblum tries at moments to restrain his outpourings of confessional Hebrew prose, he often cannot, knowing that it also brings him pleasure and relief. Like the titular autoerotic act, the act of writing the autobiography was ridden with shame and self-deprecation. Lilienblum taunts himself: "Why do I write? Why? For whose benefit? Whom will I benefit by this other than myself?"[36]

The text of the autobiography served as the ideal receptacle for its author's erotic desires in more ways than one. Paperno describes a similar self-pleasuring and self-tormenting function that diary writing served for Chernyshevsky, whose diary held "the poverty and loneliness of his student years, his life devoid of sensual gratification, his indulgence in 'feverish fantasies' desiring a woman whose nose and brow are exactly 'the way it should be,' and a woman of genius without equal in history."[37] Similarly, Dobrolyubov dreamed in his diaries: "If I had a woman with whom I could share my thoughts and feelings, and she would even read my writings, then I would be happy."[38] As for the founders of Russian nihilism, so too for Lilienblum: sexual and romantic fantasies constituted an imagined ideal mediated by the processes of reading and writing.

During the time of his persecution and excommunication from Vilkomir, Lilienblum embarked on a romance with a thoughtful and "enlightened" woman, Nehamah Navhovich, whose identity was concealed behind the initials N. N.[39] Lilienblum, who had been married against his will at the age of fifteen and subsequently fathered four children, found in N. N. a compassionate listener and a skilled conversation partner with whom he could freely share and discuss his ideas, a pleasure he had never experienced with a woman. The relationship was mediated entirely by texts. In the spirit of Rousseau, who did not want to distinguish "reading from living, nor loving from writing love letters," Lilienblum enjoyed reading the works of Mapu to his beloved.[40] Lilienblum writes: "I read to her Mapu's *Love of Zion* and the *Guilt of Samaria*, and by reading these books our feelings developed more and more and I realized that I am in love! Oh, how joyful I was then!"[41] Scenes of romantic encounters on the pastoral landscape of biblical Israel acted as a love potion on Lilienblum (and many other readers of the novel), engendering new dreams and visions of love in the heart of the Talmudist. Navhovich supported his intellectual aspirations, and the relationship, lasting for many years after Lilienblum left for Odessa, progressed as a passionate correspondence of letters and love poems. But, alas, for the ex-Talmudist, who in fact shared in *The Sins of Youth* many of his correspondences with Navhovich, "the word never became flesh," and the relationship was never consummated.[42]

Perhaps Lilienblum understood that the rewards of this textual romance would bring him much more pleasure than a real physical encounter. After all, we know that Chernyshevsky also refused (for as long as possible) to fulfill his conjugal duties in order to not "spoil" his ideal vision of his wife.[43] In the absence of the real physical relationship, it was very difficult for Lilienblum, the newly converted materialist, to dispel the illusions of romantic pain and bliss and to cease writing passionate poems and letters to his textual lover. Having the moral decency not to abandon his unloved family without whatever meager financial support he could provide (unlike other maskilim had done), Lilienblum continued to provide for them and tried to forget his dreams of a future with N. N. Using a nihilist metaphor to describe the gradual dissipation of his feelings, he writes that his life turned from "poetry to prose."[44]

The irony of Lilienblum's position is encapsulated by the fact that he was a materialist who did not know how to take pleasure in the material world. Lilienblum only came to understand this fact when it was too late: "Had I been wealthy, or someone who can enjoy this world, or if I could fill my head with the exact sciences, I would not feel so painfully the absence of the imagination—because I would have been able to enjoy the reality that I have made for myself. But I am nothing but a poor am ha-aretz [ignoramus] who knows nothing but how to undermine every pleasant thought and imagination."[45]

Even though the materialist outlook helped Lilienblum realize the importance of physicality and material life on earth, he did not know what to do with it. He was no longer bound by religious law or superstition but was not yet capable of enjoying physical pleasure. His romantic affair with N. N. proved to be a harmful illusion that he felt compelled to give up. He wanted to study the natural sciences, but he failed to make progress in the field. His life's toil of Torah learning had lost value in his eyes. Meanwhile, the material troubles in his life kept abounding. His wife and children came to live with him in Odessa, and he could barely support them. Living out his own ironic twist of the nihilist slogan that the classics of world literature are worth less than a good pair of boots, in a letter to his wife, Lilienblum reported that he was even forced to sell his precious five-volume collection of Pisarev's writings to buy, in its stead, a bag of potatoes.[46]

Materialist philosophy, it accurately seemed to him, gave him only the knowledge of "how to undermine." In the words of Bazarov, how to build "[was] none of our business."[47] Feeling a growing sense of emptiness, Lilienblum began to wonder whether perhaps the merchants and "charlatans" who frequented the brothels of Odessa were the true materialists rather than the idealistic ex-yeshiva-students who had become nihilists as he had.

Postmodern readers may appreciate the circular and self-negating character of Lilienblum's absorption in Russian materialism, which undermined his faith in literature. The texts of materialism themselves, however, escaped unscathed. Lilienblum seemed to have forgotten their textuality; that is, to say that, like the ideas of the Haskalah and the Talmud that had previously been his obsessions, materialist ideas too were articulated in books and journals. Without realizing this new entrapment, Lilienblum became a martyr of materialism and adhered devotedly to his new conviction. In moments of existential despair about the "great machine that is the universe," Lilienblum, like Bazarov, considered the possibility of suicide. But the half-nihilist decided against it because it would be too "romantic" and apologized to the reader for leaving this "Hebrew drama" without a proper denouement.[48]

Lilienblum's autobiography ended with a markedly poetic passage. Once prepared to accept the bitter truth of materialism at any cost, he now dreams of the possibility of return to the enchanted world of textuality and the imagination, even by means of deceit and intoxication:

> There is no pleasure in the world other than in the imagination. And all imagination is futile. In all my life, I found pleasure in nothing other than futility. Sometimes I wish I could forget my present convictions and to become

absorbed by some pleasant fantasy, like when I was closer to God. But then a voice startles me: "Return, o mischievous children . . . except for Aher, who knew my glory!" Only mischievous children who sin from lust while their minds are clueless can return, but not I. With all my might, I sometimes wish that I could procure an opium that would intoxicate me and move my heart like in the days of old; is there such an opium for me? But my heart is a terrible ice, and a deadly chill roams there without rest.[49]

Since Lilienblum's only source of pleasure was found in activities that were "futile," how could he ever be happy with a worldview that valued utility above all? Unable to bear the pain of meaninglessness, he wishes for an "opium" that would make him forget his materialistic convictions and enable him to reenchant his mind.

Standing at what seems to him to be the finishing line of his life, he identifies with the Talmudic archetypical heretic Elisha ben Abuya, also known as Aher, "the other one, the changed one." Elisha was a passionate scholar who once reached the mystical heights of learning and entered God's sacred orchard of textual interpretation, the pardes (paradise). For reasons that still evade scholars and interpreters, the mystical experience in the orchard of textuality proved to be a destructive one for Elisha, who in a moment of anger and despair "cut down its saplings" and become an apostate. Betrayed by his best student, who "knew his glory," God, in the Talmudic account, denies Elisha the possibility of repentance by exclaiming "return o mischievous children . . . except for Aher," thus renaming him "the changed one."[50]

Lilienblum described a similar desire for return into the paradise of rabbinic learning but felt that, if not the voice of God, then the true nature of the world according to materialism views prohibited it. Denied the possibility of spiritual transcendence and miserable in the world, Lilienblum signs the autobiographical novel with the anagram *umlal ba'aretz* ("the one who is wretched on the earth"), which is a Hebrew acronym for "I, Moshe Leib Lilienblum, the son of my father Rabbi Tzvi." As for Aher, he does return in the Talmudic account, when his Torah learning is used by his student Rabbi Meir as grounds to reintegrate him. Lilienblum also returned to practicing rabbinic textuality when he wrote his own materialist Mishnah passage through the voice of Elisha ben Abuyah.

Materialism according to Moses

The turn took place in 1877, when Lilienblum's life had changed for the better. Having completed his autobiography four years earlier, Lilienblum could not have imagined that Hebrew literature, let alone his self-indulgent emotional outpourings, would move anyone other than "naive yeshiva students from rural towns."[51] But he soon found that *The Sins of Youth* was becoming Odessa's new Jewish best seller, rivaling Mapu's *Love of Zion*. Furthermore, naive yeshiva students were becoming a powerful social and intellectual force among Russian Jews. His journalistic endeavors in the spheres of religion, Jewish nationalism, and literary criticism set Lilienblum as a spokesperson for a new generation of young post-yeshiva intellectuals and as an important voice in the Jewish press.

The success of *The Sins of Youth* partially alleviated Lilienblum's financial troubles. With Odessa being at the front of the Russo-Turkish War in 1877, Lilienblum happily sent his wife and family back to Vilkomir. He was thus free to start taking steps toward a university education and studied accounting, acquiring skills on which he later drew occasionally to support himself alongside his journalistic career. Despite his book's success, Lilienblum retained his conviction that much of Hebrew literature was useless. With the exception of the sequel to *The Sins of Youth*, a book called *The Way of Return* (alternatively, *The Way of Repentance* [*Derekh teshuva*]), published close to the end of his life in 1899, Lilienblum stopped publishing fictional and literary works.[52]

That same year of 1877, which marked the peak of Lilienblum's journalistic success, there was a new development in Jewish intellectual life: an attempt to elaborate Marxist and other socialist ideas in a Judaic idiom. The initiative came from a fellow Jewish writer and the graduate of a state-supported yeshiva, Aaron Samuel Liebermann (1843–1880). Influenced by Russian materialism like previous Jewish writers, but also among the first of the post-yeshiva Jewish writers to be familiar with the works of Marx and Engels, Liebermann began to organize a movement of Jewish socialism in eastern Europe. Together with a group of yeshiva-educated writers hungrily devouring the words of Marx and Engels, he founded the monthly journal *Ha-Emet* (*The Truth*), published in Vienna, that was devoted to disseminating Marxist and socialist ideas among Jews.[53] Liebermann and his fellow Jewish socialists wanted Lilienblum, the now-famous author and journalist, to write a propagandistic article for their journal. Lilienblum did not take interest in Marxism or Liebermann's socialist platform and repeatedly refused. When Liebermann suggested the idea of writing an article from the perspective of the Talmudic heretic Elisha ben Abuyah, who disturbs Talmud learners in the study house and urges them to take up productive occupations, however, Lilienblum accepted the proposal, though not without caveats. According to the story in the Jerusalem Talmud Hagigah 2:1, Elisha's violent act of "cutting down the saplings" in the orchard meant that he prevented people from becoming great Torah scholars by convincing the learners in the beit midrash to acquire a productive profession. Having severed these potential scholars from their source of spiritual life, the Jerusalem Talmud says Elisha was "a murderer." Despite or because of this, Elisha had figured as a romantic hero of maskilic writings since the beginning of the nineteenth century. In Lilienblum's prime years of development, Elisha's character appeared in the maskilic poet Meir Halevi Letris's 1865 Hebrew translation of Goethe's *Faust* retitled *Ben Abuyah*. This translation prompted a debate among prominent Jewish writers, such as Avraham Uri Kovner and Smolenskin, each mobilizing this rabbinic character as a representative of their nationalist or political ideologies.[54]

Liebermann had demanded a satirical and didactic article advocating socialism. Instead, Lilienblum produced what seems like a modern-day Mishnah, simulating its traditional commentaries and stylistic elements. Liebermann asked Lilienblum to hide the fact that Rabbi Meir, seen as a representative of Orthodox hegemony, revered Elisha and continued to learn the Torah with him despite his heresy, but Lilienblum ignored this. Unlike Pisarev, who misrepresented Turgenev's character Bazarov to suit his nihilist ideology, Lilienblum refused to make the Talmudic account conform to socialist propaganda and delivered the opposite of what Liebermann had requested.[55] Lilienblum, rather, delivered to Liebermann a superb example of literature, and it is worth a thorough examination. The mock Mishnah passage entitled "The Tractate of World Inhabitation" begins in a manner that would have been familiar to Jewish readers accustomed to the Mishnah:

> Upon three things the world stands: On the Torah, on labor, and on charitable deeds. And Elisha ben Abuyah says: On the Torah and on labor. The inhabitation of the world is similar to its creation. It has been created by Torah and labor; hence it must be inhabited with Torah and labor.
>
> From where do we learn that the world was created with Torah? As it says: "The Lord with wisdom has founded the earth"; [Proverbs 3:19] "He has made a limit that shall not be transgressed." [Psalms 148:6]
>
> From where do we learn that the world was created with labor? As it says: "and God has made"; [Genesis 1:7, 16, and 25] "[and He rested] from all His work which God created *to be made*." [Genesis 2:3]
>
> And they [the sages] said to Elisha: According to you, should he who is poor go to the cemetery and die? He said to them: when you are not diligent about Torah and labor, you are required to rely on charitable deeds, but when

you are diligent about Torah and labor, you do not need to rely upon charitable deeds. And they said to him: But how about the verse "and the poor shall not cease from the land"!? [Deuteronomy 15:11] He said to them: perhaps not from the entire land, but from many lands the poor will surely cease.[56]

Lilienblum's Mishnah passage was modeled on the well-known text of Pirkei Avot ("The Ethics of the Fathers"). But, instead of the established and often more contemplative ethics of the fathers, Lilienblum's Elisha, the rebel and freethinker, supersedes the old generation's ethics with a practical guide for life. The text begins by citing Avot 1:2 as its opening statement: "The world rests on three things, on Torah [traditionally interpreted as the Pentateuch], on labor [traditionally denoting temple worship], and on charitable deeds." Usually, the opening statement is followed by one or several conflicting opinions or by an elaboration. Here Lilienblum provides the rebuttal through the voice of Elisha, who subverts each concept and principle of the opening statement.

The first subversion occurs on a rhetorical level. Elisha disputes the importance of charitable deeds as one of the foundations of the world by omitting it from his repetition of the opening statement. Far from being the satirical exposure of the Orthodox positions that Liebermann had requested, Lilienblum's Mishnah is interested in conducting an honest disputation and, thus, gives the opposing side legitimate and serious arguments.[57] Elisha's rabbinic interlocutors challenge his position as radical: "According to you, they say, if there would not be any charitable deeds then, should he who is poor go to the cemetery and die?" Elisha defends himself by arguing that, when the first two founding principles of the world are observed diligently, there will be no need to rely on charity. When the rabbis challenge his position as being overly utopian by citing the verse "And the poor shall not cease from the land," however, Elisha moderates his position to argue that poverty will not cease entirely but can be greatly alleviated.

Elisha's next subversion pertains to the traditional interpretations of the concepts of Torah and labor, which he accomplishes using scriptural proof texts. In *The Ethics of the Fathers*, the term *Torah* is interpreted as the study of the written and oral law. In many places in the Midrash and Tannaitic literature, however, the definition of Torah goes beyond that. The text of the Torah, both in its physical and semantic attributes, is seen as the actual foundation, or blueprint, that God used to create the physical world; as literally imagined by the Midrash Genesis Rabbah (1:1), "God looked in the Torah and created the world." This idea that the text of the Torah forms the basis of physical reality was a central idea of mitnagdic theology as articulated by Chaim of Volozhin and was a basic principle of Lilienblum's rabbinic education. In an act of rebellion against the central textual theology of the mitnagdim, Lilienblum's Elisha brings scriptural proof from the Torah to undermine its claim to being the world's foundation. Instead, he shows that the world rests on the immutable laws of science and nature, "which shall not be transgressed." Elisha continues his homily to prove that *Torah* is synonymous with *materialism*. "What is Torah? Everything that is in the world, in the human, in the heavens, and their causes this is Torah, and all that is not in the world and is not [tangible] within human hands is not Torah." In other words, Torah is the totality of the material universe. He even integrates Pisarev's principle of "evident manifestation" when he suggests that whatever is not in the world is not Torah and thus does not exist.[58] The traditional view of a world built upon texts is thus replaced by a world that follows science and natural law in accordance with the philosophy of Russian materialism.

Lastly, Elisha subverts the understanding of labor. The traditional commentaries first interpreted the term *labor* to denote temple service, which they then replaced with prayer after the temple's destruction. Elisha, following Maimonides, interprets labor as useful physical work. Citing proof texts from the creation of the Sabbath—"the Lord has created to be made"— Elisha, whom the Talmud depicts as violating the Sabbath, shifts the texts focus from "the Lord rested" to "the Lord created" and commanded "to be made" to emphasize the productive enterprise of human beings as a necessary pillar for society's proper function.

Of equal importance to its meaning was the fictional Mishnah's form. An undeniable product of mitnagdic textual learning and practices, no stylistic or structural detail in this text escapes the intricate and delicate poetic crafting. Even the text's original appearance, preserved by the publisher of the 1912 printing of Lilienblum's collected works in Krakow, deliberately reproduces the traditional appearance of printed rabbinic texts. The main text is located in the center and surrounded on all sides by commentaries. On the far left is a fictitious commentary in the voice of Obadiah Bartenura (1445–1515), which, as commentaries in printed works did, appears in the typeface known as Rashi script and is usually twice or three times the length of the main text. On the right and left sides of the main text are traditional glosses whose function it is to reference the location of citations. To the right of the main text, notes indicate citations from rabbinic literature, including manuscript variants. To the left of the main texts, the "Torah Or" provides scriptural citations, indicated in the main texts with small circles or asterisks.

If not advocating socialist values, what prompted Lilienblum to write this work for *Ha-Emet*? The creation of the idiosyncratic "Mishnah of Elisha ben Abuyah" presented a legitimate opportunity for social benefit while engaging in rabbinic textual practices. With his Talmudic expertise, Lilienblum gathered marginal positions and proof texts in rabbinic literature that, had they made their way into modern practice, would have rewritten the structures of Jewish life. By inserting into the Mishnah the voice of Elisha advocating that Jews engage in labor, Lilienblum imagines how Jewish society might have developed differently. This time-traveling exercise could imaginatively correct what Lilienblum saw as the biggest vices in his life and the lives of fellow lomdim—namely, the denial of the physical world.

While engaging in this scholarly feat of the most extravagant poetic means, however, it seems that the pleasure of the process overpowered the end goal. Like a poet who carefully adheres to the rules of a given poetic form, Lilienblum's rigorous adherence to the literary and structural details of rabbinic conventions indicates his treatment of them as a form of poetics. In a direct departure from the utilitarian literary aesthetics of the Russian nihilists, this literary exercise represents the aesthetic engagement with literature that is for its own sake—the secular adaptation of the very notion of Torah lishmah. Perhaps to Lilienblum's great relief, "The Mishnah of Elisha ben Abuyah" was never published in *Ha-Emet* due to the government's shutting down the journal in 1879. Indeed, it remained unpublished during the author's lifetime. As Lilienblum's notebooks reveal, however, the engagement with rabbinic texts was an activity he enjoyed practicing in private, and in his old age, he worked on compiling his own interpretation to the Mishnah.[59]

Conclusion

After a troubled journey through different types of textuality, the Talmud, the Haskalah, Hebrew literature, and the writings of the Russian nihilists, Lilienblum eventually retired from his literary career and moved on to Zionist activism. *The Way of Return* (1899) details Lilienblum's path from disillusionment and meaninglessness in *The Sins of Youth* to his embrace of Zionism as the new path toward utility and benefit, finding in the latter the solution to the Jewish people's social and political plight. In 1883, Lilienblum became a founder of the Odessa committee of the Lovers of Zion and served as its secretary until his death. Despite having found in Zionism that elusive cause that could bridge idealistic transcendence with real-world implications, Lilienblum never fully abandoned rabbinic textuality and continued to engage with it in his private writings in projects like writing a commentary to the Mishnah and continuing his Talmudic study.[60]

The struggle with the value of fictional literature—be it ancient or modern, a wasteful pastime, or the one true source of meaning and pleasure—was the central question of *The Sins of Youth* and Lilienblum's other writings. The emotional adventure of *The Sins of Youth* inspired many widely read Hebrew novels, from Reuven Asher Braudes's *Religion and Life* (1878) to the story "Whither" ("Le'an," 1900) by Mordecai Feierberg (1874–1899). These works feature as their central protagonists Lilienblum-like figures, conflicted yeshiva intellectuals in search of enlightenment. At the same time, the anxieties that Lilienblum's autobiography raised about the seemingly impossible task of finding utilitarian value in the identity of a secular Jewish writer were still serious and debilitating. Lilienblum's autobiography forced post-yeshiva writers to evaluate critically their transition from Talmud learners to secular writers, asking: Is there really a difference between these two textual occupations, and, if not, is Hebrew literature a worthwhile pursuit? How future writers negotiated these anxieties in favor of remaining modern Hebrew writers is the subject of the following chapters.

Notes

1. Mintz, *Banished*; Moseley, *Being for Myself Alone*.
2. Lilienblum, *Ktavim otobiografiyim*, 2:126.
3. Klausner, *Historiyah shel ha-sifrut*, 4:193.
4. Lilienblum, *Ktavim otobiografiyim*, 1:118.
5. Lilienblum, 1:109–10.
6. Paperno, *Chernyshevsky*, 49.
7. Lilienblum, *Ktavim otobiografiyim*, 1:98.
8. Manchester, *Holy Fathers, Secular Sons*, 177.
9. Lilienblum, *Ktavim otobiografiyim*, 1:104.
10. Lilienblum, 1:110.
11. Lilienblum, 1:121.
12. Mintz, *Banished*, 32.
13. Lilienblum, *Ktavim otobiografiyim*, 1:111.
14. On this, see Etkes, "Marriage and Torah Study."

15. Maimon, *Solomon Maimon*, 30–34; Ginzburg, *Vidui shel maskil: Aviezer.*

16. Lilienblum, *Ktavim otobiografiyim*, 1:115.

17. Feingold, "Ha-otobiografiyah ke siporet"; Stanislawski, *Autobiographical Jews*, 55–65.

18. Lilienblum, *Ktavim otobiografiyim*, 1:141–48.

19. Mintz, *Banished*, 36.

20. Lilienblum, *Ktavim otobiografiyim*, 1:159.

21. Lilienblum, *Kol kitvei*, 1:9.

22. Lilienblum, 1:9.

23. Biale, *Not in the Heavens*, 148.

24. Litvak, "Revolt," 11–12.

25. Paperno, *Chernyshevsky*, 39.

26. Lilienblum, *Ktavim otobiografiyim*, 2:92.

27. Although the reputation of Odessa as "anti-intellectual" certainly improved beginning in the later part of the nineteenth century, Steven Zipperstein writes that, during Lilienblum's time there, the maskilim "still faulted Odessa for the supposed vacuity of its intellectual life and the restless hedonism of its Jewish middle class." Zipperstein, *Jews of Odessa*, 70.

28. Lilienblum, *Ktavim otobiografiyim*, 2:52.

29. Lilienblum, 2:134.

30. Lilienblum cites these critics and writers explicitly by name in Lilienblum, 2:72, 96.

31. This remark by Dostoyevsky, often mistakenly attributed to Pisarev, is taken from a satirical novel entitled *Shchedrodarov*, which pokes fun at the nihilists. The original version is from Zola, and the Pushkin version is from Saltakov-Schadrin. Terras, *Handbook of Russian Literature*, 303.

32. Lilienblum, *Ktavim otobiografiyim*, 2:73.

33. Lilienblum, 2:97.

34. Mintz, *Banished*, 38–39.

35. Lilienblum, *Ktavim otobiografiyim*, 2:51.

36. Lilienblum, 2:125.

37. Paperno, *Chernyshevsky*, 161.

38. Paperno, 80.

39. On Lilienblum's romance with Navhovich, see Klausner, *Historiyah shel ha-sifrut*, 4:207–17; Mintz, *Banished*, 46–47.

40. Darnton, "Readers Respond to Rousseau," 228.

41. Lilienblum, *Ktavim otobiografiyim*, 2:103.

42. Mintz, *Banished*, 45.

43. Paperno, *Chernyshevsky*, 101.

44. Lilienblum, *Ktavim otobiografiyim*, 2:116.

45. Lilienblum, 2:134.

46. Lilienblum, 2:162.

47. Turgenev, *Fathers and Sons*, 84.

48. Lilienblum, *Ktavim otobiografiyim*, 2:134.

49. Lilienblum, 2:134.

50. Talmud Bavli Hagigah 14b.

51. Klausner, *Historiyah shel ha-sifrut*, 4:238.

52. *The Way of Return* was completed in 1899, but Lilienblum wanted it to be published as the third part of *The Sins of Youth* so that it could be read as a "happy ending" in which

Lilienblum finds a solution to his existential crisis in Zionism; however, scholars treat this as a completely separate work. See Mintz, *Banished*, 32.

53. E. Stern, *Jewish Materialism*, 56–84.

54. Natkovich, "Elisha Ben Abuya."

55. Joseph Klausner, who edited Lilienblum's collected works, reports that Liebermann covered the original manuscript of "The Mishnah of Elisha ben Abuyah" with corrections of mistakes in socialist-Marxist ideology, which Lilienblum did not know well. Klausner, *Historiyah shel ha-sifrut*, 4:245.

56. Lilienblum, *Kol kitvei*, 2:192.

57. On the depictions of Elisha, see Natkovich, "Elisha Ben Abuya."

58. See the essay entitled "Nineteenth-Century Scholasticism" in Pisarev, *Selected Philosophical*, 104.

59. Gafni, *Peshutah shel mishnah*, 73–76.

60. Epstein, *Lilienblum*, 38.

5

READERS' PARADISE

Hebrew Literature in the Volozhin Yeshiva

WHAT WAS TO BECOME OF MODERN HEBREW LITERATURE after it was declared to be useless? The utilitarian critique of literature dealt a powerful blow to the prestige of Hebrew literature among the maskilim and cast doubt on its future for the new postmaskilic generation of writers. Lilienblum, the first post-Haskalah writer, had likened Hebrew literature to masturbation because it seemed to give its writers and readers nothing more than a fleeting and inconsequential moment of pleasure. By the 1880s, however, the futile pleasure of Hebrew verse and prose—art, in other words—was no longer considered a legitimate pursuit for the Hebrew writer. The new ethical imperative that literature should be of some practical use, although previously foreign to Jewish culture, gradually outgrew in its iconoclastic status and precipitated important ideological shifts among the Jewish literary intelligentsia.

This transformation in Jewish writers' literary attitudes was accompanied by the important developments that took place in the 1870s and 1880s. The first of these developments was the rise of Yiddish as a vehicle for socially conscious literature in the 1870s. Unlike Hebrew, the narrow operating sphere of which limited its successful implementation as an instrument of social change, Yiddish was the perfect medium for reaching the Jewish masses, being the one universally spoken language among eastern European Jews. The utilitarian guidelines for the valuation of literature based on in its ability to respond to the needs of people on the ground served to reverse the long-standing bias against Yiddish as a supposedly ugly and impure language—a bias inherited from the Berlin Haskalah's notions of language. Now, under the literary precepts of a socially oriented realism, Yiddish's alleged aesthetic shortcomings were discovered as its strengths.

The 1870s thus saw a new wave of Yiddish literary creativity in the form of satirical fiction geared toward reaching ordinary Jewish folk.[1]

The second development was the adoption of Zionism as the social and political agenda, which would justify the otherwise completely disadvantageous production of Hebrew letters in Russia. After the pogroms of 1881–1882 that swept across the southwestern provinces of the Russian Empire, many maskilic writers were left disillusioned about the possibility of Jewish emancipation in Russia. Thus, the period after the pogroms saw the flourishing of Zionism and Jewish nationalism under the aegis of Hibat Tziyon, founded in 1884.[2] The founders of this movement, who called themselves Hovevei Tziyon (the Lovers of Zion), were some of the most prominent writers and intellectuals of the period. Among them were Lilienblum, Ahad Ha'am (Asher Ginsberg, 1856–1935), Eliezer Ben Yehuda (1858–1922), and Leon Pinsker (1821–1891). These individuals, who were otherwise ideologically variegated, shared a common vision that saw Jews united not only by the religious framework of Judaism but as a physical people and nation, *am* and *le'om*. As such, they could flourish physically only in the land of Israel, where they had been a nation once before and where they would reclaim Hebrew as the national language of culture and daily interaction.[3]

Hibat Tziyon ended up becoming a haven for young writers who still aspired to become maskilic poets. These young writers were romantic lovers of Hebrew, scorned by the nihilists for their aesthetic attachment to Hebrew. Having had their hopes for Jewish integration in the Russian Empire shattered by the pogroms, they discovered their new calling to Zion under the auspices of Hibat Tziyon. The most prominent among them were Mordechai Tzvi Maneh (1859–1886) and Naftali Hertz Imber (1856–1909), whose poem "Ha-tikvah" (1878) was later cast as the Israeli national anthem.[4] The group was stationed in Odessa, which had become the new leading center, after Vilna and St. Petersburg, for Jewish writers and intellectuals.[5] Odessa was also the center of Jewish publishing, where influential writers controlled a robust Hebrew publishing activity.[6] Ahad Ha'am presided as editor over the successful literary journal *Ha-Shiloah* for which he carefully selected works whose goal it was to discuss the agenda of Zionism and Jewish culture.

The influence of the nihilists' instrumentalist modes of thinking and the rising interest in Zionism and nationalism created important ideological shifts that were felt inside the lives of ordinary Jews in Russia. The Jewish memoirist Pauline Wengeroff (1833–1916) wrote of the 1870s that "these years of inner change" saw the development of new household terms like "nihilism, materialism, assimilation, antisemitism, and decadence," which suddenly surfaced in Russia and made themselves into the everyday vocabulary of Jewish youth. Traditional modes of study were falling by the wayside. The gymnasium and university now became the goals of young people, and it was considered "a shocking exception" when a wealthy man sent his gifted son to a yeshiva.[7]

While Jewish culture was rapidly transforming, absorbing, and adapting to the currents of its time, there remained places that lagged the flow of modern ideas. On the periphery of urban centers, Jewish life still revolved around religious mores, governed by already transforming yet nonetheless traditional institutions. There, the learners, the high priests of textuality, flourished in yeshivas, consumed by the study of the Talmud. Some of these were Jewish writers in the making—young men who were freshly discovering the developments of secular Jewish literature and thought of the past thirty years. They would begin by reading, as literature, the Hebrew Bible and its language rather than focusing entirely on the Talmud. These writers-to-be would study Hebrew grammar and then Russian; they would read maskilic poetry, history, and philosophy written by German and Russian Jewish thinkers. Then they moved on to contemporary Hebrew writers, reading Lilienblum's *The Sins of Youth* as their own autobiographies. Through old Hebrew journals, they relived all the debates in the intellectual sphere up to the most current periodical in their possession. Within the span of a few years, these forbidden literary adventures would lead them away from the world of the yeshiva, only to return to it in literary recollections. This at least was the story of the two most important Hebrew writers of the late 1800s and early 1900s, Berdichevsky and Bialik, who were students in the Volozhin Yeshiva between 1885 and 1891.

Berdichevsky, Bialik's senior by seven years, was one of Hebrew's first and most prolific modernist prose writers. He was also a scholar, essayist, translator, and writer of Yiddish and German. Berdichevsky, Hebrew's first modernist, left his mark on Hebrew literary and intellectual history as a revisionist of Jewish values. Credited with the introduction of Nietzschean ideas to a Jewish audience, in his later oeuvre, Berdichevsky drew on Nietzsche's critique of slave morality as an admonishment against Jewish culture's book-bound preference for spiritual achievement over the "Greek" values of physical vitality, strength, and beauty.[8] Berdichevsky's revolt against Jewish textuality and his simultaneous attachment to it, however, were both products of his early immersion in the Jewish texts and of his early experience as a student in the yeshiva, where Berdichevsky first became a Hebrew writer.

The work that began Berdichevsky's literary career was a novella entitled *The World of Nobility* (1888), written during his time at the Volozhin Yeshiva. Weaving together a new Hebrew literary dialect from the use of yeshiva jargon, Aramaic Talmudic expressions, and the subversive use of textual allusions—the work is a remarkable example of how the rabbinic sphere of learning served as a cultural foundation for the development of the Hebrew literary language, also known as the nusach. The novella tells the story of five yeshiva students for whom the yeshiva is the closest thing to paradise on earth. These characters are the book lovers who leave behind their poor and troubled lives to study in the Jewish world's most prestigious institution. Central to the novella is the observation that the textual practices of Torah lishmah, the autotelic engagement with texts of the Jewish tradition, facilitate the translation of textual devotion from its originally religious subject matter to secular literature. Textual adventures take each of Berdichevsky's characters from the Talmud to Spinoza and to Hebrew periodicals as the practice of autotelic learning propels creativity and advancement into other intellectual spheres. Torah for its own sake thus becomes literature for its own sake, and the yeshiva, ironically, is the only place that shields those who pursue disinterested intellectual pursuits from the practical utilitarian demands rampant in the world at large.

Life in the yeshiva turns out to be far from paradise, however. The young men's idealistic abandonment of reality takes a toll on their mental and physical health and threatens to lead to their demise and, perhaps, as the author suggests, to that of Jewish culture at large. Integrated into this closed circle of textual transformations is the personal life of the author. Like Lilienblum before him, the author/narrator struggles to break free from the seductions of a textual existence, but his attempts to do so seem only to bind him closer to it.

First Loves

Berdichevsky was born in 1865 in Medzhibizh to a Hasidic family of rabbinic lineage on his father's side and of merchant descent on his mother's.[9] Although Berdichevsky's Hasidic origins set him apart from other writers, the difference was mitigated by his father's rabbinic and scholarly lineage.

From his early childhood, Berdichevsky was brought up to be a scholar. He was taught by private teachers under his father's guidance. Like Lilienblum, Berdichevsky quickly gained the title of Talmudic prodigy, and his father began preparing Berdichevsky to take over his post as one of the prominent Hasidic rabbis of the town.

From his early youth, Berdichevsky was enamored with texts and scholarship. Alongside Talmud study, the young Berdichevsky enjoyed reading rabbinic tales (Aggadot), Hasidic stories of righteous men, works of Hasidic thought, and Kabbalistic texts.[10] Thus, as was the case with prior writers, religious learning smoothly transitioned Berdichevsky to Haskalah literature. Facilitating this transition was Berdichevsky's discovery of Jewish historical writings. He first began with the religiously sanctioned reading of the *Sefer Yosipon*, a medieval history based loosely on Josephus. That this book made a great impression on Berdichevsky is clear; he later took the name Ben Goryon as a penname for his own Hebrew compositions; Yosef ben Goryon is the name by which *Yosipon* refers to Josephus. Berdichevsky's Jewish history reading finds expression in *The Volozhin Chapters*, where he depicts yeshiva students passionately engaged in reading the works of the German Jewish historian Graetz. Berdichevsky particularly enjoyed the latter's multivolume *History of the Jews*, which, the historian Amos Bitzan argues, represents a modern genre of Jewish history writing imbued with the sentimental affect of European Romantic literature.[11] Berdichevsky was likewise engaged by Krochmal's *Guide to the Perplexed of the Time* (published posthumously in 1851), which he acquired secretly, as well as the prose writers and poets Levinsohn, Mapu, and Gordon.

At first, Berdichevsky's ventures into the forbidden literature of the Haskalah remained unnoticed, and the young scholar, aged seventeen, was considered an eligible scholastic suitor versed in most of the Talmudic tractates and commentaries. In 1882, his father arranged for him a kest marriage with a wealthy merchant's daughter, who was only a year younger than the groom. The match was surprisingly consensual, an autobiographical detail that separated Berdichevsky from many of his contemporaries. Berdichevsky's literary works often recalled the love between him and his first wife. His love for textuality and scholarship, however, came between them.[12]

Soon after his marriage, Berdichevsky, who, under the kest arrangement, was expected to study the Talmud exclusively, was caught red-handed by his father-in-law in the study of forbidden books. Fearful of having a heretic for a son-in-law, the father-in-law demanded that Berdichevsky grant his wife a divorce. While waiting for reconciliation with the father-in-law, Berdichevsky went to study at the Volozhin Yeshiva in 1885–1886, when he was twenty-one years old. There he began writing profusely. His first work was none other than a history of the Volozhin Yeshiva, entitled *The History of the Etz Hayim Yeshiva*, followed by the novella *The World of Nobility* and the epistolary collection "Letters from a Yeshiva Student," published in 1888 in *Ha-Tzefirah* and later compiled as *The Volozhin Chapters* (*Pirkei Volozhin*).

Berdichevsky was soon forced to choose, however, between his devotion to texts and knowledge on one hand and his marriage on the other. He chose the former. Upon his return from the yeshiva, Berdichevsky accepted the six hundred rubles of the dowry his father-in-law offered him for granting the divorce to the merchant's daughter. With this money he hoped to begin an independent life in which he would materialize his literary dreams.[13] The early divorce, depicted by the author as a fatal choice of the text over reality, was a defining experience that Berdichevsky continued to relive in many short stories scattered throughout his writing career, and one of its first iterations appears in the novella *The World of The Nobility*.[14]

Literature and the Yeshiva

Berdichevsky's *The World of the Nobility* begins with the observation that the Volozhin Yeshiva is perhaps the most concentrated expression of Jewish identity, in which textual study is synonymous with "life": "In all other schools, students designate times for study so that they do not forget to live, and, when their lessons are over, they leave *olam ha-atzilut* [the world of nobility] and enter *olam ha-hayim* [the world of life] for a stroll, a laugh, or just for enjoyment. But the young Jew, a child of the nation of the book—a nation whose Torah is its life—this young man puts aside all worldly life and occupies himself with a life of learning."[15] In contrast to the theological seminary or the gymnasium, at least in Berdichevky's imagination, in the Volozhin Yeshiva, intellectual activity never stopped.[16] Its student, "a child of the nation of the book," never left the world of intellectual "nobility" as he rejects the "world of life." Berdichevsky introduces the reader to a familiar dichotomy between the intellectual or textual life of the mind and the life of the body—a dichotomy that we have already encountered in Lilienblum's *The Sins of Youth* with the distinction between "the world of contemplation" and "the world of action." Berdichevsky portrays this dichotomy—a consequence of Volozhin's devotion to the study of the Torah for its own sake—as a national characteristic integral to the "nation of the book," for whom textual study takes the place of physical life.

The title of Berdichevsky's text is a key concept taken from Chaim of Volozhin's magnum opus and panegyric to Torah study *Nefesh Ha-Hayim* (*The Soul of Life*), whose language and philosophy permeated the culture of the yeshiva. Using the term *nobility* to describe the yeshiva reflected Jewish culture's attribution of the highest status to the "elite of the mind," which did not concern itself with worldly affairs. But the esoteric dimension of the term *world of nobility* refers to a metaphysical realm beyond the physical world, a supernatural realm of inertness, a sphere utterly disconnected from mundane considerations. By creating a safe haven where students could study the Torah without a care in the world, the yeshiva brings this supernatural world down to earth.

The twist is that the Volozhin students, despite being aloof from all worldly affairs, are not always occupied with the Torah, for they have transformed this magical realm of Torah study into a sanctuary for secular literature. And this was why intellectual life at Volozhin was so rewarding. Berdichevsky portrays the Volozhin Yeshiva as a brewing ground for new ideas cultivated through book exchange: "Because of the various students from different lands, numbering four hundred young men, it is unavoidable to find maskilim, knowledgeable in various matters, who will encourage the others to enlighten themselves. . . . There are several books in the hands of each student; everyone exchanges them with one another, and the books add up to one great account."[17] As a result of the relatively lax (albeit negative) policy against reading nonreligious materials, Berdichevsky depicts the yeshiva as a place of a thriving book exchange. Secular and religious books are being passed from already satiated maskilim to yeshiva students thirsty for knowledge; students exchange Hebrew periodicals and even attempt to found a secret literary club.

The growing interest in secular literature in the yeshiva is the unwitting result of the expansion of the notion of Torah study from its original restriction to Jewish religious texts to secular intellectual pursuits. Berdichevsky writes of the Volozhin student: "All day, he roars like a lion in the profound sanctuary of the Talmud. But, at the day's end, when midnight strikes and the entire city is fast asleep, he does not rest. After he has finished studying, he is still awake. To soothe his weary soul, he reads *Ha-Shachar* and *Ha-Melitz*, *Dor dor ve-dorshav*, Jewish history, and sometimes Spencer and Haeckel, or just sits and writes."[18]

The enthusiasm for the Torah during the day becomes even greater enthusiasm for secular literature at night. The magical hour of midnight is an hour most susceptible to the power of evil spirits, as this liminal moment signifies the transition between the physical and spiritual realms. This was when the lust for secular literature was at its strongest.[19] Hebrew journals, a maskilic scholarly work on Jewish law,[20] books by German Jewish historians and European Social Darwinist philosophers—the same forbidden books that caused Kovner, Lilienblum, and Berdichevsky so much trouble—were commonplace in the yeshiva and became the substitutes for the students' nightly Torah vigil.[21] And, of course, the student did not fail to try his own hand at the production of texts; he "sits and writes."

By using a term reserved solely for Torah study to describe the Volozhin students' secular literary adventures, Berdichevsky depicts how textual engrossment for its own sake takes the place of what used to be a purely religious ideal. The result of the secularization of Jewish literacy is ambiguous. On one hand, expanding Torah lishmah to include secular fields of knowledge and art contributes to the advancement of Jewish intellectual achievement. Berdichevsky certainly celebrates Volozhin as an incubator of prominent Jewish leaders and intellectuals. At the same time, however, the secularization of Torah lishmah creates a dangerous subversion of both religion and life. The transformation of the religious worship of the Torah into the secular worship of textuality entraps the Torah lishmah practitioner in an endless web of texts, leading to his physical and psychological demise.

Picking up where Lilienblum's novel left off, Berdichevsky offers a compelling new explanation for the text centeredness of rabbinic Jewish culture. Whereas the Jewish nihilists saw this focus on texts as a "bad habit" instilled by the values of traditional education and perpetuated by the social order, Berdichevsky's characters choose Talmud study over material productivity not because it is a bad habit but because it is a better bargain than reality—and certainly more pleasurable.

The diligent Talmud student's disregard for the beauty of the natural world is not due to the lack of sentiment or aesthetic refinement; rather, Berdichevsky writes, "he forsakes a life of beauty, pleasure, and comfort and chooses a life of study and spirit because he loves the Talmud with the fiercest love. . . . He delights in Talmudic literature, knowing how to compare its various contexts and situate them side by side. He does not seek a goal in this pursuit, for he finds it in his study. He once said to me in a letter: 'You ask me for my goal? My goal is study itself.'"[22]

The trouble with yeshiva students, Berdichevsky's novella suggests, is that they prefer textual study to the world. It is precisely that purposeless devotion to textuality—which the Jewish nihilists like Kovner so disparaged and which many Jewish writers saw as the source of the Jews' material and political problems—that is the yeshiva student's solution for reality. In this particular sketch, what the character delights in is Talmudic literature and its various rich cultural and historical intersections.[23] This practice of world denial comes at a price, however, and that price is the characters' physical well-being.

Texte Fatale

Reservations about the life-denying engrossment in texts are to be found in the rabbinic substructure of Berdichevsky's allusion-rich prose.[24] The following sketch depicts another yeshiva student's dangerous love affair with textuality:

> The last sound of footsteps had long vanished from the marketplace, but you can still hear one man's footsteps coming from the yeshiva, treading through mud and mire. His shoes, torn and broken, are filled with water. His bones shiver from the cold under a shabby hat borrowed from charity. What is the reason for this trepidation with which he runs out at midnight, undeterred by the rain, the cold, and the holes in his shoes? Could he be running to meet his beloved for a midnight tryst? Surely a son of Israel knows that it is not his place to seek love. No, he is going to borrow the journals *Ha-Melitz* and *Ha-Tzefirah*, *Di yidishe frage* and *Autoemancipation*, or just a book to read. . . .[25]
>
> We return to his room in an hour to find him lying on a bed of broken bricks, a straw sack under him, and a thin torn covering on top. The walls are raven-black, and rain is leaking in at the corners. With his right arm tucked under his head, he lies reading *Ha-Melitz*. Now he finished it, folded it and tucked it under his head. It is 2 AM. The candle burns, and the book is open. Let's see what book it is. Today it is *Geschichte der Juden* by Graetz, and tomorrow—Zunz, Herzfeld, Jost, Frankel. . . . Why does he forget his sorrows and sacrifice himself for study and knowledge? Because of the fierce lust for contemplation in the heart of the Jewish boy. Here, dear reader, is a true picture of one who kills himself in the tent of knowledge.[26]

In this passage, the engagement with texts figures as the yeshiva student's only form of jouissance and as a substitute for the erotic experience. In the late evening hours, the nameless character is found skipping out on his nightly Talmud study vigil. Instead, he runs to borrow secular journals with the excitement and "trepidation" with which a "normal" young man would be expected to run to a rendezvous. But the rendezvous here is with Hebrew journals and books of Jewish history by the somber scholars of *Wissenschaft des Judentums*. Nevertheless, for the scholarly Talmudist, this is his pleasure of choice. Berdichevsky takes the reader into the yeshiva student's bedroom, where he is spending the night hours secretly, lustfully, indulging in forbidden books, literally under the covers. In a clever subversion of Song of Songs 2:6, where the male lover's left hand is similarly tucked under his head while his right hand is locked in an embrace, the yeshiva student is positioned, hands reversed, in an autoerotic embrace with a book.

Berdichevsky is drawing on the well-known Talmudic topos termed by Daniel Boyarin "Torah as the Other Woman," in which the pleasures of Torah study are so highly exalted that Torah study becomes portrayed as a substitute for the erotic.[27] In Talmudic stories, rabbis often leave their wives for prolonged periods to study the Torah and use sexual language to speak about the intellectual pleasures of Torah study, as the example of Ben Zoma shows.[28] Here, for instance, the "fierce lust for contemplation" is an allusion to Song of Songs 8:6: "For love is fierce as death." Juxtaposing attraction to textuality with death, Berdichevsky's text begins sending the ominous message that the eroticized attitude of yeshiva students toward literature is damaging to one's health. The caveat here, however, is that, while in the traditional context sexual lust becomes replaced by lust for the Torah, here it becomes replaced by lust for literature—Jewish periodicals and books of history and scholarship. This depiction is a familiar one; as we have seen, writers who emerged out of highly literate religious cultures often preferred texts over reality—be it Lilienblum, who preferred an epistolary correspondence to a physical one, or Chernyshevsky, who, despite holding the most sexually liberated views of his time, refused to consummate his marriage for as long as he could manage.

Continuing with the examination of Berdichevsky's allusions, we find that the theme of textuality being fatal is embedded in the text at every turn. By concluding that the yeshiva student "kills himself in the tent of knowledge," Berdichevsky is making a connection with the dictum of the Talmudic sage Reish Lakish, which draws on the verse, "This is the law: when a man dies in a tent, every one that comes into the tent, and every thing that is in the tent, shall be unclean seven days" (Numbers 19:14): "Reish Lakish said: From where do we learn that words of Torah are only fulfilled by one who kills himself for it? Because it says, "This is the Torah [law or teaching]: when a man shall die in the tent [a reference to Numbers 19:14]" (Talmud Bavli Berakhot 63b).

Reish Lakish's original interpretation of the verse maps the laws of handling a dead body in the tabernacle onto the context of Torah study—already a strange and macabre analogy. Berdichevsky's broader audience would understand that "to kill oneself in the tent" means to study the Torah arduously under difficult material conditions in the study house, for which the word *tent* serves as a cultural metaphor.[29] Furthermore, the description of the character's impoverished and recklessly ascetic lifestyle points the reader to recall a famous passage from Pirkei Avot: "Such is the way of Torah: Bread with salt you shall eat, water in small measure you shall drink, and upon the ground you shall sleep; live a life of suffering while you toil in Torah" (Mishna Avot 6:4).

Berdichevsky's character enacts almost every part of this dictum of asceticism prescribed for Torah study. He is sacrificing his life for intellectual achievement, but he has holes in his shoes, sleeps on a bed of brick in a damp room, and is shivering from cold. What if he becomes ill and dies? The narrative seems to be either foreshadowing or seeding the reader with the anxiety that the ascetic conditions under which this yeshiva student fulfills "the way of the Torah" will result in human sacrifice.

Berdichevsky's slight alteration of Reish Lakish's dictum, substituting "knowledge" for "Torah," defamiliarizes the traditional context, yielding a new interpretation. While figuratively "killing oneself" for a life of Torah study was a religiously sanctioned ideal held up for centuries as the cornerstone of Jewish survival in exile, Berdichevsky asks what happens when Jews begin dedicating their lives to the worship of secular textuality. Replacing traditional Jewish literature with secular literature is uncharted territory. Culture and art do not hold within them the promise of Jewish preservation and are, therefore, both attractive and threatening.

The mixture of pleasure and danger associated with the intellectual endeavor, be it secular or still part of the religious tradition, is one of the central themes running through Berdichevsky's work. In the novella, this combination features in Berdichevky's retelling of his early marriage and subsequent coerced divorce while he was in Volozhin. In the following autobiographical sketch, a young Berdichevsky, a yeshiva student forced to divorce his wife after his zealous father-in-law catches him reading "heretical" books, drowns out his sorrows by continuing to immerse himself in forbidden literature at Volozhin.

> When most of the inhabitants of the city of Volozhin went for a stroll in the forest to hide from the heat, only one wretched yeshiva student diligently sits and studies Talmud by the sweat of his brow. . . . His face, white as chalk, emits

a terrible anguish. His small forehead wrinkles up from time to time, and his protruding eyes convey despair.

He recalls the joyful days he spent in the shade of his beloved wife, an enlightened soul in a magnificent vessel, a wife who loved him, whose soul was tied to his own. For three years he lived as a hired worker in the shade of happiness, a life of peace and comfort. But, suddenly, the lust for knowledge jumped on him. The desire for knowledge grew in his heart, made him decrease his Torah study as he began to secretly toil at the gates of enlightenment. . . . He was exiled from his home, his beloved wife and daughter were taken away, and all his money too, and now he is here at Volozhin. . . . The head of the yeshiva looks down at him because his father-in-law said that he gazed and was harmed. Soon his fate shall be decided.[30]

The discontents of the protagonist begin when he becomes a "hired worker" of his father-in-law, who has figuratively hired him to study the Torah full-time in exchange for marriage to his daughter and a dowry. The kest arrangement ceases to be the institution that enables the study of the Torah for its own sake but rather monetizes Torah study, thus making it a burden. It is not surprising then that the turn to forbidden books of knowledge and enlightenment are the exciting and intellectually liberating avenues for the young Talmudist, who reports that, "suddenly, the lust for knowledge jumped on him," erotically displacing his interest in both his marriage and in Torah study.

Incidentally though, the particular forbidden book for which the character is caught was not exactly heretical. It is a book by a Zionist writer entitled *Eternal Hatred for an Eternal Nation*, a book about the origins of antisemitism.[31] But the father-in-law, blinded by religious zealotry, misunderstands it to be a book promoting antisemitism and demands a divorce for his daughter from the son-in-law. In the interim, the youthful character escapes to Volozhin, where he is free to engage with forbidden literature to his heart's desire. Yet this freedom in Volozhin begins taking a toll on both his physical and mental health. His own father, Berdichevsky describes, was angry with him because, as a Hasidic rabbi, he did not approve of his son going to a yeshiva of their opponents, the mitnagdim. Hence, Berdichevsky's father refused to send him a penny to sustain himself. To make matters worse, in the yeshiva, the young outcast gained a bad reputation after the father-in-law informs the head of the yeshiva that his son-in-law was a heretic.[32]

Scholars have usually understood the story as a maskilic polemic against the forces of tradition. For instance, Avner Holtzman interprets the entire episode as a typical maskilic drama representative of the militant Haskalah authors, "akin to Gordon's 'Tip of the Yud,' where the message that Berdichevsky internalized was that the enlightened ones are defeated by the forces of darkness." Denying the story any traces of the author's self-reflection, Holtzman concludes that "the then-young writer did nothing that would push the reader to undermine the sharp opposition between the evil father-in-law and himself."[33]

A close reading attuned to Berdichevsky's subliminal use of literary allusions, however, yields a different interpretation in which Berdichevsky's interest in textuality is front and center. The key words here are "gazed and was harmed," which are used to describe the nature of the character's "heresy." These words serve as a textual marker of the famous Talmudic story "The Four Who Entered the Orchard": "Four entered the orchard [*pardes*]— Ben Azzai, Ben Zoma, Aher [Elisha ben Abuyah] and Akiva. Ben Azzai gazed and died; Ben Zoma gazed and was harmed [i.e., lost his sanity]; Aher cut the saplings. Akiva entered in peace and left in peace" (Talmud Bavli Hagigah 14b, emphasis added). In Berdichevsky's allusion to this story, we first note that he is mapping the mystical orchard of the Torah (pardes) onto the heretical orchard of Haskalah texts, a comparison we have already encountered in this work. And while Lilienblum identified himself with Aher, who "cut the saplings," Berdichevsky chose to reenact the experience of a different Talmudic sage, Ben Zoma, who "gazed and was harmed" by his excursion into the mystical orchard of textuality, driving him to madness.

The choice of modeling the character on his experience and identifying him with the sage Ben Zoma is meaningful and relevant to Berdichevsky's retelling, throughout the author's works, of the story of his early marriage. Berdichevsky's imagined Talmudic reader knows Ben Zoma as the sage who rejected the commandment of marriage and procreation in favor of Torah learning. "What can I do if my soul desires the Torah? Let the world be procreated by others," they would recall Ben Zoma saying (Talmud Bavli Yevamot 63b). Berdichevsky's story adopts the same language of lust and sexual desire that Ben Zoma used for Torah study to refer to "the lust for knowledge" that "grew in his heart," "jumped on him," and essentially seduced him away from his wife. Unlike the Torah in the story of Ben Zoma, it is secular textuality here that possesses such a vital sexual force that it pulls the yeshiva student away from reality. Like Ben Zoma, this character had a choice between living a productive, sexual life with his wife and studying enlightenment literature; he chose literature.

With this reading, the story becomes a deep and self-critical reflection on the seductions of a textual existence for the Jewish man of letters. That is, it is not the religiously oppressive father-in-law who is to blame, as scholars have suggested, but the character himself, for it was his own choice to forgo sexuality for texts. Replacing marriage and sexuality with texts leads to the character's demise: "His face is white as chalk, his small forehead wrinkled, his protruding eyes convey despair."[34] This character becomes the image of the walking dead and, like his Talmudic counterpart Ben Zoma, is profoundly harmed by his venture into the world of texts. Bringing this insight back to the original Talmudic story of the orchard, we see that even the learned sages of the Talmud could not withstand the ultimate pull and danger of textuality. For three of the four Talmudic sages who entered pardes—the one who died, the other who went mad, and the third who became destructive—the encounter with the most intense form of textuality in the mystical orchard of the Torah proved a dangerous and harmful adventure.

Citing a poem by the Hebrew poet Y. L. Gordon, Berdichevsky concludes the novella with the ominous message that, however attractive and pleasurable it may be, the autotelic commitment to textuality presages death:

> O, the lust for knowledge! How much you have grown
> in the hearts of Jewish youth, that nation of worms,
> standing on Mir's, Eysishok's, Volozhin's roads.
> But where are you going? To sleep on the ground,
> to live a life of wretchedness and torment,
> for such is the Torah that men die in its tent.[35]

Berdichevsky draws on Gordon's image of the Jewish nation as a nation of worms. This grotesque connotation of being a nation of "bookworms" implies a sense of degeneracy and rot associated with real worms as with excessive intellectualism. This degenerate condition, the lust for books and knowledge, Berdichevsky implies, grew and multiplied precisely in the heart of Jewish learning, Lithuanian yeshivas of Mir, Eysishok, and Volozhin. The last lines combine Reish Lakish's dictum that "the words of the Torah are only fulfilled by one who kills himself for it," with the ascetic prescription of Avot 6:4: "This is the way of the Torah. . . . Sleep on the ground, and live a life of hardship, while you toil in Torah study." The result is the poet's devastating realization in the last line: "Such is the Torah, that a man dies in its tent." Through the use of Gordon's poem, Berdichevsky ends his novella by suggesting that, in national terms, the excessive textuality of the yeshiva system is the harbinger of doom.

Between Texts

After the publication of Berdichevsky's account of text-intoxicated yeshiva students in his 1886 *The World of Nobility*, great changes took place in his life. By the time he left the yeshiva in 1889, he was twice divorced, no longer devout, and growing more and more disillusioned with the possibility of harmonizing traditional Judaism with Enlightenment and secular learning as his characters enjoyed doing in the yeshiva. Following in the footsteps of Lilienblum, who was every late-nineteenth-century ex-yeshiva student's hero, Berdichevsky traveled to Odessa, the city of broken maskilic dreams. Berdichevsky's move from the insular world of textual scholarship of his early childhood and the yeshiva to Odessa, a move that so profoundly figured in Lilienblum's account of his disillusionment and turn toward materialism, was similarly disillusioning. Like Lilienblum, Berdichevsky expected to find among the inhabitants of this western European city "the spirit of enlightenment, idealism, an aspiration for knowledge and aesthetic sensibility" but was surprised to discover "apathy, spiritual frozenness, and a ceaseless chase after instant gratification in personal and material comforts."[36] Berdichevsky poignantly wrote in his diary that "the city made *sheimos* [i.e., the ritual burial of sacred books] in my soul"—poignantly, because the expression reveals how the writer saw his inner world as completely composed of texts, albeit ones condemned to a proper burial.[37]

Shortly after his unsuccessful attempt to find spiritual and intellectual fulfillment in Odessa, Berdichevsky, age twenty-five in 1890, embarked on his dream of a university education, a dream that Lilienblum never succeeded in materializing. In 1891, Berdichevsky enrolled at the University of Breslau. He later attended the University of Berlin and University of Bern, where, in 1896, he eventually completed his doctoral work in philosophy. His studies at the University of Breslau exposed him to new cultural movements and ideas. He was fascinated by decadence and modernism and expressed his high regard for the dramatist Henrik Ibsen and the painter Edvard Munch. Berdichevsky read Tolstoy and Dostoyevsky in German translation. The strongest source of inspiration to take hold of Berdichevsky during his studies in Europe, however, was his exposure to a new "life-affirming" set of ideas. Starting in 1893, his writings begin to be filled with the mention of Nietzsche. "This summer, I read much of Friedrich Nietzsche," wrote Berdichevsky in a letter to a friend, something he subsequently recorded in his diary. At the time, Berdichevsky was indeed trying to acquire a copy of *On the Genealogy of Morals.*[38]

Berdichevsky's life story adds another branch to the genealogical tree of Jewish writers struggling with textuality. The milestones involved in Berdichevsky's "coming of age" as a secular Jewish writer—which began with a yeshiva education, then a maskilic one, followed by a move to Odessa and its subsequent disillusionment, all proceeding to his immersion in the writings of Nietzsche—parallel the emotional and intellectual struggles experienced two decades earlier by Lilienblum, whose replacements for the Talmud became the writings of Pisarev and Chernyshevsky. Berdichevsky did not stray far from this familiar trajectory. From the way in which Berdichevsky spoke about his "Nietzschean studies" in letters, Holtzman concludes that Berdichevsky studied Nietzsche's works in their German original, poring over them like the traditional study of Talmud folios. "If you were only *baki* [fluent] in Nietzsche like myself," Berdichevsky wrote to Ahad Ha'am in the manner of one haughty Talmudist to another, "you would be able to find explicit proof texts regarding the Jewish nation's moral genius."[39]

At this point, one must ask, why did Nietzsche and his works function as the next substitute for Talmud study for Hebrew writers after Chernyshevsky and the Russian materialists? Aside from a general iconoclasm, disregard for tradition, and an attempt to undermine a religious-textual tradition of the West—the writers of these two camps are distinct ideologically, culturally, chronologically, and stylistically. Their unlikely juxtaposition at the hands of Jewish writers struggling to find meaning in their identity as men of texts in the late nineteenth century, however, sheds light on how both thinkers were driven by a similar struggle.

Just like the priestly creators of Russian nihilism, Nietzsche, too, was the son of a clergyman—a Lutheran pastor. Was Nietzsche not, likewise, a man of texts, a classical philologist, and a philosopher poet? His entire oeuvre is permeated with a desire to reclaim a physically inspired existence and to rise, despite his struggle with illness, from the wretchedness of false spiritual comfort. He bemoaned his own "decadence"; he rejected his "idealism"—a shattered idealism that was the driving force of the work and thought of the nihilists, formerly religious men of texts who preached "earth" but dreamed of heaven. Nietzsche too devoted his life's work to literature, which, like Chernyshevsky, he found irresistibly attractive but claimed not to value. He frequently pondered a question still relevant to scholars and students of literature today, asking himself: Why on earth did he become a man of texts, and "why not at least a physician or something else that opens one's eyes?"[40] Nietzsche's experience of the world and its struggles from his perspective as a literary man is precisely what made him appealing and relatable to Berdichevsky.

The late 1890s was a time when Nietzsche's ideas were read by Jews and Russians almost simultaneously in the Russian Empire. Berdichevsky, who read Nietzsche in the German original, became one of his foremost popularizers among Russian Jews, translating his ideas into Hebrew with the first article appearing in 1894.[41] Russian-fluent Jews could also read about Nietzsche in thick Russian journals beginning in 1892; his popularization, along with a proper translation of his complete works, continued well into the twentieth century.[42] In the Jewish context, Nietzsche was not being read on his own terms, but his ideas were being mobilized by writers to intervene in ongoing debates about Jewish literature, culture, and identity. Although ideologically distant from the Russian nihilists and certainly not a utilitarian, the ideas of Nietzsche at the fin de siècle served for Jewish writers the same role as did those of Chernyshevsky and Pisarev almost half a century earlier—namely, to provide Jewish writers with a new philosophical framework of "life-affirming" ideas with which to counter their identity as superfluous men of texts.[43]

Berdichevsky's importation of Nietzsche onto the Jewish literary stage, which began a revolution in the Jewish intellectual sphere and inspired many other writers, movements, and debates, is a well-studied topic that features in works by Holtzman, Brinker, Golomb, and others. Unlike Lilienblum's distant admiration of Chernyshevsky, however, Berdichevsky had an almost personal acquaintance with the eccentric and brilliant thinker. Berdichevsky moved to live in Weimar during the last years of Nietzsche's life and used to frequent the house where the then mad philosopher resided. Nietzsche was confined in the upper floors of his house by his sister, without anyone being allowed to see him. Berdichevsky somehow managed to become friendly with Nietzsche's sister, however, and reports that she even agreed to read and comment on Berdichevsky's German works that he was writing at the time.[44]

Beginning in 1893, Berdichevsky began publishing his "Nietzschean articles" in Ahad Ha'am's journal *Ha-Shilo'ah* and quickly defined himself as the editor's ideological opponent. Ahad Ha'am, like Berdichevsky and Bialik, came from a Hasidic background. A child prodigy, Ahad Ha'am taught himself secular subjects; was able to read Russian, English, French, and German; and considered himself a maskil. Moving to Odessa, initially to work at his family business, he quickly gained the status of a leading Jewish intellectual and publicist. Integrating himself into Hovevei Tziyon, he assumed its helm after the death of Leon Pinsker in 1891 and soon became the editor of *Ha-Shilo'ah*.[45] At the height of his influence in the 1890s, Ahad Ha'am was using his political and literary platform to debate the essence of Jewish culture, literature, and Geist (spirit), seeking a Jewish national renewal on his idiosyncratic Zionist platform.

Berdichevsky, on the other hand, blamed the rabbinic establishment for cementing Jewish law and repressing the vital forces of pagan and antinomian movements present in Judaism since antiquity. Invoking an apocryphal Nietzschean phrase, "to build a house (temple) one must destroy a house (temple)," he provocatively argued that the temple of the book based on the Torah of Moses, prophets, and rabbinic literature must be destroyed to make a new temple of the sword and the will to power.[46] Berdichevsky denied the national limits for literature imposed by Ahad Ha'am, arguing that such censorship would lead to the further impoverishment of Jewish culture. These clashes led to Berdichevsky eventually parting ways with Ahad Ha'am and his journal, leading to the formation of distinct literary groups around the two intellectuals, with writers like Shaul Tchernichovsky (1875–1943) and Yosef Hayim Brenner (1881–1921) uniting around Berdichevsky's group of "young" writers, the *tze'irim*, whereas the older generation of writers, including Bialik, centered on the thought and literary agenda of Ahad Ha'am.

Despite these differences regarding the agenda by which Jewish literature and culture should be revived, whether based on Ahad Ha'am's model of the morality of the prophets or Berdichevsky's model of the vitality of premonotheistic ancient Israel and paganist Hellenism—scholars rarely mention that the two writers were ideologically united on one crucial front. Both were trying to locate a new source of Jewish vitality in which a renewal of Jewish culture and literature would take place—a revival that was necessary in the face of the degeneration and decay both saw in Jewish culture of the time. Both writers laid the blame for this denegation on none other than traditional Jewish textuality.

In a collection of articles, the sum of which later became known as "Transvaluation of Values," Berdichevsky crafted a poetic polemic against the Jewish tradition's obsession with the study of texts and the denial of physicality and nature inherent to it. These were themes that Berdichevsky had been contemplating since his days in Volozhin. The following passage appears in the first installment of Berdichevsky's Nietzschean articles, titled "To Be or To Cease": "The intangible book had swallowed up the nation's strength, power, and life, through its long history. Now this nation no longer has a connection to life and nature. It had become a book itself—everything emerges from it and is contained within it. And a Jew has nothing left to do but to turn its pages; to interpret, to clarify and to study it; for it is the essence of life and the purpose of mankind, which was not created other than for it [i.e., the book] alone."[47]

Referencing Nietzsche at times by name, at other times by his initials F. N., or using the phrase "one sage said," Berdichevsky draws on Nietzsche's articulations to advance a familiar critique of the ill effects of rabbinic textuality on Jewish life and literature. In Berdichevsky's time, the same problem was still on the table. Once again, the book—a metonymy for rabbinic textuality—was to blame for severing the Jewish connection to life. For Berdichevsky, however, Nietzsche has a different solution to the problem of textuality. Instead of utility, Berdichevsky proposes vitality.

Conclusion

Moving into the European intellectual landscape, Berdichevsky established himself at the forefront of a new "vitality" discourse, becoming the first modernist Hebrew author to experiment with innovative depictions of physicality and sexuality in novels like *A Raven Flew, Miriam*, and his many short stories. In his everyday life, however, he lived the monastic lifestyle of "a typical scholar among books and manuscripts, just like his rabbinical predecessors," succumbing to the same performative contradiction as did his fellow post-yeshiva writers, as well as the Russian nihilist critics and even Nietzsche himself.[48] Berdichevsky's early work, the novella *The World of Nobility*, was only the beginning of the struggle with and, ultimately, transformation of his attitude toward Talmudic textuality that would inform his future works. The recognition that the autotelic devotion to the textual pursuit was both the creative force of a secular literary endeavor and the recipe for its destruction was what defined the fragile path of Hebrew literature in the Russian Empire against the backdrop of uncompromising material and utilitarian considerations. The next chapter continues to track the transformations of Hebrew literature under the new trends of aestheticism and decadence, which finally moved the Jewish intellectual discourse away from the demands of both utility and vitality in the writings of Bialik and in the context of the Russian Empire at large.

Notes

1. See the notion of the "aesthetics of ugliness" in Miron, *Traveler Disguised*, 67–69.

2. Although some scholars have challenged the significance of the pogroms' role in the formation of Zionist movements in the Russian Empire, literary accounts suggest that they were powerful motors behind the growth in the movement's appeal to Jews. Shumsky, "Leon Pinsker and 'Autoemancipation!'"

3. Stanislawski, *Zionism*, xviii; Zipperstein, *Elusive Prophet*.

4. Hibat Tziyon poetry has generally been neglected by readers and scholars. Barzel, *Shirat ha-tehiyah*, 98.

5. See Zipperstein, *Jews of Odessa*, 154.

6. In 1886 Ahad Ha'am established the journal *Ha-shilo'ah*, which became the most prestigious Hebrew journal of the time and was later edited by Bialik and Klausner. Other prominent Odessan Hebrew journals were *Kaveret* (Beehive, 1890) and *Pardes* (Orchard, 1892–1896), edited and published by Ravnitzky. S. Pinsker, *Literary Passports*, 43.

7. Wengeroff, *Memoirs of a Grandmother*, 144.

8. Holtzman, *Mikhah Yosef Berdichevsky*, 8.

9. Holtzman, *El ha-kera sheba-lev*, 302.

10. Holtzman, *Mikhah Yosef Berdichevski*, 29, 32.

11. Bitzan, "Problem of Pleasure," 110.

12. Holtzman, *Mikhah Yosef Berdichevsky*, 34.

13. Holtzman, 36.

14. The second, titled "He Peeked and Was Harmed" (1888), was followed by "Apostrophes" (1890) and "Across the River" (1898). See Holtzman, *Ha-sefer ve-ha-hayim*, 40.

15. All the translations in this chapter are mine unless otherwise indicated. Berdichevsky, *Pirkei Volozhin*, 17.

16. Stampfer writes, "Volozhin differed from most yeshivas in that students were encouraged to study at all hours of the night. In other words, students never stopped learning in the study hall except for prayer. This unceasing study is a remarkable expression and application of R. Hayim's view that the very existence of the world was dependent on Torah study." Stampfer, *Lithuanian Yeshivas*, 38.

17. Berdichevsky, *Pirkei Volozhin*, 15. Berdichevsky also describes the dissemination of ideas and languages, writing that "some boys would teach each other Jewish history, and students who came from Courland would teach the rest German."

18. Berdichevsky, 17.

19. Holtzman shows that Berdichevsky's view of the Torah included literature as well. Holtzman, *El ha-kera sheba-lev*, 65.

20. This was a five-volume work by Yitzhak (Aizik) Hirsch Weiss: *Dor ve-dorshav* (*Each Generation and Its Scholars*). As its German title, *Zur Geschichte der jüdischen Tradition*, shows, it is a history of halacha (Jewish law).

21. Stampfer writes, "In Volozhin there was no clear line between the permitted and forbidden; it was not obvious to students that Talmud study was totally incompatible with other studies." Even the heads of the yeshiva themselves read secular newspapers. Stampfer, *Lithuanian Yeshivas*, 163.

22. Abridged translation. Berdichevsky, *Pirkei Volozhin*, 23.

23. The position of trying to merge the study of the Talmud with secular literature was known in learned Jewish circles of the late nineteenth century as *maskil torani*, a "Torah-learning maskil." Holtzman writes that Berdichevsky identified himself as a maskil torani at an early point in his career. Shortly after Berdichevsky's departure from Volozhin, he published a single issue of a literary journal that would realize his dream of starting a literary club at Volozhin. In his desire to make "literature into a living beit midrash," he named his journal *Beit Midrash*. As its editor and main contributor, Berdichevsky expressed there an appreciation for literature for its own sake—without having any beneficial applications. Holtzman, *Mikhah Yosef Berdichevski*, 60–62.

24. Pomyalovsky, *Seminary Sketches*, 200n9. Continuing with the comparison of yeshiva students to Russian Orthodox seminarians, it is useful to compare the intertextual devices that the two groups used. The Slavic scholar Alfred Kuhn observes, for instance, that "the seminarians liked to lace their speech with words and phrases that reproduced or imitated the solemn archaic language of church Slavonic in which the Bible and divine liturgy were written." The clash between the elevated language of the church and the "vulgar colloquialism of the school boys" is what gave Pomyalovsky's work its subversive edge.

25. Berdichevsky, *Pirkei Volozhin*, 15.

26. Berdichevsky, 20.

27. Boyarin, *Carnal Israel*, 134.

28. Rubenstein, *Culture of the Babylonian*, 18–19; Boyarin, *Carnal Israel*, 134.

29. The association between tents and houses of learning comes from such verses as Genesis 25:27, containing the reference to "Jacob, dweller of tents," and Genesis 9:27, referencing "the tents of Shem." In both instances, tents have been agadically interpreted as houses of study.

30. Berdichevsky, *Pirkei Volozhin*, 22.

31. This treatise was written by the Zionist writer, poet, and translator Nachum Sokolov (1859–1936).

32. Holtzman describes the story of Berdichevsky's forced divorce in Holtzman, *Mikhah Yosef Berdichevski*, 35–40. Moseley also writes that at the time of his writing this piece, Berdichevsky "still did not establish a sufficient distance for him to enter into an autobiographical relation with the events he describes." Moseley, *Being for Myself Alone*, 227.

33. Holtzman, *Mikhah Yosef Berdichevsiy*, 38.

34. Berdichevsky, *Pirkei Volozhin*, 21.

35. Berdichevsky misquoted and compiled this poem from different parts of Gordon's poem titled "Mehei kever." Berdichevsky, *Pirkei Volozhin*, 36.

36. Holtzman, *Mikhah Yosef Berdichevski*, 45.

37. From a diary entry of 1889 written in Odessa, cited in Holtzman, 45.

38. Holtzman, *Ha-sefer ve-ha-hayim*, 201.

39. Holtzman is citing this from an archival source in Beit ha-sefarim ha-le'umi in Jerusalem. Holtzman, 203.

40. Nietzsche, *Genealogy of Morals*, 241.

41. The works of Nietzsche that Jewish writers were aware of, either through translation or in the original, were *The Birth of Tragedy, On the Use of and Abuse of History for Life, Human, All Too Human, Genealogy of Morals, Beyond Good and Evil,* and *Zarathustra.* On the reception and popularization of Nietzsche among Russian Jews, see Brinker, "Nietzsche's Influence," 394–95.

42. Nietzsche was first introduced to a Russian readership through thick journals in 1892, only two years before Berdichevsky first made mention of him in his articles. A Russian articulation of Nietzsche first appeared in a highly respected journal titled *Problems of Philosophy and Psychology* (*Voprosy filosofii i psikhologii*) in V. D. Preobrazhensky's article "Friedrich Nietzsche: The Critique of the Morality of Altruism." On the reception of Nietzsche among Russian writers in the late nineteenth century, see Rosenthal, *Nietzsche in Russia,* chap. 1.

43. Biale, *Eros and the Jews,* 170.

44. Holtzman, *Ha-sefer ve-ha-hayim,* 203; Golomb, "Al ha-pulmus ha-nitshe'ani bein Ahad Ha-am le-Mikhah Yosef Berdichevsky."

45. Zipperstein, "Ahad Ha-Am." For a detailed account of Ahad Ha'am's own textual upbringings, see Zipperstein, *Elusive Prophet,* 7–20.

46. Biale, *Not in the Heavens,* 86.

47. Micah Joseph Berdichevsky, *Kitve Mikhah Yosef Berdichevsky (Bin-Goryon),* ed. Avner Holtzman and Josef Kfakhfi, vol. 3 (Tel Aviv: ha-Kibbutz ha-me'uhad, 1996), 138.

48. Holtzman, *Mikhah Yosef Berdichevski,* 8.

6

THE TALMUDIC PASSION

Rabbinic Aesthetics in Modern Hebrew Poetry

H EBREW WRITERS IN LATE IMPERIAL RUSSIA WROTE AGAINST an intellectual backdrop that, in changing iterations, saw the artistic engagement with texts as the antithesis to action in the world. Between the focus on materialist utility of the 1860s and onward and the subsequent quest for "vitality" beginning in the 1890s, the seemingly unreachable expectation for Hebrew literature to matter led many of its writers to adopt an ideological target for it or to give up on it altogether. With Bialik's work, however, we open a new chapter in the life of modern Hebrew letters. Bialik's unapologetic treatment of Talmudic textual culture as a form of art enabled him to finally break free of the anxieties about Hebrew's irrelevance that had plagued Jewish writers since the beginnings of Hebrew literature in the Russian Empire. Transcending the pragmatic definition of value, both artistically and philosophically, the poet's primary concern became not what was useful but rather what was beautiful and meaningful to the human experience, as expressed through the eyes of a Hebrew writer. Renewing the focus on the aesthetic features of literature without the previous substratum of the didacticism and self-deprecation prevalent among his senior contemporaries, Bialik succeeded in breathing new and lasting life into the pursuit of Hebrew literature in Russia, bringing it unprecedented acclaim, even among non-Jewish residents of the empire.[1]

Scholars have long attributed Bialik's overwhelming literary success and the recognition that he brought to Hebrew as a national literature to his alignment with the central Zionist figure of Ahad Ha'am.[2] Even a cursory glance at Bialik's oeuvre, however, reveals that Bialik was not a simple champion of the national cause and expressed disillusionment and despair with Zionism at every stage in its development.[3] Many of his poems—marked by diasporic nostalgia and individualistic depictions of weakness, loneliness, orphanhood, and decay—were of little service to the image of strength that the early Zionist movement was trying to cultivate in the first decades of the twentieth century.[4] Moreover, his national persona often clashed with his artistic voice and even silenced it.[5] Whatever Bialik's relationship to Zionism may have been, his poetry came to epitomize the modern Hebrew canon and remains widely translated, read, and studied to this day.

The departure from the utilitarian criterion for literature and the move toward aesthetics took place in the context of a late Russian Empire brewing with new artistic and apocalyptic energies. At the turn of the twentieth century, Russian writers took part in the rising decadence movement, which, across Europe, sought to reinstate art for art's sake as a viable aesthetic ideal. Appearing in French, German, Polish, English, and Russian literatures, decadence made its way into Jewish writings through different avenues beginning in the early 1890s. Undoing the aesthetic equation between what is beautiful and what is natural and healthy, decadent literature celebrated decay, degeneration, immorality, and artificiality, offering these as rival aesthetic themes. Russian writers of the early 1900s, such as Mikhail Kuzmin (1872–1937), Vasiliy Rozanov (1856–1919), and Fyodor Sologub (1863–1927), began their search for "beauty in Sodom," looking for aesthetic inspiration in the darker corners of Russian culture and society.[6]

Already in the 1890s, however, as a reaction to the destruction of cultural meaning brought about by nihilism, Russian writers from Dostoevsky to Vladimir Solovyov (1853–1900), began reinventing the forms and practices of Russian Orthodoxy as an inspiration for art. The aestheticization of religion and religious practice—which did not imply a return to orthodox religiosity—saw its beginnings in the writings of Dostoevsky and inaugurated a religious renaissance in the early 1890s, paving the way for Russia's Silver Age.[7]

In a cultural climate well attuned to Russia's religious renaissance, Bialik drew on his immersion in Talmudic culture as a reservoir of language, meaning, and aesthetic expression for a new Hebrew poetics. The creative and intellectual interest in the world of Talmud learning spanned Bialik's entire oeuvre. It found its culmination in his work *Sefer ha-Aggadah* (*The Book of Legends*), an encyclopedic anthology of stories from the entirety of the rabbinic canon, compiled and adapted together with his close friend Yehoshua Ravnitzki (1859–1944). In Bialik's poetry, inspirations from the Jewish world of traditional Jewish learning found their most particular expression in a set of poems known as "the poems of the beit midrash." The first poem in this subset is the long narrative poem titled "Ha-matmid" ("Ha-masmid" in Ashkenazi pronunciation), usually rendered as "The Diligent Talmud Student." *Matmid* is a paradigmatic term for Talmudic textual culture that means "diligent scholar." The word also shares a root with *tamid*, meaning "perpetual" or "everlasting": the scholar's study is constant. Embedded in the title of the poem is Bialik's symbolic equation of Jewish textual and intellectual culture with Jewish survival. Bialik began writing the poem in 1888 while still a student in the Volozhin Yeshiva and continued to revise it for the next ten years until its final version appeared in the 1902 anthology of his collected poems.

Bialik's "Ha-matmid" depicts a young yeshiva student in an arduous struggle to remain loyal to his prohibitive lifestyle of constant study despite the allures of nature, physicality, and the tempting freedoms of secularity. Bialik's keen artistic sensitivity and Hebrew virtuosity enabled him to showcase the passion and vitality of the matmid amid his decaying cultural milieu. Transforming the Talmud student's repetition of the words of long-dead Talmudic sages into hauntingly beautiful verse, Bialik's poem recasts the all-consuming devotion to the texts of the Jewish tradition as a powerful source of artistic inspiration for secular Jewish literature and culture. Undermining the reigning view that Jewish textuality was useless and antithetical to the revival of Jewish culture—a premise unanimously articulated by figures as ideologically distant as Berdichevsky and Ahad Ha'am—Bialik's poem recast the supposedly unnatural and degenerate process of Talmud study as the ultimate source of Jewish cultural vitality. Examining Bialik's early biography, his experiences as a student in the Volozhin Yeshiva, and the compositional history of the poem, this final chapter details how Bialik was able to bring the artistic engagement with textuality, inspired by Talmudic culture, to bear on Hebrew letters.

Textual Upbringings

Bialik was born in 1873 in Radi, a small village near the Ukrainian town of Zhitomir. His family was of Hasidic origins, but not from a distinguished rabbinic lineage like that of Berdichevsky. His father was a devout and moderately learned tavern owner, who, according to Bialik, used to study the Torah at work. Though seemingly incongruous, this was not an unusual habit for Jewish tavern owners.[8] Aged seven when his father passed away, Bialik was placed in the care of his scholarly grandfather in Zhitomir, who supervised his education. Noticing Bialik's early talent for reading and his excellent memory, Bialik's grandfather entertained high hopes for him to become a rabbinic scholar. Under his grandfather's tutelage, Bialik studied an eclectic mix of religious texts. Some of this material consisted of the standard works of Jewish law, Aggadah compilations, and a few Kabbalistic texts. Other types of works were books on *musar* (pious ethical works), such as *Shevet Musar* (*The Discipline Rod*) by Eliyahu ha-Kohen and a work of Kabbalistic ethical literature called *Reshit Hokhmah* by Eliyahu de Vidas, both works of the late-sixteenth-century Ottoman Sefarad. Bialik also read Hasidic works about the lives of righteous men in this period. In his grandfather's bookcase, which later become the inspiration for his poem "Lifnei aron ha-sefarim" ("Before the Bookcase," 1909), Bialik found works of Jewish medieval philosophy, such as Yehuda Halevi's *Kuzari* and Maimonides's *Guide to the Perplexed*. Most of his time, however, was spent learning Talmud by himself in an old study house in Zhitomir, which too would later feature in his well-known poem "Al saf beit ha-midrash" ("On the Doorstep of the Beit Midrash," 1893).[9]

Zhitomir was a moderate-sized city with a thriving Jewish publishing business, a state-run rabbinic seminary (in which the maskilic Hebrew writer Gottlober had taught) and a center for the Haskalah. Bialik discovered Hebrew Haskalah literature when he was still a child, finding in his neighbor's attic an old version of the journals *Ha-Tzefirah* and *Ha-Melitz*. Whereas in the 1860s maskilic literature had cost Lilienblum an excommunication and in the early 1880s led to Berdichevsky's banishment and divorce, by the end of the 1880s, formerly forbidden books were not considered as dangerous as before. In fact, secular Hebrew writings were openly available for Bialik to read in none other than the Zhitomir study house. There, Bialik came across poetry by Isaac Baer Levinsohn (1788–1860), books of Hebrew grammar, the novels of Mapu, the poetry of Gordon, and of course Lilienblum's *The Sins of Youth*. From these readings, Bialik learned about all the issues being discussed in Jewish circles—ideas about nationalism and assimilation, Jewish education, modern debates about rabbinic authority, Zionism, and the settlement of Palestine.[10] Through the journals, he also encountered the writings of Russia's prime Jewish voices, such as Ahad Ha'am and the young Berdichevsky, who had just published his feuilletons about the Volozhin Yeshiva in *Ha-Tzefirah* in 1888.[11]

Berdichevsky's passionate descriptions of yeshiva students rejoicing in both religious and secular pleasure reading in Volozhin led—or more accurately, misled—the young Bialik to venture there with the hope that Volozhin would expose him to a world of secular literature and enlightenment.[12] We know, of course, from Bialik's later remarks, of his disappointment upon finding out that "Volozhin was no haven for the seven wisdoms and the seventy languages promised by Berdichevsky." Instead, Bialik only found there "fellows like myself, who sit and study nothing but gemara, gemara," and eventually, he too resigned himself to doing the same.[13] Despite Bialik's disappointment at the lack of secular learning in Volozhin, however, the yeshiva fueled his literary career.

Bialik arrived at the Volozhin Yeshiva at the age of seventeen, already a maskil and freethinker, whose religious observance was waning. His initial dream, he later wrote to Klausner, was to obtain a doctorate in Judaic studies from the acclaimed rabbinical seminary of Azriel Hildesheimer (1820–1899) in Berlin, where Berdichevsky had studied, and he viewed Volozhin as an initial stepping-stone for getting to Berlin.[14] When he arrived at the yeshiva, however, its overwhelming vibrancy of Talmud learning captivated him.

It is difficult to render with historical accuracy how Volozhin appeared to its students during its heyday, but the memoirs of Jewish intellectuals and religious leaders who studied in Volozhin are filled with exuberant descriptions. For instance, the scholar, writer, and rabbi Moshe Eliezer Eisenstadt (1869–1943), who began his studies at Volozhin in 1886 and likely overlapped with Berdichevsky and Bialik there, invites the reader of his memoirs to "imagine a large hall filled with tables and benches. The tables are covered in a tablecloth, and on it are thick books with thick great covers. And the benches are occupied by 300–350 young men swinging and moving back and forth, absorbed in the sing-song study of the Talmud."[15] The repetitive back-and-forth movement and the "sing-song" manner of students repeating Talmudic passages in order to memorize them made its way directly into the heart of Bialik's poem "Ha-matmid" as the quintessence of Talmud study. The extant memoirs of Volozhin almost unanimously describe it as an intellectually open and stimulating environment and as a place where, despite immense economic and physical hardships, the pursuit of learning truly took place "for its own sake," as per the ideal of Torah lishmah.

This stimulating atmosphere of Volozhin seemed, at least at first, to act on the young Bialik as he experienced a period of invigorated religious zealousness. In a letter to friends in Zhitomir, shortly after his arrival in

Volozhin, the poet wrote that he had rejected his previous preoccupation with the Haskalah in favor of traditional learning: "I have distanced myself from all my previous distractions. All things that amused me in the past are far from me now. I consider the Haskalah artificial and avoid its books like the plague. I do not regret this loss and shall do my best to blot it out of memory because I know they have harmed me and were a *satan* on my path."[16]

Deciding to which set of texts to declare one's allegiance was an important coming-of-age experience that Bialik shared with the writers examined in previous chapters. Unlike previous writers, however, for whom the texts of the Haskalah defeated their earlier devotion to the Talmud, Bialik's priorities developed in the reverse direction. His newfound interest in the Talmud overtook his previous devotion to Haskalah literature. Describing his interest in the Haskalah as a "satan," a deceiver on his path, Bialik vowed to "distance himself from all previous distractions" and dedicate himself exclusively to religious study.

The renunciation of all distractions, however, did not very last long. Memoirs of Bialik's time in Volozhin as well as the poet's own recollections reveal that he was quickly integrated into a politically active group of students. These were not the studious *matmidim*, but rather they were the freethinkers who were members of an underground Zionist organization called Bnei Menasheh. The head of the yeshiva at the time, Naftali Tzvi Berlin, also known as the Netziv (1816–1893), was himself a Zionist and supported Hovevei Tziyon, so he likely knew of the student organization and did not actively suppress it, even though it was not officially permitted. A satellite of the Odessa Hovevei Tziyon, this student group recruited Bialik to serve as their official writer. It was during his involvement with this group that he published his first work: a religious Zionist manifesto of the yeshiva students entitled "The Idea of Settlement" ("Ra'ayon ha-yishuv").[17] Literature and politics, it seems, were interwoven, not necessarily harmoniously, from the very beginning of Bialik's career, for it was among these fellow members of the Zionist organization that he also found his first audience and circulated drafts of his first poems, "El ha-tzipor" ("To the Bird") and "Ha-matmid."[18]

Bialik's Materialism

Like many intellectuals in late imperial Russia, the young Bialik was captivated by materialist ideas. The brief period of Bialik's flirtation with the didactic norms of a socially oriented realism can be gleaned from the early drafts of "Ha-matmid," whose composition dates to 1888.[19] Bialik's choice for the poem's original title, "From among the Poor Folk," is quite telling; it is a direct reference to the title of Dostoyevsky's first novel, *Poor Folk* (1845). Bialik's initial idea for his first long poem was to be an exposé on the social and economic plight of poor students in the world of the rabbinic elite. The first drafts of what was later to become "Ha-matmid" offered a damning utilitarian critique of Talmudic culture, familiar to us from the works of Berdichevsky, Lilienblum, and the Kovner brothers. Its final stanzas, which Bialik eliminated from the final version of the poem, contain a poignant example of Bialik's early materialism:

> For whom do you toil, lost, miserable brother?
> Your labor is belated; your work's hour has passed.
> Your field is scorched; your meadow, a salt flat.
> Who will praise your conquests on the great earth?
> Who will desire your work under the sun?
> Your charity is for the dead,
> Your reward is in the world-to-come,
> But the faith of our time is in the land of life.[20]

אַךְ לְמִי אַתָּה עָמֵל, אָח אֹבֵד, חַלָּכָה?!

עֲמָלְךָ מְאָחָר, עֲבֹדְתְךָ פְּגֵרָה.

תְּנִיר נִיר רָאשִׁים, שַׂדְמָתְךָ מְלַחָה.

גַּם נַפְשְׁךָ הַתְּמִימָה לָבֹא אַחֲרָה,

מִי יְבָרֵךְ חֵילְךָ עַל אֶרֶץ רַבָּה?

מִי יִרְצֶה פָעָלְךָ תַּחַת הַשָּׁמַיִם?

חַסְדְּךָ לַמֵּתִים וּשְׂכָרְךָ בָעוֹלָם הַבָּא,

וֶאֱמוּנַת עִתָּנוּ—בְּאֶרֶץ חַיִּים.

Drawing on Gordon's well-known lines from the poem "For Whom Do I Toil?"—in which the exasperated maskilic poet predicts the demise of Hebrew literature—Bialik directs the same poetic address to yeshiva students engaged in an occupation that is likewise facing extinction. Its "toils" are not physical but textual. Yet they are depicted with physical actions, drawing on rabbinic metaphors linking Talmud study to such hyperphysical activities as *hayil* (conquest, war making, or valor) and *amal* (labor). These are followed by agricultural metaphors (the scorched field and the salt flat) that convey the fruitlessness of Talmud study according to a materialist value framework. Bialik then invokes the nihilists' utility argument, asking: What is the use of this metaphorical labor of Talmud study "on the great earth" and "under the sun"? By suggesting that this intellectual and spiritual toil is only good "for the dead"—that is, good for nothing—Bialik articulates a heretical rejection of the traditional belief in reward and punishment in favor of an atheistic, materialistic conception of the world. Strongly articulated by the last line, Bialik affirms the materialist credo that "the faith of our time" resides not in some imagined reward in the "world-to-come" but in the real world of the living.

Bialik continued to rework the poem for the next ten years, and remarkably, by the time of the publication of "Ha-matmid" in 1898, all traces of materialism had disappeared from the poem entirely. The transformation of the poem, which reflects the intellectual shifts that took place in Bialik himself and in Russia at large, occurred after the defining experience of Bialik's move to Odessa in 1891 and his confrontation with the so-called real world. As for the previous protagonists in this book, Bialik's experience of Odessa was one of hardship and disillusionment. "For six months," Bialik wrote, "I wandered in Odessa like a lost sheep. I knew hunger and torment . . . and no one knew my plight. I was bashful and fearful of knocking on doors of people who might be willing to help a lad like myself."[21]

The first person on whose door Bialik did knock was none other than Lilienblum, to whom Bialik brought the draft of his first short poem, "El ha-tzipor." Written in the medieval Hebrew style of Yehuda Halevi's hymns to Zion, the poem appealed to the aging Hebrew writer. Lilienblum, who, at the time, was the secretary of Hovevei Tziyon, sent Bialik to see his colleague Ahad Ha'am, who was then the editor of the Hebrew literary journal *Ha-Shilo'ah*. Ahad Ha'am, the influential Zionist leader, conducted his journal according to a utilitarian agenda and only accepted submissions of "purposeful poetry projecting a philosophical and ideological message to its readers."[22] Ironically, Bialik's first poem did not meet the standards of his hero Ahad Ha'am, who criticized it for excessive emotionality. The young poet found better luck with Ravnitzki, who published Bialik's first poem, "El ha-tzipor," in *Ha-pardes* in 1892, becoming his life-long friend and collaborator.

Following his first Odessa adventures, Bialik returned to Zhitomir, married, and took up his father-in-law's failing timber business. It was during this intermediary period that Bialik reworked "From among the Poor Folk" into the final version of "Ha-matmid" and successfully submitted it for publication in 1898 to Ahad Ha'am's journal. The final draft of "Ha-matmid," despite its unpopular aggrandizement of the very culture that Jewish writers were then trying to escape, enjoyed wide acclaim, marking the beginning of Bialik's rise to prominence as a Hebrew poet.

The Phantom of the Study House

Taking on the rhetoric of degeneration, Bialik embraced the image of the living dead as a poetic subject for his first long poem, "Ha-matmid." Developing in it a distinct poetics that rebel against both Ahad Ha'am's new spiritual Zionism and Berdichevsky's Nietzschean cult of strength, Bialik located the essential qualities of the Jewish spirit in the living-dead figure of the matmid, to whom we are carefully introduced in the first stanza:

> There are still abandoned corners of our exile,
> Remote, forgotten cities of dispersion,
> Where our ancient candle gives off smoke,
> Where God has saved a remnant from peril,
> Where embers glimmer in a ruin of ash.
> There, as meager flints exhausting their last smoke,
> Wretched and unhappy souls maintain the vigil—
> Spirits grown old beyond the reckoning of time;
> Grown old beyond the numbering of days.
> And, when you go out alone at night
> In one of these forsaken towns,[23]
> When sky above is quick with breaking stars,
> And grass below, with whisperings winds,
> Your ear will hear the murmur of a voice,
> Your eye will catch the twinkle of a light,
> Set in a window, and a human form—
> A shadow, like the shadow of the dead—
> Scurrying and swaying back and forth,
> Emitting death-like groans,
> Will come toward you on the waves of silence.
> It is the matmid in his prison-house,
> late in the night, that you shall find.[24]

עוֹד יֵשׁ עָרִים נְכָחָדוֹת בִּתְפוּצוֹת הַגּוֹלָה
בָּהֶן יַעְשַׁן בַּמִּסְתָּר נֵרֵנוּ הַיָּשָׁן;
עוֹד הוֹתִיר אֱלֹהֵינוּ לִפְלֵיטָה גְדוֹלָה
גַּחֶלֶת לוֹחֶשֶׁת בַּעֲרֵמַת הַדָּשָׁן.
וּכְאוּדִים מֻצָּלִים זְעֵיר שָׁם תֶּעְשַׁנָּה
הַנְּפָשׁוֹת אֻמְלָלוֹת וּנְשָׁמוֹת עֲלוּבוֹת,
הַחַיּוֹת בְּלִי יוֹמָן וּבְלִי עֵת תִּזְקַנָּה
כֶּחָצִיר הָעוֹלֶה בְּאֶרֶץ תַּלְאֻבוֹת.

וּבְצֵאתְךָ יְחִידִי לְעִתּוֹת בַּלַּיְלָה

בְּאַחַת מֵאַלֶּה הֶעָרִים הַבְּרוּכוֹת,

בְּשָׁעָה שֶׁנּוֹצְצִים כּוֹכָבִים מִלְמָעְלָה,

הַדְּשָׁאִים מִתְלַחֲשִׁים וּמְסַפְּרוֹת הָרוּחוֹת,

וְשָׁמְעוּ אָזְנֶיךָ מֵרָחוֹק קוֹל הוֹמֶה,

וְרָאוּ עֵינֶיךָ מֵרָחוֹק אוֹר נוֹצֵץ

בַּחַלּוֹן, וּבַעֲדוֹ דְּמוּת אָדָם הַדּוֹמֶה

לְצִלּוֹ שֶׁל-מֵת מִתְנוֹעֵעַ, מִתְרוֹצֵץ,

מִתְרוֹצֵץ, מִתְנוֹדֵד, וַהֲמִית הֲגְיוֹן נְכָאִים

תִּנָּשֵׂא עַל-נִבְכֵי הַשֶּׁקֶט עָדֶיךָ—

אָז מַתְמִיד בְּאֶחָד מִבָּתֵּי הַכְּלָאִים

מֵאַחַר בַּגֶּשֶׁף—רְאֵינָה עֵינֶיךָ.

Bialik begins by taking the reader on a poetic journey to a secluded ye-shiva town, where the reader can glimpse a specimen of an endangered spe-cies, the matmid, a sole remnant of its kind, a keeper and representative of a long-standing Jewish tradition.[25] Bialik imagines this remnant of an en-dangered people as a candle or flint that neither burns nor is extinguished but is perpetually emitting its last smoke. He describes the creatures that belong to this haunted setting of the yeshiva as "wretched souls" that nei-ther age nor follow the normal flow of life but have "grown old beyond the numbering of days" and, thus, appear to be leading an immortal and, hence, somewhat inhuman existence. No longer alive, yet existing among the living, the matmid embodies the description of the exilic living-dead Jew also portrayed in Leon Pinsker's 1882 essay "Autoemancipation," dis-cussed further below.[26]

Bialik's opening stanza introduces the matmid through a series of end-less deferrals in a deliberate effort to distance his poetics from naturalistic description. Like the exilic Jew who figured in Pinsker's essay, the matmid is but an image of a person, a shadow of a swaying dead being. His sway-ing motion, *mitnoded*, like the endless wandering of the wandering Jew (as implied by the root form *n-d-d*), is limited to the repetitive back-and-forth swaying of traditional Talmud study. While his mind may travel the breadth and depth of the Talmud, his body is imprisoned by the text, rejecting na-ture and the outside world. Harmonizing with the matmid's description as a living-dead creature is a sinister pastoral landscape of stars, night, and whispering winds—all elements of Romantic and decadent aesthetics.

Returning to reality, however, Bialik makes it clear that this supernat-ural creature is actually a young man or boy. Following the conventions of seminary and yeshiva memoir genres, Bialik lightens the dark mood by describing the different personalities of the students in the yeshiva and their boyish shenanigans. While the other students devote their time in the yeshiva to playing cards, smoking, carousing, or reading forbidden books, the matmid alone rejects all pleasures and never ventures out from his self-inflicted prison. Alone, unchanging, and unaware of the passage of time, the matmid sees only the wall and his books.

Even the most steadfast matmid, however, is not impervious to the pleasures of life. In a famous passage that Bialik added to the poem in the mid-1890s, after his exposure to the writings of Berdichevsky and Ahad Ha'am, Bialik responds directly to their assertion that "the book" has alienated the Jewish nation from nature and caused them to "cease feeling." In it, he depicts the matmid in a passionate temptation scene:

> It happens that a playful wind,
> Out of the blue, just like the tempter comes.
> It dances, curls his side-locks with a playful hand,
> Seduces secretly, arousing thoughts of madness.
>
> The wind descends unto the garden green,
> It whispers, coaxes, in the voice of thin silence:
> "See, sweet youth, how verdant is my cradle"
> . . .
>
> He lifts his weak hands to the wind,
> As pleading: "Take me, wind!
> Carry me away to a place where we may find rest,
> I am too weary here, too confined!"
> But a great blow from the garden fence,
> Reminds him that he has strayed from the path.[27]

אָז יֵשׁ אֲשֶׁר-יְרַקֵּד כְּשָׂטָן לִקְרָאתוֹ
הָרוּחַ הַפּוֹחֵז מִשִּׁפְעַת הַתְּכֵלֶת,
וְשָׁת לוֹ בַּחֲלָקוֹת וְסִלְסֵל פֵּאָתוֹ,
יְפַתֶּנּוּ בַּסֵּתֶר, יָפִיחַ הוֹלֵלוּת.
אָז יֵרֵד הָרוּחַ אֶל יֶרֶק הַגַּנָּה,
הוּא לָחֵשׁ, הוּא מְפַתֶּה בְּקוֹל דְּמָמָה דַקָּה:
"רְאֵה, עֶלֶם חֲמוּדוֹת, מָה עַרְשִׂי רַעֲנַנָּה"

. . .

וְשָׁלַח לָרוּחַ אֶת-יָדָיו בְּלִי-כֹחַ
כִּמְבַקֵּשׁ: "קָחֵנִי, הָרוּחַ, שָׂאֵנִי!
נָעוּפָה מִזֶּה וּמָצָאנוּ מָנוֹחַ,

פֹּה צַר לִי הַמָּקוֹם, פֹּה עָיֵף הִנֵּנִי!"
אַךְ חֲבָטָה גְדוֹלָה בִּמְשׂוֹכַת הַגִּנָּה
מַזְכִּירָה לַנַּעַר כִּי-סָר מִן הַנְּתִיבָה.

In this striking passage, Bialik describes the wind as a dancing devil (*satan* in the Hebrew) that tempts the matmid away from his studies by playing with his side locks and arousing lustful thoughts. Nature attempts to seduce the Talmud student away from his living-dead textual existence with the love poetry of Song of Songs, inviting him to its "verdant cradle," urging him to join the refreshing world of the senses. The matmid's susceptibility to the temptations of nature portray him as a passionate and sensitive person, perhaps also a *ba'al tayve* (a traditionally pejorative expression for an overly sensual person), who is far from the unfeeling and atrophied textual Jew imagined by Ahad Ha'am and the German Jewish physician, literary critic, and Zionist visionary Max Nordau (1849–1923), discussed further below. The seducing wind, in this passage, functions as a metaphor for the attractive pull of secular Jewish culture.[28] The matmid's cry of "Tzar li ha-makom" (I am too confined) implies that Talmudic culture is too confining. The line is an explicit reference to Berdichevsky's revisionist motto, articulated on the pages of *Ha-Shilo'ah*, in which he too insisted, "Tzar lanu ha-makom."[29] Despite the matmid's fantasy of straying from the path, however, a sharp confrontation with the garden fence—a metaphor for the "fence" of Jewish law—functions as a crude reminder of his vow of self-denial.

Returning to his dark corner in the study house after this ordeal, the matmid is overcome by a dark mood. Here, the motif of the living dead returns, as do the descriptions of darkness and decay that we encountered in the opening stanza, as Bialik attempts to portray how the matmid's repeated rejection of nature and the suppression of his desire for freedom lead him to becoming "sick of heart":

And then a spider appears out of its den
To pitch his tent above the boy.
There's darkness in the room and
All the corners of his heart are chill and dread.

. . .

His voice sounds as though ascending from
A weary man, who knows that he is dying,
A voice of a heart laid low, a sick heart

Filled with supplication and overpouring bitterness,
And all his Talmud-learning then appears to him
A bitter keening song.[30]

וּשְׁמָמִית יְרוֹקָה אֵי מִזֶּה תָּבֹא
לִתְקֹעַ מַסַּכְתָּהּ בְּקִירוֹת הַפִּנָּה,
וּמִשְׁנָה אֲפֵלָה בַּפִּנָּה, בִּלְבָבוֹ,
וּבְכָל חַדְרֵי נַפְשׁוֹ רְעָדָה וְצִנָּה –

. . .

וְנִשְׁמַע קוֹלָהוּ כְּאִלּוּ הוּא עוֹלֶה
מִנֶּפֶשׁ עֲיֵפָה שֶׁלָּמוּת הוֹלֶכֶת:
קוֹל לֵב הוּא הַמְּכֶּה כָעֻשָּׁב, לֵב חֹלֶה
הַמָּלֵא תַחֲנוּנִים וּמְרֵרֶה נִשְׁפָּכֶת.
וַיְהִי-לוֹ תַלְמוּדוֹ לְקִינַת תַּמְרוּרִים

The matmid suffers intensely from feelings of abandonment and ennui, which he feels both for himself and on behalf of the Jewish collective. The appearance of the *shemamit,* a rare biblical word translated here as "spider," following the medieval commentator Rashi's gloss on Proverbs 30:2 and based on the creature pitching a tent, accompanies the matmid in his suffering. According to Hamutal Bar-Yosef, it is a deployment by Bialik of European decadent tropes, since it shares the same root as the word for the matmid's depression and ennui, *nafsho shomemah.*[31] The repression of his natural urges and the unhealthy preoccupation with Talmudic learning have indeed resulted for the matmid in the "sickness of the heart" Nordau diagnosed as the symptom of degeneration. It is in this moment of intense suffering, however, that the matmid also realizes that his Talmud study is a song, an art form, however bitter it may be.

Decadence and Degeneration in the Russian Empire

The decade of the 1890s, in which Bialik was revising "Ha-matmid" into its final form, saw the development of a new discourse centered on the notion of degeneration. Nordau, who employed the term as a cultural diagnosis, saw it as encroaching on every sphere of Jewish life in Europe and harming nationalist hopes of revival.[32] Although originally a medical term, the concept of degeneration had always had a close association with art. The term was first introduced in the medical community by the French physician Augustin Morel in his book *The Physical, Intellectual and Moral Degeneracies of the Human Species,* which appeared in 1857, the same year as Baudelaire's harbinger of decadence, *Les Fleurs du Mal*.[33] Nordau took degeneration theory, as Olga Matich poignantly describes, right out of the psychiatric hospital (where he had worked) and "applied it to the literary and philosophical avant-garde."[34] In his magnum opus, *Degeneration* (1892), Nordau attempted to warn Europe about the moral, psychological, and physical threats inflicted on European culture by immoral and unhealthy literature and art, which were the fruits of the allegedly unhealthy psyches of their creators. In a new twist on materialist utilitarianism, Nordau argued that "morality is not connected with metaphysical truth or an inner quest for sincerity, but rather with what is 'useful' in terms of the progress of the species." Despite his new bet on "utility," in an ironic twist of fate, Nordau became remembered as the "philosopher of decadence" for having devoted hundreds of pages to a meticulous literary analysis of the works that he found most useless and harmful—among them Nietzsche, Tolstoy, Wilde, and the greatest artists of the nineteenth century.[35]

Nordau, who was in correspondence with Ahad Ha'am, began to take an active interest in Russian Jewish literature. After sampling the leading Russian Jewish literary journals, and in particular Ahad Ha'am's *Ha-Shilo'ah*, Nordau rushed to diagnose the "degeneration" of modern Hebrew literature.[36] Most likely referring to the young writers associated with Berdichevsky, Nordau characterized the literary efforts of Russian Hebrew writers as "the ramblings of Haskalah-intoxicated youths who have escaped from the beit midrash and believe themselves to be the latest word in all of Europe," casting the blame for the degenerate quality of Hebrew literature on yeshiva education.[37]

With mounting anxieties about degeneration, prevalent both in Jewish culture and in Russian intelligentsia circles, Hebrew writers attempted to deal one final blow to their connection with the image of the Jew as a degenerate textual creature and to recreate it, as well as themselves, into the "New Hebrew Man."[38] The term *New Men* was first conceived by Chernyshevsky and the Russian nihilists as the unsentimental and hyper-rational heroes who would transform Russian society. The term, however, took on new meanings under Nietzschean Jewish writers and continued to resonate in modernist Hebrew literature well into the first three decades of the twentieth century. Tchernichovsky, a celebrated poet and a translator of Babylonian and ancient Greek poetry, envisioned his New Hebrew Man as the Hellenistic antithesis to the traditional portrayal of masculinity under Talmudic culture in his 1900 poem, "Facing the Statue of Apollo":

> I bow to life, to strength, and to beauty,
> To all the precious things of which we were robbed
> By living corpses, a rotten seed of man,
> Rebels against life given by my rock Shaddai,
> The God of gods who stormed Canaan in conquest—
>
> . . .
>
> But they have bound him with the straps of the phylacteries.[39]

אֶכְרַע לַחַיִּים, לַגְּבוּרָה וְלַיֹּפִי,

אֶכְרַע לְכָל שְׂכִיּוֹת-הַחֶמְדָּה, שֶׁשָּׁדְדוּ

פִּגְרֵי אֲנָשִׁים וּרְקַב זֶרַע אָדָם,

מוֹרְדֵי הַחַיִּים מִיַּד צוּרִי שַׁדַּי,

אַל אֱלֹהֵי כּוֹבְשֵׁי כְּנַעַן בְּסוּפָה . . . ,,

וַיַּאַסְרוּהוּ בִרְצוּעוֹת שֶׁל תְּפִילִין . . .

Bowing to life, strength, and beauty—instead of the traditional values of textual study, self-restraint, and piety—Tchernichovsky attempts to distance Jewish culture from rabbinic tradition and its values. He describes its representatives as "living corpses" and" "rebels against life," who shackled Jewish culture with the straps of the phylacteries. Tchernichovsky's poem aimed to transgress every threshold of tradition both semantically and linguistically. Even in his use of the Hebrew language, he drew on the archaic pagan registers of the Bible so that his language would sound more foreign to the eastern European Jewish ear.

The notion of the Jewish nation as "living corpses," existing in a state of deep sleep somewhere between life and death, permanently degenerating but never properly dying, accosted Russian Hebrew writers from all directions. The strongest articulation of this image was given in the influential essay "Autoemancipation" by Pinsker, a Russian Jewish physician and the first head of Hovevei Tziyon. This essay was originally published as a German pamphlet in 1882 and then translated into Yiddish and Russian. It instantly became extremely influential among Jewish writers and intellectuals, owing partially to Pinsker's reputation as an acclaimed physician. Moved by the pogroms of 1881, Pinsker offered a psychological and medical explanation for Europe's disdain of the diasporic Jew. He proposed that the anti-Jewish sentiments so ubiquitous among Russians and other Europeans were the natural psychological effects that come from viewing the Jewish nation in exile as a living-dead creature:

> Thus the world saw in this people the frightening image of a dead being walking among the living. That image from the world of the ghosts, the image of the wandering dead, an image of a people that is not united in a body of organs and limbs, that is not tied to a particular land, that is no longer alive but nonetheless walks among the living; this strange image, which has no precedent in the history of the nations and unlike anything before and after it—could not but create a strange and astonishing impression in the imagination of the nations.[40]

Drawing on a medicalized view of the Jews as a dysfunctional body and on the grotesque image of a wandering corpse, Pinsker attempted to describe gentile perceptions of Jewish degeneration. In Ahad Ha'am's Hebrew translation from the German, Pinsker's essay became the political manifesto for Russia's early Zionists seeking a cure to the degenerative malady of the body and spirit afflicting Jews of the Diaspora.

The common theme among these intersecting discourses was that the identity of the Jew as a textual rather than a bodily being was perceived as the central obstacle to Jewish political and cultural revival. Ahad Ha'am was the one to articulate the link between rabbinic textuality and degeneration in his essay "Torah sheba-lev" ("Law of the Heart," 1893). "The book," he wrote, "had ceased to be a source of new inspirations and moral strength; on the contrary, its function became to weaken and, finally, crush all the spontaneity of life and emotion, until people become wholly dependent upon the written word and incapable of responding to any stimulus in nature or life without its permission and approval."[41] Ahad Ha'am blamed the degeneration of Jewish culture on the unhealthy attraction to the written word. Combining the cultural critique of degeneration with Pinsker's political one, Ahad Ha'am called on Zionism for the renewal of Jewish culture and spirit in the land of Israel as the only solution to degeneration.

The Talmudist as an Artist

The alternating motifs of religious passion and emotional anguish point to the influence of decadence on Hebrew writers. Bar-Yosef dates Jewish writers' explicit awareness of decadence as a literary movement to 1894, the year when Berdichevsky popularized the writings of Nietzsche. In that same year, the Yiddish writer Y. L. Peretz (1852–1915) published his Hebrew poetry collection *Ha-Uggav* (*The Lyre*), giving an explicit articulation to the rise of decadence in Russia and the West. In an essay titled "On Mental Illnesses among Writers," Peretz draws on the link that Nordau made between decadent literature and mental illness as he describes his allegiance to this new movement: "The sun of realism has already set on the literary world, and, likewise, the sun of materialism. But decadence is on the rise. Yet, among us [Jewish writers] who are far from the battlefield, realism is still a new slogan that excites many hearts. Let them [i.e., the Jewish writers] add a few more drops of myrrh to *The Love of Zion* and a few drops of dew on their nationalism. Drink up and tell me, how does it taste?"[42]

Defending his Hebrew poetry collection against materialist critics who accused it of being a "degenerate" celebration of the unnatural and unhealthy facets of the human experience, Peretz takes a stab at Mapu's *Love of Zion*, whose saccharine pleasures, he claimed, were continually being recycled by Hebrew writers. Peretz points particularly toward such writers as Lilienblum and Ahad Ha'am, accusing them of lagging the latest developments of the greater literary world. The old generation of writers, Peretz argues, is still bound up with the utilitarian aims of Russian materialism, while also producing bad literature in the service of Zionism.

Peretz, who had a strong identification with Polish culture and nationalism, was one of the first writers to move away from the Russian brand of utilitarian social realism that had occupied Yiddish literature since the 1870s. Instead, he aligned himself with the decadent movement, which was rapidly gaining underground momentum in Poland in the work of such writers as Stanisław Przybyszewski (1868–1927) and Stanisław Wyspiański (1869–1907). These writers, who served as literary models for Peretz, often drew on Polish folk motifs to explore decadent themes like the artistic counterpoint between religion and transgression, sexuality, and art.[43]

In 1888, roughly the same year Bialik wrote the first draft of "Ha-matmid," Peretz published a long poem in Yiddish titled "Monish" (revised up until 1908), which, for the first time, attempted to describe a decadent sexual encounter in plain Yiddish. For the poem's romantic hero, Peretz cast the unlikely figure of a young matmid named Monish, whose arduous devotion to the Talmud provokes the demonic Lilith to seduce him in the guise of a non-Jewish woman. Peretz describes his portrait of a new Jewish hero, the matmid, in Yiddish rhyme and meter:

> Drinking Torah like a sponge,
> His mind is lightning,
> Which could plunge from highest peak,

To lowest depth,
Maimonides—no matter how complex—
Monish could crack.
Like water, he consumes the *Taz*,
And sails the ocean of the *Shas*.

And what a beauty, a delight!
His curls are black like night,
Red lips like roses,
Black brows like bows,
And like the sky, blue eyes
In which a little fire glows.[44]

Toyre zapt er vi a shvom;
un a kelp—vi a blits,
tsi aroyf—tsum hekhstn shpits,
tsi arop—in tifstn thom!
Vi a vaser zupt er Taz;
meg der Rambam zayn, vi harb,
treft er bald arayn in karb,
un a boki shoyn in shas . . .

Un a sheyner yung—a prakht:
shvartse lokn, vi di nakht;
royte liplekh—royzn tsvey,
shvartse bremen, vi di boygn,
vi der himl bloye oygn,
un dos fayerl in zey!

In the character of Monish, Peretz develops his Yiddish portrayal of a devout young Talmudist. Monish is the perfect rabbinic bridegroom, and, by the same token, he is the perfect specimen of fin de siècle cultural ridicule. Since childhood, he has been abnegating the physical world for texts, studying them day and night. Peretz gratuitously summons for the secular Jewish reader the obscure textual world of Talmud study by describing the specific commentaries that Monish is reading. For instance, he knows how to crack Maimonides, no matter how difficult it might be; he studies the *Taz* (the *Turei Zahav*), the exhaustive commentary to the Jewish Code of Law, the *Shulchan Arukh*, and he is an expert in the "Shas" (i.e., the Talmud).

Monish is the irresistible embodiment of the scholarly ideal as dictated by Talmudic tradition. As women swoon and blush when Monish passes them by on the street, Peretz's poem performs a folkloric admiration for the femininely beautiful, genteel scholar as the favored object of female desire. Monish's appearance is a farcical cliché of romantic female beauty standards: he has black curls like the night and red lips like roses. But, while his beauty is indeed feminine, it does not render him weak. On the contrary, there is a fire in his eyes—a Talmudic metaphor for eros, a mental virility and intellectual prowess that are characteristic of the Talmudic portrayal of seasoned scholars.

This reversal of values and aesthetic conventions that Peretz's poem performs by bringing back the allegedly disembodied textual Jew as an erotic subject is comical but also serious, for it represents, as Daniel Boyarin has suggested in other contexts, not an ignorance of Western constructions of masculinity but rather a deliberate reversal of those norms in favor of the values of Talmudic culture.[45] In what has been described as the most risqué passage in nineteenth-century Jewish literature, Peretz depicts the sexual encounter between the yeshiva student and his demonic seductress:

> Love is burning in the ruins;
> Bats and spiders lend their ear
> To their singing, to their laughing,
> How they kiss and how they swear.
>
> And he vows to her his love,
> By his rabbi, and his mother, and his father,
> And by all of the above.
> "Say! What else is there, God willing?"
> And she whispers "More!" and "More!"
> And he swears away his *peyes*,
> and his *tzitzis*, and his *tefillin*,
> Vows more fevered and outrageous,
> And she smiles at him and begs him,
> "Swear on further, swear on further,"
> And she cries out "higher, higher,"
> And her eyes, they are on fire;
> And her lips, they are bewitching.[46]
>
> Un in khurve brent di libe;
> fleder-mayz un shpinen hern
> zeyer zingen, zeyer lakhn,
> zeyer kushn, zeyer shvern!
> Un er shvert ir bay zayn rebn,
> bay dem tatn, bay der mamen

un bay ale nokh tsuzamen! . . .
—"Zog, vos nokh? Um gotes viln!"
Un zi sheptshet: "Veynik, veynik!"
Un er shvert ir bay di peyes,
bay di tsitses, bay di tfiln,
alts farbrenter un farshayter,
un zi shmeykhlt un zi bet zikh:
"Shver nokh vayter, shver nokh vayter!"
Un zi ruft alts, "Hekher, hekher!"
Zi vil zikher zayn ingantsn,
un zi kisheft mit di liplekh,
un di oygelekh—zey glantsn.

Scholars have interpreted Lilith's seduction of Monish as a metaphor for the one-sided defeat of Western culture and its literary modes of expression over the Yiddish language, which Peretz bemoaned in the poem's 1888 version as having "no single word for love, for feeling." They have focused mainly on Monish's succumbing to these foreign temptations.[47] The context of the decadent and religious renaissance in the Russian Empire and in Poland, however, suggests that what Peretz is describing is an exchange of sacred objects between the world of rabbinic learning and the realm of the erotic. While Monish is indeed giving in to temptation, Lilith is being seduced no less by receiving these sacred objects of value—his *peyes* (ear locks), his tzitzis (ritual fringes), and his tefillin (phylacteries). The swearing away of each object only intensifies Lilith's desire for further exchange. The phylacteries, which Tchernichovsky's Hebrew poem cursed for binding Jewish culture, become a valuable object in this unholy exchange, where climactic shouts of "more and more" and "higher, higher" eventually culminate in Monish's fall. Once the exchange is complete, however, we realize that it is a loss for Monish—but a gain for Lilith. The fire that was once in Monish's eyes, that Talmudic symbol of intellectual vitality, now appears in Lilith's eyes. Perhaps rather than trying to corrupt him, the "dark forces" of European culture are trying to steal for themselves Monish's Talmudic fire and jouissance as an antidote for their own creative decline.

A similar reversal of values and aesthetic conventions is undertaken by Bialik in "Ha-matmid." Bialik, who took the long road from the materialist pragmatism of the poem's original draft, ends in a similar process of aestheticizing the religious textual practices of the Volozhin Yeshiva. The last section of the poem shows how it is precisely the matmid's unhealthy, "anti-life" tendencies that constitute, in Bialik's new recognition, the source of his power and vitality:

"Oy, Oy omar Rava, hoy omar Abbayye!"
Is this the fountain of the nation's soul?
Is this its quick-flowing blood source which plants
In her seeds of everlasting life,
Infusing her with heat and flame?
Is this the source of the great ones of the past,
The spring of heroes yet unborn,
Chiseling the nation's spirit from a stone,
What voices, then, what flames are these
That carry the soul to the heart of heaven!
Who hid enchantments in these withered scrolls,
Who granted power to these mildewed words,
To chisel flames from perished souls,
To issue sparks from dimming eyes?
"Oy, Oy, omar ravah,"—can you hear and sense
The expiration of the soul, the fiercest love—
Before each fiery speech, each bleeding word,
Will tear your devastated heart.[48]

"—!הוֹי, הוֹ אָמַר רָבָא, הוֹי אָמַר אַבַּיֵּי!"
הֲפֹה בֵּית הַיּוֹצֵר לְנִשְׁמַת הָאֻמָּה?
הֲפֹה מְקוֹר דָּמֶיהָ, הַנּוֹטְעִים בָּהּ חַיֵּי
עוֹלָמִים, הַשֹּׁפְעִים בָּהּ אִשָּׁהּ וְחֻמָּהּ?
הֲפֹה אַדִּירֶיהָ—מְאוֹרוֹת עֲתִידִים,
הַיּוֹצְרִים אֶת-רוּחָהּ עַל הָאֲבָנִים?—
כִּי מָה הֵם הַקּוֹלוֹת וּמָה הַלַּפִּידִים
הַנּוֹשְׂאִים הַנֶּפֶשׁ עַד לֵב הַשָּׁמָיִם!
מִי צָפַן הַקְּסָמִים בַּגְּוִילִים הַבָּלִים,
מִי נָתַן הַכֹּחַ לַאֲמָרוֹת עֲבֵשׁוֹת,
לַחְצֹב לֶהָבוֹת מִלְּבָבוֹת חֲלָלִים
וּלְהַתֵּז נִיצוֹצוֹת מֵעֵינַיִם עֲשֵׁשׁוֹת?
"הוֹ, הוֹ אָמַר רָבָא!"—הֲתִשְׁמַע, הֲתָחוּשׁ
אֶת-כִּלְיוֹן הַנֶּפֶשׁ, הַחִבָּה הָעַזָּה?
הֲטֶרֶם יִקְרָעוּ לְבָבְךָ הַנָּחוּשׁ
כָּל-אֹמֶר אֵשׁ חֹצֵב, כָּל מִלָּה דָם מַזָּה?

The matmid's familiar song—"Oy, Oy omar Rava, hoy omar Abbaye!" ("Thus says Rava in the name of Abbaye")—is no longer a repetitive chant of the words of long-dead sages. This refrain becomes Bialik's testament to the continued vitality of the rabbinic intellectual endeavor, its irreducible value, and its artistic merit. Bialik sees the timeless conversation between learners of the Talmud, past and present, as the essence and "fountain" of the Jewish spirit (*beit ha-yotzer le-nishmat ha-umah*), endowing that spirit with immortality. This immortality, however, is not one of eternal decay, as in Pinsker's image of the exilic Jew, but is, rather, infused with "heat" and flame," the quintessential markers of life. The vitality of rabbinic textual culture is illustrated by paradoxical images: a love as fierce as death, magic in withered pages, strength in decaying words, and flames in the souls of the perished.[49] While the matmid's grip on life may indeed be dubious, it is the words of Jewish texts themselves, described as bleeding, that undergo an incarnation into material existence in the final lines of the poem.

Conclusion

Invested in portraying the artistic counterpoint between vitality and decay at the heart of the Jewish textual endeavor, Bialik refused to offer a resolution for these opposing qualities and discouraged others from finding one. Bialik's intimate familiarity with the yeshiva and his deep appreciation for its intellectual and cultural achievements allowed him to be simultaneously critical and proud of this culture without falling into sentimentalism. And although, toward the poem's conclusion, Bialik attempts to imagine a possible future where the prohibitive "way of the Torah" would be reconciled with the freedom of a secular life, he does not choose to follow along that path. The ending of the poem suggests that, perhaps like art, which tends to flourish the more the artist suffers, greatness in learning cannot be achieved without great sacrifice. Drawing on the expression "ki yafim la-torah hayei tza'ar" ("a life of suffering is beautiful for the Torah"), Bialik concludes with the recognition that there is beauty in the tensions inherent to the Jewish textual endeavor that make it no different from art.

Notes

1. Bialik became the best known Hebrew writer among Russians after Vladimir Jabotinsky (1880–1940) translated his poem "In the City of Slaughter" about the Kishinev pogrom in 1904. Stanislawski, *Zionism*, 183–93.
2. Miron, *Ha-predah min*; Rubin, "'Like a Necklace.'"
3. Moss, *Jewish Renaissance*, 26–27; Hutchinson, "Artist as Nation-Builder," 503.
4. Mosse, "Max Nordau"; Biale, *Eros and the Jews*, 176–203.

5. Penkower, "Silences of Bialik."

6. The phrase is from Dimitry Karamazov's monologue "Confessions of an Ardent Heart" in Dostoyevsky, *The Brothers Karamazov*, 108; Dostoyevsky, *Bratia Karamazovy*, 14:100. Cited in Kelly, "An Unorthodox Beauty," 20, 123n49.

7. Lachover, *Bialik: hayav vi-yetzirotav*, 1:115.

8. Klausner, *H. N. Bialik*, 3.

9. Klausner, 3, 13–14.

10. Holtzman, *Hayim Nahman Bialik*, 43.

11. Klausner, *H. N. Bialik*, 15.

12. Feinstein, *Sunshine, Blossoms and Blood*, 26.

13. Bialik, *Igrot Bialik*, 1:21.

14. Aba Blosher's memoir recalling his time with Bialik in Volozhin, cited in Etkes and Tikochinski, *Yeshivot Lita*, 171.

15. Cited in Etkes and Tikochinski, 108.

16. Bialik, *Igrot Bialik*, 1:22–27.

17. Holtzman, *Hayim Nahman Bialik*, 55.

18. Aba Blosher claimed that, when he saw Bialik's poems published in *Ha-Zeman*, he recognized "From among the Poor Folk" (the first draft of "Ha-matmid") as one of the poems he had already seen in Volozhin. Etkes and Tikochinski, *Yeshivot Lita*, 168.

19. Bialik attributed the poem to his time in Volozhin, but the poem, in its original draft, was only published in 1896 in *Ha-Zeman*. Bialik, *Ha-Matmid*, 14.

20. My translation. Hebrew text from Bialik, 84.

21. Bialik, *Igrot Bialik*, 4:195. Cited in Feinstein, *Sunshine, Blossoms and Blood*, 64.

22. Feinstein, 71.

23. I have rendered "he-arim ha-berukhot" as "forsaken towns." "Berukhot" here could denote both "blessed" and "cursed" in biblical Hebrew, and Bialik undoubtedly takes advantage of this ambiguity.

24. My translation, adapted from Bialik, *Selected Poems*, 51.

25. Miron refers to the idea of Bialik as a "guide" in *Ha-predah min*, 174.

26. The image of the living-dead exilic Jew also draws on the European myth of the Wandering Jew, who is believed to be immortal. According to one legend, the Wandering Jew's immortality consisted of him being reborn every month. Isaac-Edersheim, "Ahasver," 210, 212, 218.

27. My translation adapted from Bialik, *Selected Poems*, 62.

28. In the poem "Levadi" (1905), which begins with the line "the wind carried everyone away," Bialik mourns the fact that the "winds" of change have taken away from the Shechinah her last sons, the matmidim of the yeshiva, and only he alone is left.

29. Shamir, *Ha-nigun shebi-levavo*, 193.

30. Translation adapted from Bialik, *Selected Poems*, 80.

31. Bar-Yosef, *Maga'im shel dekadens*, 86–129.

32. See the multifaceted analysis of Nordau and his works in Stanislawski, *Zionism*.

33. Matich, *Erotic Utopia*, 11.

34. Matich, 13.

35. Mosse, "Max Nordau," xxiii.

36. Holtzman, *Ha-sefer ve-ha-hayim*, 208.

37. Nordau, *Paradoksim*, 280.

38. On the physical turn of Hebrew literature and the image of the New Hebrew, see Gluzman, *Ha-guf ha-tsioni*; Biale, *Eros and the Jews*, 186–87; S. Pinsker, *Literary Passports*, 155–60.

39. My translation; Hebrew text from Tchernikhovsky, *Kol kitvei Shaul Tchernikhovsky*, 1:86.

40. This translation into English is of Ahad Ha'am's Hebrew translation of Pinsker's German original. Pinsker, "Auto-emantsipatsiya." A frequently cited English translation is L. Pinsker, *Auto-Emancipation*, 3. "The world saw in this people the uncanny form of one of the dead walking among the living. This ghostlike apparition of a people without unity or organization, without land or other bond of union, no longer alive, and yet moving about among the living—this strange form, hardly paralleled in history, unlike anything that preceded or followed it, could not fail to make a strange, peculiar impression upon the imagination of the peoples."

The original German passage can be found in L. Pinsker, *Autoemanzipation*, 7. "Die Welt erblickte in diesem Volke die unheimliche Gestalt eines Toten, der unter den Lebenden wandelt. Diese geisterhafte Erscheinung eines wandelnden Toten, eines Volkes ohne Einheit und Gliederung, ohne Land und Band, das nicht mehr lebt und dennoch unter den Lebenden umhergeht; diese sonderbare Gestalt, welche in der Geschichte ihresgleichen kaum wiederfindet, die ohne Vorbild und ohne Abbild ist, konnte nicht verfehlen, in der Einbildung der Völker auch einen eigentümlichen, fremdartigen Eindruck hervorzubringen. Und wenn die Gespensterfurcht etwas Angeborenes ist und eine gewisse Berechtigung findet im psychischen Leben der Menschheit—was Wunder, daß sie sich auch angesichts dieser toten und dennoch lebenden Nation in hohem Grade geltend machte?"

41. Cited in Zipperstein, *Elusive Prophet*, 88.

42. The article was published in Warsaw in 1894 as "Ha-Hetz" ("The Arrow"). Cited in Bar-Yosef, *Maga'im shel dekadens*, 20.

43. For example, Peretz's Yiddish play *Bay nakht oyfn alten mark* (*At Night in the Old Marketplace*, 1922) appears to be an homage to Wyspiański's drama *Wesele* (*The Wedding*, 1901).

44. My translation; Peretz, *Ale Verk*, 1:273.

45. Boyarin, *Unheroic Conduct*, 72.

46. Peretz, *Ale Verk*, 1:283.

47. Miron, *Traveler Disguised*, 60–63.

48. Translation adapted from Bialik, *Selected Poems*, 71.

49. The expression *amarot aveshot* (dry words) is a play on the "dry bones" (*atzamot yeveshot*) of Ezekiel's vision of resurrection.

EPILOGUE

Reflections on the Value of Literature

MOVING INTO THE TWENTIETH CENTURY, HEBREW WRITERS FROM Bialik to S. Y. Agnon (1888–1970), who drew heavily on the tradition of Jewish textual learning, championed Hebrew literature's development as a literature for its own sake, as an art independent of both ideological and practical ends. Jewish culture's foundational struggle, however, with the impracticality of the Judaic and Hebrew textual enterprise—or, in other words, its resistance to political mobilization—had itself become a literary trope in Jewish fiction. One such example appears in the 1904 Russian novella *Pioneers*, by the Jewish writer and revolutionary S. An-sky (1863–1920). The novella depicts a young yeshiva dropout who leaves home with eight rubles in his pocket to begin a new life of secular wisdom and enlightenment in the big city. The young hero's first order of business upon his arrival, before tending to any practical matters, is a stop at a Jewish bookstore. There, among shelves lined with sacred texts, he spots a "great and extremely dangerous" Hebrew novel—none other than Lilienblum's *The Sins of Youth*.[1] To the young protagonist's great shock, he finds this heretical materialist novel lying openly in broad daylight.[2] Quickly recognizing that the young visitor is a naive self-styled freethinker, the shop owner devises the perfect sales pitch for the novel for which there is apparently little demand. He tells the young yeshiva student a blown-up tale of the novel's persecution by zealous rabbis who have offered to pay the exorbitant sum of "two rubles, *in cash*" to buy out and destroy each remaining copy.[3] The young hero now finds himself faced with a dilemma: to save his beloved Hebrew novel that articulates his deepest trials and aspirations or to save himself from going hungry. The short moment of hesitation, however, comes to a quick resolution. "Could the worth of *The Sins of Youth* really be assessed in rubles?" wonders the young hero, as he reaches for the money to buy the novel.[4]

Writing in the early 1900s, at a time when the materialist propagandistic vision of literature was beginning to gain social and political power in Russia, An-sky's *Pioneers* was an homage to an earlier consciousness in Jewish culture in which the written word was more real than anything else. The "pioneers" of An-sky's novel are a group of yeshiva dropouts living together in an abandoned apartment. Though they are dressed in tatters and suffer from cold and hunger, their minds aspire to the heights of enlightenment—which entails reading works by Hebrew writers and mastering Russian literature and cultural criticism. Despite tasting pork and smoking pipes on the Sabbath, they are still deeply entrenched in the textual universe and habits of their old yeshiva days, applying rabbinic numerology (gematria) to prove that Pisarev's materialist doctrines were given to Moses at Sinai and memorizing the latter's articles "*afn finger* [by the finger]."[5] The characters' use of numerologies, pseudocanonical verses, and mock blessings, which the boys utter to mediate every new aspect of their experiences as the secular champions of the Jewish Enlightenment, represents their deliberate retention of rabbinic textual practices and reinvention in secular forms. The boys even carry out a rabbinically flavored enactment of Chernyshevsky's *What Is to Be Done?* in which they try to save their friend Sonya (whom they imagine as Chernyshevsky's protagonist Vera Pavlovna) from an unwanted marriage, by marrying her to one of them with the instant rabbinic formula *harei at mekudeshet li* (behold you are consecrated unto me) in front of unsuspecting witnesses.

In gratuitously indulgent passages, An-sky's novella critically portrays the failure of these Don Quixote–like characters, whose lives are dictated by texts, to begin new lives that reckon with material problems, while at the same time celebrating that failure as a creative force. Interestingly, among the novella's most appreciative readers was the Russian realist writer Maxim Gorky. Having clearly understood the novel well, Gorky praised An-sky's representation of the Jews as "great martyrs" on behalf of the word, who continually chose to live a life that revolved around texts and literature at the expense of their material existence.[6]

As depicted more abstractly by *Pioneers*, as well as by the texts that this book has examined, the lives and works of the creators of Hebrew literature in the late nineteenth century were marked by a recurrent return to the world of Talmudic textuality from which they had so painstakingly tried to escape. They imagined that in leaving the yeshiva they were transforming themselves from Talmudists and men of texts into enlightened men of deeds who would act in the world.[7] Yet they had left one life of textual study only to begin another. They substituted the veneration of religious texts with secular ones, exchanging their Talmud volumes for Hebrew novels, journals, and the works of Chernyshevsky, Pisarev, and, later, Nietzsche.

And, though in these new secular texts they saw a call to action—an invocation to wield a tool or a weapon and to wage war on behalf of earthly life—the only weapons they dared wield were their old books, pens, papers, and words. Their new lives continued to be devoted to the study and production of texts.

The emergence of modern Hebrew literature in Russia would certainly have been impossible without what scholars have described as the breach that tore through "the fortified walls of the old religious and cultural foundations" to give rise to a modern intellectual endeavor.[8] More importantly, however, the emergence of modern Hebrew literature was equally a story of the renewal of an unconditional devotion to textuality that lay at the core of those breached cultural foundations. Hebrew writers' choice to remain writers was the product of their creative negotiation with the Jewish tradition of textual study, which, unlike religion, they were reluctant to leave behind. In an important sense, the success of Hebrew literature during this crucial incubatory period of its development sprang from the failures of these former students of religious texts to begin new lives grounded in material existence.[9]

The rise of modern Hebrew literature in nineteenth-century Russia, this book has argued, was shaped by the productive encounter between competing philosophical visions of the literary endeavor that played themselves out against the backdrop of Jewish life in Russia. The early works of modern Hebrew literature produced by the efforts of the Haskalah movement in Russia were the products of its writers' faith in the morally and spiritually improving power of Hebrew letters and the importance of Hebrew as a quintessential component of the Jewish national essence. With the rise of Russian nihilism in the 1860s, however, and the critique of literature in the name of utility advanced by the nihilists, a new generation of Jewish writers moved on to redefine literature's benefits in material and instrumental terms—terms that the nascent sphere of Hebrew letters was fundamentally unable to meet. Instead of disintegrating into oblivion, however, Hebrew literature thrived.

From the 1860s, multiple generations of Jewish writers and intellectuals expressed the idea that "the time for words has passed."[10] Nevertheless, Hebrew literature persisted to be, by its very nature, a continual affirmation of art in the face of an ideology of utility on one front and market forces on the other. Perhaps more than that of Jewish literature written both in Russian and in Yiddish, Hebrew literature resisted identification with any particular ideological goal, including that of Zionism, and favored, instead, individualism, aestheticism, and the free play of ideas.[11] The argument of this book has been that what enabled Jewish writers to make the case for Hebrew literature in a world defined by ideological and materialist interests was the ethos of Torah lishmah taken from the Talmudic culture of learning, whose freedoms and pleasures, though they were impractical, nonetheless made Hebrew literature worthwhile.

The question of literature's value, of whether the worth of a book could be assessed in rubles, shekels, dollars, or any other metric category, remains no less relevant today than during the time and context in which it was posed. In metrics-driven times as ours, when quantitative analyses have come to be relied on to represent the value of most of our experiences, scholars continue to search for new ways of defending the study of literature against the charge of its impracticality. Struggling with faltering enrollments and literature's apparent inability to compete with the hard benefits of the so-called objective disciplines, many scholars and teachers of literature have risen to the field's defense with an age-old argument—a defense of literature on ethical and ideological grounds. The leading response to the concern of "uselessness" characteristic of the past several decades of literary studies has been the embrace of ideological ends as a justification for literature and its study. In a recent work on literary and critical theory, Paula Moya has argued, "If literature were not fundamentally ideological—if it were not so revealing of the ways in which our diverse cultural ideas inform and motivate our equally-diverse practices and behaviors—there would be little reason to retain it as a field of study in the academy."[12]

At the other end of the discussion, scholars have too willingly relied on the social and medical sciences to prove the ways in which literature contributes to society.[13] Contemporary cultural thinkers have championed the notion that literary fiction produces desirable social outcomes, while articles published in scientific journals have heralded the various benefits of reading literary fiction, from the improvement of brain function and memory to the reduction of stress.[14] The pitfall of such arguments to rescue literature from the accusation of impracticality in contemporary times, however, is that the advantages that these findings confer to the literary endeavor are in no way intrinsic to it. There are much simpler and more effective ways of achieving the benefits of relaxation, memory enhancement, and the improvement of one's social skills than through the reclusive, intellectually taxing, and time-consuming activity of reading literary fiction, not to mention the unprofitability of studying it as a major at a university.

The continuing efforts to pinpoint literature's positive action in the world amid the ever-growing assault on its value belong to a long tradition in the West at whose heart is the firm belief that the role of literature is to teach, to edify, and to fight for the social good. But it is equally accepted that if literature fails to deliver on the well-delineated expectations that society has put in place for it in a given era and ideological paradigm, then what it has to offer, as sharply put by the English literature scholar Corey McEleney, may be deemed "pointless at best, poisonous at worst, and profitless either way."[15] The fact is that in the absence of pragmatic or ideological ends, our culture struggles with defining the essential value of the literary enterprise.

The reason that the attempts by literary scholars to defend the value of literature in today's climate have largely failed is precisely because they have attempted to do so from inside a paradigm that accepts its value as determined by either pragmatic or ideological utility. Thus, to rephrase the question posed earlier, in the absence of utility, what is it about the pursuit of literature that makes it valuable?[16]

When reflecting on the success story of Hebrew literature in Russia from today's vantage point, what appears most striking is the unlikelihood and unpredictability of its success. In attributing this success to the practices of Torah lishmah, however, this book has not been arguing against goals or the need for literature to have a socially conscious purpose and responsibility but only about the way to achieving those aims without compromising the very freedoms that make the pursuit of literature worthwhile. What the remarkable story of the rise of Hebrew literature in nineteenth-century Russia teaches is that we can never predict which ideas might become useful, when, and in what ways nor judge the pursuit of literature by metric categories. Thus, despite the pressing needs of economic and political transformations that took place in the late nineteenth century and the allures of a secular social purpose, Jewish writers continued to be drawn to the artistic and intellectual freedoms of Torah lishmah as they continued to experiment with rabbinic textual practices in Hebrew poetry and prose.

What did the future of Hebrew literature hold beyond the nineteenth century? By the end of its founding period in the nineteenth century, the period of revival (tehiyah), Hebrew literature flourished to create and participate in the avant-garde of literary modernisms in Russia, western Europe, and British Mandate Palestine. With new access to education and the development of Hebrew into a spoken language, a new generation of women began to innovate on Hebrew's literary front. Although at first Hebrew poetry and fiction was limited to a handful of pioneers, such as Esther Raab (1894–1981) and Devorah Baron (1887–1956), toward the mid-twentieth century, the number of leading female voices in Hebrew literature increased significantly. Male and female Hebrew writers on these three fronts continued to develop their aspirations for literature alongside the economic and material demands of their lives. At the same time, they held on to the hopes that their new identity as modern writers would be reconciled of its former contradiction and would grow to embody an organic union between the literary and the material—a new poetic identity the poet Avraham Shlonsky (1900–1973) brilliantly described in his 1928 poem "Toil" as *paytan solel be-yisra'el,* or "a road-paving Jewish bard."

Continuing its development into the literary movements and directions of the twentieth century, the language of Hebrew poetry and prose has retained its appreciation for the textual subtleties characteristic of Talmudic culture and its love for hermeneutics. From the sexual manipulation of Hebrew verse by Yona Wallach (1944–1985), to the scholarly and restrained poetics of Dahlia Ravikovitch (1936–2005), the textual practices ridiculed as "useless" by materialist Jewish writers in Russia were perfected into indispensable aesthetic instruments in Hebrew's modern literary toolkit. Intertextual games and allusions to the Jewish religious canon continued to produce the minimalist and exact poetics of Yehuda Amichai (1924–2000), Nathan Zach (1930–2020), and Dan Pagis (1930–1986), while the advances in literary fiction produced by the novels and short stories of Berdichevsky and Brenner gave way to the conceptual and linguistic innovation of contemporary Hebrew prose.

Since its development in nineteenth-century Russia, Hebrew literature never abandoned its commitment to reflect, interpret, and undermine the various social and political causes under which it was written in each given time. Hebrew literature was never identical with these causes, however, but an end among them. The path taken by Hebrew literature in the twentieth century was one of "art, aesthetic experience and cultivation of individuality as exalted ends in themselves."[17] Hebrew literature's productive yet elusive relationship to ideology, as Harshav argued, was never linear but rather marked by intellectual and cultural diversity. Ideologically, geographically, and linguistically diverse landscapes—in which Leninist socialism competed with Hasidic ecstasy, Russian futurism comingled with rabbinic influences, the Zionist struggled with the diasporic—combined in unpredictable ways to create new intertextual landscapes that would be at the disposal of future generations of Hebrew writers.[18]

Mikhail Bakhtin long ago pointed out that while practical and ideological motives no doubt shape the creative enterprise, they are never able to fully define it.[19] I have argued here that this was the case with Hebrew literature. Although the ideological and political landscape that gave birth to a literary work may change beyond recognition, and the urgency of its utilitarian aims may dissipate over time, the need for the art and process of the literary endeavor has, much like the Judaic literary tradition, a proven way of enduring.

Notes

1. An-sky, *Pioneers*, 5–6.
2. Lilienblum, "Olam ha-tohu."
3. An-sky, *Pioneers*, 5–6.
4. An-sky, 6.
5. An-sky, 128.
6. Maxim Gorky also noted with approval that "[*Pioneers*] acquaints us with the Jews better than the tear-soaked works of [other Jewish writers]." Safran, *Wandering Soul*, 168; An-sky, *Pioneers*, x; Krutikov, "Russian Jew," 135.
7. The dichotomy between men of words and men of deeds, or, alternatively, the world of contemplation and the world of action, was one that Lilienblum employed. It is analyzed in Roskies, "Maskil as Folk Hero," 219–35; Mintz, *Banished*. See also the notion of "this-worldniks" in Veidlinger, *Jewish Public Culture*, 1–5.
8. Roskies, "An-Sky, Sholem Aleichem," 35.
9. David Roskies summarized this observation regarding the literature of the Haskalah: "Despite all the efforts invested in him, the young Man of Words never grew into a mature and believable Man of Deeds, and yet in this failure to mature was the success of maskilic prose." Roskies, "Maskil as Folk Hero," 223.
10. Moss, *Jewish Renaissance*, 13, 27.
11. Kenneth Moss notes that "Yiddishists in particular obediently began to remake their culture—and themselves—in accordance with the Revolution's ideological imperatives" Moss, 8.
12. Moya, *Social Imperative*, 7.
13. Landy, *How to Do Things*, 29.
14. The headlines of the following two *New York Times* pieces from 2014 and 2106 exemplify this tendency: Belluck, "For Better Social Skills"; Hipps, "To Write Better Code."
15. McEleney, *Futile Pleasures*, 4.
16. Pleasure has long been proposed as the purpose of the literary pursuit, as argued by scholars from Roland Barthes to Robert Alter. Alter has argued, however, in setting the goal of literary studies to be something other than literature, the language of criticism has

alienated itself both from pleasure and from the "imaginative life of the text." This has been the case since the second part of the twentieth century, when it has become the standard for contemporary works of literary studies to mirror the dense, gratuitously technical writing of the "objective disciplines," albeit without any added objectivity. Alter, *Pleasures of Reading*, 15.

17. Moss, *Jewish Renaissance*, 5.

18. Harshav, *Language in Time*, 177–180.

19. Bakhtin, *Problems of Dostoevsky's Poetics*, 90.

BIBLIOGRAPHY

Alter, Robert. *The Pleasures of Reading in an Ideological Age*. New York: W. W. Norton, 1996.

An-sky, S. *Pioneers: A Tale of Russian-Jewish Life in the 1880s*. Translated by Michael R. Katz. Bloomington: Indiana University Press, 2014.

Bakhtin, Mikhail. *Problems of Dostoevsky's Poetics*. Translated by Caryl Emerson. Theory and History of Literature 8. Minneapolis: University of Minnesota Press, 1984.

Bar Asher, Moshe. "Mekomah shel ha-aramit ba-ivrit ha-hadashah." In *Ha-lashon ha-ivrit be-hitpat'hutah uve-hithadshutah*, 14–76. Edited by Joshua Blau. Jerusalem: Ha-akademiah ha-le'umit ha-yisraelit le-mada'im, 1996.

Bar-Yosef, Hamutal. *Maga'im shel dekadens: Bialik, Berdichevsky, Brenner*. Be'er Sheva, Israel: Ben Gurion University of the Negev Press, 1997.

Barzel, Hillel. *Shirat ha-tehiyah: Hayim Nahman Bialik*. Tel Aviv: Sifriyat po'alim, 1990.

Belliustin, I. S. *Description of the Clergy in Rural Russia: The Memoir of a Nineteenth-Century Parish Priest*. Ithaca, NY: Cornell University Press, 1985.

Belluck, Pam. "For Better Social Skills, Scientists Recommend a Little Chekhov." *Well* (blog). *New York Times*, October 3, 2013. https://well.blogs.nytimes.com/2013/10/03/i-know-how-youre-feeling-i-read-chekhov/.

Berdichevsky, Mikhah Yosef. *Kitve Mikhah Yosef Berdichevsky (Bin-Goryon)*. Vol. 6. Tel Aviv: ha-Kibbutz ha-me'uhad, 1996.

———. *Pirkei Volozhin*. Holon, Israel: Bet Devorah ve-Imanuel, 1984.

Berdyaev, Nikolai. *The Origin of Russian Communism*. Ann Arbor: University of Michigan Press, 1960.

Biale, David. *Eros and the Jews: From Biblical Israel to Contemporary America*. Berkeley: University of California Press, 1997.

———. *Not in the Heavens: The Tradition of Jewish Secular Thought*. Princeton, NJ: Princeton University Press, 2011.

Bialik, Hayim Nahman. *Ha-Matmid: bi-livyat hiluk nusah ve-nispahot*. Edited by Dan Miron. Tel Aviv: Ha-Kibbutz ha-me'uhad, 1977.

———. *Igrot Bialik*. Edited by Fishel Yeruham Lachover. 5 vols. Tel Aviv: Dvir, 1938.

———. *Selected Poems by Chaim Nachman Bialik*. Translated by Maurice Samuel. New York: Union of American Hebrew Congregations Press, 1972.

Bitzan, Amos. "The Problem of Pleasure: Disciplining the German Jewish Reading Revolution, 1770–1870." PhD diss., University of California, Berkeley, 2011. http://www.escholarship.org/uc/item/20c378fm.

Boyarin, Daniel. *Carnal Israel: Reading Sex in Talmudic Culture*. Berkeley: University of California Press, 1993.

———. "The Gospel of the Memra: Jewish Binitarianism and the Prologue to John." *Harvard Theological Review* 94, no. 3 (2001): 243–84.

———. *Unheroic Conduct: The Rise of Heterosexuality and the Invention of the Jewish Man*. Berkeley: University of California Press, 1997.

Brinker, Menachem. "Nietzsche's Influence on Hebrew Writers of the Russian Empire." In *Nietzsche and Soviet Culture: Ally and Adversary*, edited by Bernice Glatzer Rosenthal, 393–441. Cambridge: Cambridge University Press, 1994.

Brower, Daniel R. *Training the Nihilists: Education and Radicalism in Tsarist Russia*. Ithaca, NY: Cornell University Press, 1975.

Chernyshevsky, Nikolai. *Chto Delat'? Iz Rasskazov o Novykh Liudiakh*. Edited by Tamara I. Ornatskaia and Solomon A. Reiser. Leningrad: Nauka, 1975.

———. *What Is to Be Done?* Translated by Nathan Dole and Simon Skidelsky. Ann Arbor, MI: Ardis, 1986.

Chernyshevsky, Nikolay, and N. A. Alekseev. *Dnevnik*. Moscow: Tiporafia gozety "pravda," 1931.

Cohen, Tova. "The Maskil as Lamdan: The Influence of Jewish Education on Haskalah Writing Techniques." In *Jewish Education and Learning*, edited by Glenda Abramson and Tudor Parfitt, 61–75. Langhorne, PA: Harwood Academic, 1994.

———. "The Maskilot: Feminine or Feminist Writing?" In *Jewish Women in Eastern Europe*, edited by Paul Hyman, Antony Polonsky, and ChaeRan Y. Freeze, 57–86. Oxford: Littman Library of Jewish Civilization, 2007.

Curtius, Ernst Robert. *European Literature and the Latin Middle Ages*. Princeton, NJ: Princeton University Press, 1953.

Darnton, Robert. "Readers Respond to Rousseau: The Fabrication of Romantic Sensitivity." In *The Great Cat Massacre and Other Episodes in French Cultural History*, 215–56. New York: Basic Books, 1984.

Dauber, Jeremy Asher. *Antonio's Devils: Writers of the Jewish Enlightenment and the Birth of Modern Hebrew and Yiddish Literature*. Stanford, CA: Stanford University Press, 2004.

Dobrolyubov, Nikolai. "What Is Oblomovism?" In *The Cambridge History of Russian Literature*, translated by Charles Moser, 261–62. Cambridge University Press, 1992.

Dostoyevsky, Fyodor. *Bratia Karamazovy: knigi I–X*. Vol. 14. Leningrad: Nauka, 1976.

———. *The Brothers Karamazov*. Translated by Richard Pevear and Larissa Volokhonsky. New York: Random House, 1992.

Epstein, Zalman. *Moshe Leib Lilienblum*. Tel Aviv: Dvir, 1935.

Etkes, Immanuel. "Haskalah." In *The YIVO Encyclopedia of Jews in Eastern Europe*. Accessed March 30, 2021, http://www.yivoencyclopedia.org/article.aspx/Haskalah.

———. "Marriage and Torah Study among the Lomdim in Lithuania in the Nineteenth Century." In *The Jewish Family: Metaphor and Memory*, edited by David Charles Kraemer, 153–78. New York: Oxford University Press, 1989.

Etkes, Immanuel, and Shlomo Tikochinski, eds. *Yeshivot Lita: pirkei zikhronot*. Jerusalem: Merkaz Zalman Shazar, 2004.

Feiner, Shmuel. Introduction to *Sefer ha-matsref*, by Itzhak Isaac Kovner. Jerusalem: Mosad Bialik, 1998.

———. *Milhemet tarbut: tenu'at ha-haskalah ha-yehudit ba-me'ah ha-19*. Jerusalem: Carmel, 2010.

Feingold, Ben-ami. "Ha-otobiografiyah ke siporet: iyun behatot ne'urim li-lilienblum." *Mehkarei-yerushalayim besifrut 'ivrit* 4 (1984): 86–111.

Feinstein, Sara. *Sunshine, Blossoms and Blood: H. N. Bialik in His Time, a Literary Biography*. Lanham, MD: University Press of America, 2005.

Feuerbach, Ludwig. *The Essence of Christianity*. Translated by Marvin Evans. 2nd ed. London: Kegan, 1893.

Finkin, Jordan D. *A Rhetorical Conversation: Jewish Discourse in Modern Yiddish Literature.* University Park: Penn State Press, 2010.

Frede, Victoria. *Doubt, Atheism, and the Nineteenth-Century Russian Intelligentsia.* Madison: University of Wisconsin Press, 2011.

Freeze, Gregory L. Introduction to *Description of the Clergy in Rural Russia: The Memoir of a Nineteenth-Century Parish Priest,* by I. S. Belliustin, 13–62. Translated by Gregory L. Freeze. Ithaca, NY: Cornell University Press, 1985.

———. *The Parish Clergy in Nineteenth-Century Russia: Crisis, Reform, Counter-Reform.* Princeton, NJ: Princeton University Press, 2014.

Gafni, Chanan. *Peshutah shel mishnah: Iyunim be-heker sifrut haza"l ba-et ha-hadashah.* Bnei Brak, Israel: ha-Kibbutz ha-me'uhad, 2011.

Ginzburg, Mordechai Aharon. *Vidui shel maskil: Aviezer.* Edited by Shmuel Werses. Jerusalem: Mosad Bialik, 2009.

Gluzman, Michael. *Ha-guf ha-tsioni.* Tel Aviv: ha-Kibuts ha-me'uhad, 2007.

Golomb, Jacob. "Al ha-pulmus ha-nitshe'ani bein Ahad Ha-am le-Mikhah Yosef Berdichevsky." In *Misaviv la-nekuda: meh'karim hadashim al berdichevsky,* 69–93. Be'er Sheva, Israel: Ben Gurion University of the Negev Press, 2007.

Gordon, Y. L. "Kotso shel yud." Edited by S. Nash. *CCAR Journal* 53, no. 3 (2006): 113–88.

Gottlober, A. B. *Igeret tsa'ar ba'alei hayim.* Zhitomir: A. Sh. Sharazov, 1868.

Harris, Jay. *How Do We Know This? Midrash and the Fragmentation of Modern Judaism.* Albany: State University of New York Press, 1995.

Harshav, Benjamin. *Language in Time of Revolution.* Berkeley: University of California Press, 1993.

———. *Shirat ha-tehiya ha-ivrit.* Tel Aviv: Open University of Israel, 2000.

Hartman, Geoffrey. *Scars of the Spirit: The Struggle against Inauthenticity.* New York: St. Martin's, 2002.

Hever, Hannan. *Be koakh ha-el.* Tel Aviv: ha-Kibbutz ha-me'uhad, 2013.

Hipps, Bradford J. "To Write Better Code, Read Virginia Woolf." Opinion, *New York Times,* May 21, 2016. https://www.nytimes.com/2016/05/22/opinion/sunday /to-write-software-read-novels.html.

Holtzman, Avner. *El ha-kera sheba-lev: Mikhah Yosef Berdichevsky, shenot ha-tsemihah.* Jerusalem: Mosad Bialik, 1995.

———. *Ha-sefer ve ha-hayim: masot al Mikhah Yosef Berdichevsky.* Jerusalem: Karmel, 2003.

———. *Hayim Nahman Bialik.* Jerusalem: Merkaz Zalman Shazar, 2008.

———. *Hayim Nahman Bialik: Poet of Hebrew.* Translated by Or Scharff. New Haven, CT: Yale University Press, 2017.

———. *Mikhah Yosef Berdichevsky.* Jerusalem: Merkaz Zalman Shazar le-toldot Yisrael, 2011.

Hutchinson, John. "The Artist as Nation-Builder." *Nations and Nationalism* 5, no. 4 (1999): 501–21.

Isaac-Edersheim, E. "Ahasver: A Mythic Image of the Jew." In *The Wandering Jew: Essays in the Interpretation of a Christian Legend,* edited by Galit Hasan-Rokem and Alan Dundes, 195–210. Bloomington: Indiana University Press, 1986.

Katz, Dovid. *Lithuanian Jewish Culture.* Vilnius: Baltos Lankos, 2004.

Kelly, Martha McCrummen Fraser. "An Unorthodox Beauty: The Use of Orthodox Rite in Russian Modernist Literature and Culture (1889–1965)." PhD diss., Stanford University, 2006.

Klausner, Joseph. *H. N. Bialik ve-shirat hayav.* Tel Aviv: Dvir, 1950.

———. *Historiyah shel ha-sifrut ha-ivrit ha-hadashah*. Vol. 4. Jerusalem: Ahiasaf, 1952.

Kovner, Avraam Uri. "Yeshibotnaia Bursa." *Den*, June 20, 1869.

Kovner, Avraham Uri. *Kol kitvei Avraham Uri Kovner*. Edited by I. Zemorah. Tel Aviv: Mahbarot le-sifrut, 1947.

Kovner, Itzhak Isaac. *Sefer ha-matzref*. Edited by Shmuel Feiner. Jerusalem: Mosad Bialik, 1998.

Krutikov, Mikhail. "The Russian Jew as a Modern Hero: Identity Construction in An-Sky's Writings." In *The Worlds of S. An-Sky*, edited by Gabriella Safran and Steven J. Zipperstein, 119–36. Stanford, CA: Stanford University Press, 2006.

Kurzweil, Baruch. *Sifrutenu ha-hadashah: hemshekh o-mahpekhah*. Jerusalem: Schocken, 1971.

Lachover, Fishel Yeruham. *Bialik: hayav vi-yetzirotav*. Vol. 1. Tel Aviv: Mosad Bialik Dvir, 1964.

Lamm, Norman. *Torah lishmah be-mishnat R' Hayim mi-Volozhin uve-mahshevet ha-dor*. Jerusalem: Mosad ha-Rav Kook, 1972.

———. *Torah Lishmah: Torah for Torah's Sake in the Works of Rabbi Hayyim of Volozhin and His Contemporaries*. New York: Michael Sharf Publication Trust of the Yeshiva University Press and Ktav, 1989.

Lampert, Evgenij. *Sons against Fathers: Studies in Russian Radicalism and Revolution*. Oxford: Clarendon, 1971.

Landy, Joshua. *How to Do Things with Fictions*. New York: Oxford University Press, 2012.

Lasman, Tzofiyah, ed. *Ha-lashon ha-ivrit be-hitpat'hutah u-ve-hithadshutah*. Jerusalem: Ha-akademiah ha-le'umit ha-yisraelit le-mada'im, 1996.

Levin, Joshua Heschel, and David ben Judah Luria. *Sefer Aliyot Eliyahu*. Vilna: Shtetin bi-defus E. Shrentsil, 1855.

Lilienblum, Moshe Leib. *Hatot ne'urim*. Tel Aviv: Tel Aviv University Press, 1966.

———. *Kol kitvei Moshe Leib Lilienblum*. Edited by Joseph Tseitlin. 7 vols. Krakow: J. Fisher, 1912.

———. *Ktavim otobiografiyim*. Edited by Shlomo Braiman. 3 vols. Jerusalem: Mosad Bialik, 1970.

———. "Olam ha-tohu." *Ha-shahar* 4, Vienna, 1873.

Litvak, Olga. *Haskalah: The Romantic Movement in Judaism*. New Brunswick, NJ: Rutgers University Press, 2012.

———. "The Revolt of the Study House: M. L. Lilienblum and the Origins of Zionism in Russia." Public lecture presented at Stanford University, April 19, 2013.

Lucretius. *On the Nature of Things*. Translated by Martin Ferguson Smith. Indianapolis: Hackett, 2001.

Magnus, Shulamit. "Sins of Youth, Guilt of a Grandmother: M. L. Lilienblum, Pauline Wengeroff and the Telling of Jewish Modernity in Eastern Europe." In *Jewish Women in Eastern Europe*, edited by ChaeRan Y. Freeze, Antony Polonsky, and Paula Hyman, 87–120. Oxford: Littman Library of Jewish Civilization, 2007.

Maimon, Salomon. *Solomon Maimon: An Autobiography*. Translated by Moses Hadas. New York: Schocken, 1947.

Manchester, Laurie. *Holy Fathers, Secular Sons: Clergy, Intelligentsia, and the Modern Self in Revolutionary Russia*. Dekalb: Northern Illinois University Press, 2008.

Matich, Olga. *Erotic Utopia: The Decadent Imagination in Russia's Fin de Siecle*. Madison: University of Wisconsin Press, 2007.

McEleney, Corey. *Futile Pleasures: Early Modern Literature and the Limits of Utility*. New York: Fordham University Press, 2017.

McLean, Hugh. "Realism." In *Handbook of Russian Literature*, edited by Victor Terras, 363–67. New Haven, CT: Yale University Press, 1985.

Meir, Natan M. *Kiev, Jewish Metropolis: A History, 1859–1914*. Bloomington: Indiana University Press, 2010.

Mendele Moykher-Sforim. *Kol Kitvei Mendele Moykher-Sforim*. Tel Aviv: Dvir, 1958.

———. *The Nag*. Translated by Moshe Spiegel. New York: Beechhurst, 1955.

———. *Tales of Mendele the Book Peddler, Fishke the Lame and Benjamin the Third*. Edited by Dan Miron and Ken Frieden. Translated by Ted Gorelick and Hillel Halkin. New York: Schocken Books, 1996.

Mintz, Alan L. *Banished from Their Father's Table: Loss of Faith and Hebrew Autobiography*. Bloomington: Indiana University Press, 1989.

Miron, Dan. *A Traveler Disguised: The Rise of Modern Yiddish Fiction in the Nineteenth Century*. Syracuse, NY: Syracuse University Press, 1996.

———. *Ha-predah min ha-ani he-ani*. Tel Aviv: Open University of Israel, 1986.

Moseley, Marcus. *Being for Myself Alone: Origins of Jewish Autobiography*. Stanford, CA: Stanford University Press, 2006.

Moss, Kenneth B. *Jewish Renaissance in the Russian Revolution*. Cambridge, MA: Harvard University Press, 2010.

Mosse, George L. "Max Nordau and His Degeneration." In Max Nordau, *Degeneration*, xv–xxxiv. Reprint of 1892 edition. New York: Howard Fertig, 1968.

———. "Max Nordau, Liberalism and the New Jew." *Journal of Contemporary History* 27, no. 4 (1992): 565–81.

Moya, Paula. *The Social Imperative: Race, Close Reading, and Contemporary Literary Criticism*. Stanford, CA: Stanford University Press, 2015.

Murav, Harriet. *Identity Theft: The Jew in Imperial Russia and the Case of Avraam Uri Kovner*. Stanford, CA: Stanford University Press, 2003.

Nadler, Allan. *The Faith of the Mithnagdim: Rabbinic Responses to Hasidic Rapture*. Baltimore: Johns Hopkins University Press, 1997.

Nathans, Benjamin. *Beyond the Pale: The Jewish Encounter with Late Imperial Russia*. Berkeley: University of California Press, 2002.

Natkovich, Svetlana. "Elisha Ben Abuya as a Hero of the Haskalah." MA diss., Ben Gurion University of the Negev, 2006.

———, ed. *Kazanova mi-Vilnah*. Modi'in, Israel: Kineret Zemorah Bitan, 2017.

Nietzsche, Friedrich. *On the Genealogy of Morals and Ecce Homo*. Translated by Walter Kaufmann. New York: Random House, 1989.

Nordau, Max. *Paradoksim: prakim be-torat ha-nefesh*. Translated by Reuven Brainin. Pietrokov, Poland: Tushiyah, 1900.

Paperno, Irina. *Chernyshevsky and the Age of Realism: A Study in the Semiotics of Behavior*. Stanford, CA: Stanford University Press, 1988.

Parush, Iris. "Another Look at 'The Life of "Dead" Hebrew': Intentional Ignorance of Hebrew in Nineteenth-Century Eastern European Jewish Society." *Book History* 7, no. 1 (2004): 171–214.

Penkower, Monty Noam. "The Silences of Bialik: Zionism's Bard Confronts Eretz Israel." *Modern Judaism* 26, no. 3 (2006): 240–73.

Peretz, Isaac Leib. *Ale Verk*. Vol. 1. New York: Tsiko Bikher Farlag, 1947.

Pinsker, Leon. *Auto-Emancipation: An Admonition to His Brethren by a Russian Jew.*
Translated by D. S. Blondheim. New York: Maccabaean Publishing Company, 1906.
———. "Auto-emantsipatsiya." Translated by Ahad Ha'am. Ben Yehuda Project, 1882. http://
benyehuda.org/ginzberg/pinsker_autoemancipation.html.
———. *Autoemanzipation.* Berlin: Jüdischer Verlag, 1919.
Pinsker, Shachar. "Intertextuality, Rabbinic Literature, and the Making of Hebrew
Modernism." In *Jewish Literatures and Cultures: Context and Intertext,* edited by
Yaron Z. Eliav and Anita Norich, 201–28. Brown Judaic Studies, no. 349. Providence,
RI: Brown Judaic Studies, 2008.
———. *Literary Passports: The Making of Modernist Hebrew Fiction in Europe.* Stanford, CA:
Stanford University Press, 2011.
Pisarev, Dmitry. "Bazarov." In *Fathers and Sons,* trans. Michael Katz, 197–219. New York:
Norton Critical Edition, 1996.
———. "Bazarov." In *Polnoe Sfobranie Sochinenii,* 201. Vol. 3. Nauka: Moscow, 2000.
———. *Kritika Literaturnaia v Trekh Tomakh.* Edited by Sorokin. Leningrad:
Khudozhestvennaia literatura, 1981.
———. *Selected Philosophical, Social, and Political Essays.* Moscow: Foreign Languages
Publishing House, 1958.
Pomyalovsky, Nikolai. *Seminary Sketches.* Translated by Alfred R. Kuhn. Ithaca, NY: Cornell
University Press, 1973.
Rosenthal, Bernice Glatzer. *Nietzsche in Russia.* Princeton, NJ: Princeton University Press,
1986.
Roskies, David G. "An-Sky, Sholem Aleichem, and the Master Narrative of Russian Jewry." In
The Worlds of S. An-Sky: A Russian Jewish Intellectual at the Turn of the Century, edited
by Gabriella Safran and Steven Zipperstein, 31–43. Stanford, CA: Stanford University
Press, 2006.
———. "The Maskil as Folk Hero." *Prooftexts* 10, no. 2 (1990): 219–35.
Rubenstein, Jeffrey L. *The Culture of the Babylonian Talmud.* Baltimore: Johns Hopkins
University Press, 2003.
Rubin, Adam. "'Like a Necklace of Black Pearls Whose String Has Snapped': Bialik's 'Aron
Ha-Sefarim' and the Sacralization of Zionism." *Prooftexts* 28, no. 2 (2008): 157–96.
Rzhevsky, Nicholas, ed. "Life of Alexis, Holy Man of God." In *Anthology of Russian
Literature,* 33–38. New York: M. E. Sharpe, 1996.
Safran, Gabriella. *Wandering Soul: The Dybbuk's Creator, S. An-Sky.* Cambridge, MA:
Harvard University Press, 2010.
Scholem, Gershom. *Origins of the Kabbalah.* Edited by R. J. Zwi Werblowsky. Translated by
Allan Arkush. Princeton, NJ: Princeton University Press, 1990.
Seidman, Naomi. *The Marriage Plot, or How Jews Fell in Love with Love, and with Literature.*
Stanford, CA: Stanford University Press, 2016.
Shaked, Gershon. *The New Tradition: Essays on Modern Hebrew Literature.* Cincinnati:
Hebrew Union College Press, 2006.
Shamir, Ziva. *Ha-nigun she-bilvavo: ha-shir ha-liri ha-katsar shel H. N. Biyalik.* Tel Aviv: ha-
Kibbutz ha-me'uhad, 2011.
Shumsky, Dimitry. "Leon Pinsker and 'Autoemancipation': A Reevaluation." *Jewish Social
Studies* 18, no. 1 (2012): 33–62.
Smith, Oliver. "Anagogical Exegesis: The Theological Roots of Russian Hermeneutics." In
Thinking Orthodox in Modern Russia: Culture, History, Context, edited by Judith

Deutsch Kornblatt and Patrick Lally Michelson, 196–214. Madison: University of Wisconsin Press, 2014.

Stampfer, Shaul. *Lithuanian Yeshivas of the Nineteenth Century: Creating a Tradition of Learning*. Oxford: Littman Library of Jewish Civilization, 2012.

Stanislawski, Michael. *Autobiographical Jews: Essays in Jewish Self-Fashioning*. Seattle: University of Washington Press, 2012.

———. *For Whom Do I Toil? Judah Leib Gordon and the Crisis of Russian Jewry*. New York: Oxford University Press, 1988.

———. *Zionism and the Fin de Siècle: Cosmopolitanism and Nationalism from Nordau to Jabotinsky*. Berkeley: University of California Press, 2001.

Stern, David. *Midrash and Theory: Ancient Jewish Exegesis and Contemporary Literary Studies*. Evanston, IL: Northwestern University Press, 1996.

Stern, Eliyahu. *The Genius: Elijah of Vilna and the Making of Modern Judaism*. New Haven, CT: Yale University Press, 2013.

———. *Jewish Materialism: The Intellectual Revolution of the 1870s*. New Haven, CT: Yale University Press, 2018.

Tchernikhovsky, Saul. *Kol kitvei Shaul Tchernikhovsky*. Vol. 1. Tel Aviv: Am Oved, 1990.

Terras, Victor. *Handbook of Russian Literature*. New Haven, CT: Yale University Press, 1985.

———. *A History of Russian Literature*. New Haven, CT: Yale University Press, 1991.

Turgenev, Ivan. "Hamlet and Don Quixote." Translated by Moshe Spiegel. *Chicago Review* 17, no. 4 (1965): 92–109.

———. *Otcy i deti*. Vol. 7. Nauka: Moscow, 1981.

Turgenev, Ivan Sergeevich. *Fathers and Sons*. Translated by Constance Garnett. New York: Grosset & Dunlap, 1900.

Veidlinger, Jeffrey. *Jewish Public Culture in the Late Russian Empire*. Bloomington: Indiana University Press, 2009.

Verhoeven, Claudia. *The Odd Man Karakozov: Imperial Russia, Modernity, and the Birth of Terrorism*. Ithaca, NY: Cornell University Press, 2015.

Volozhiner, Hayim ben Yitzhak. *Nefesh Ha-Hayim*. Bnei Brak, Israel: I. D. Rubin, 1989.

Weber, Max. *From Max Weber: Essays in Sociology*. Translated by Hans Heinrich Gerth and Bryan S. Turner. New York: Oxford University Press, 1977.

Weiner, Leo, trans. *Anthology of Russian Literature from the Earliest Period to the Present Time*. Vol. 2. New York: G. P. Putnam's Sons, 1903.

Weinreich, Max. *History of the Yiddish Language*. Edited by Paul Glasser. Translated by Shlomo Noble and Joshua A. Fishman. 2 vols. New Haven, CT: Yale University Press, 2008.

Weissman, Anat. *Mendele ha-ivri*. Tel Aviv: Hargol, 2013.

Wengeroff, Pauline. *Memoirs of a Grandmother*. Translated by Shulamit Magnus. Stanford, CA: Stanford University Press, 1997.

Wolfson, Elliot R. *Language, Eros, Being: Kabbalistic Hermeneutics and Poetic Imagination*. New York: Fordham University Press, 2005.

Zierler, Wendy I. *And Rachel Stole the Idols: The Emergence of Modern Hebrew Women's Writing*. Detroit: Wayne State University Press, 2004.

Zipperstein, Steven. "Ahad Ha-Am." In *YIVO Encyclopedia of Jews in Eastern Europe*. Accessed December 23, 2020. https://yivoencyclopedia.org/article.aspx/Ahad_Ha-Am.

———. *Elusive Prophet: Ahad Ha'am and the Origins of Zionism*. Berkeley: University of California Press, 1993.

———. *The Jews of Odessa: A Cultural History, 1794–1881*. Stanford, CA: Stanford University Press, 1991.

———. "Transforming the Heder: Maskilic Politics in Imperial Russia." In *Jewish History: Essays in Honor of Chimen Abramsky*, edited by Ada Rapoport-Albert and Steven Zipperstein, 87–109. London: P. Halban, 1988.

INDEX

MARINA ZILBERGERTS (PhD, Stanford) is Assistant Professor of Jewish Literature and Thought at the Mosse/Weinstein Center for Jewish Studies and the Department of German, Nordic, and Slavic at the University of Wisconsin–Madison. This is her first book.

CPSIA information can be obtained
at www.ICGtesting.com
Printed in the USA
LVHW101304120522
718615LV00003B/36